TELEFANTASY

Catherine Johnson

 Publishing

First published in 2005 by the
BRITISH FILM INSTITUTE
21 Stephen Street, London W1T 1LN

The British Film Institute's purpose is to champion moving image culture in all its richness and
diversity across the UK, for the benefit of as wide an audience as possible, and to create and
encourage debate.

Set by Fakenham Photosetting Limited, Fakenham, Norfolk
Printed in the UK by St Edmundsbury Press, Bury St Edmunds, Suffolk

Cover design: Mark Swan
Cover illustrations: *The X-Files*, 20th Century Fox Television/Ten Thirteen Productions; *Buffy
the Vampire Slayer*, 20th Century Fox Television/Mutant Enemy Inc./Kuzui Enterprises/San-
dollar Television; *Star Trek*, Desilu Productions Inc./Norway Corporation/Paramount Television;
The Prisoner, Everyman Films/ITC

British Library Cataloguing-in-Publication Data
A catalogue record for this book is available from the British Library

ISBN 1–84457–076–2 (pbk)
ISBN 1–84457–075–4 (hbk)

CONTENTS

ACKNOWLEDGMENTS

As I've been working on this book for nearly six years acknowledgment is due to a wide range of people who have provided me with inspiration and support. My thanks must firstly go to Jason Jacobs and Charlotte Brunsdon who supervised the doctoral thesis that formed the basis of this book and who have been a source of intellectual inspiration, academic insight and emotional support. Thanks also to the rest of the staff in the Department of Film and Television Studies at the University of Warwick, particularly Jon Burrows, Elaine Lenton and Rachel Moseley, the Midlands Television Research Group, and my fellow doctoral candidates, Helen Wheatley and Natalie Mercer for making my time as a doctoral student intellectually engaging and fun. In addition, Lynn Spigel and Jonathan Bignell were excellent examiners who gave me advice on developing the thesis into a book. My colleagues at the University of Southampton were a great source of support and inspiration as I was completing the thesis, and put up with me talking about *Buffy* – a lot. Thanks also to the Arts and Humanities Research Board, who funded the thesis upon which this book is based, and to the staff at the BBC Written Archive Centre. Over the past two years, the staff and students at Royal Holloway, University of London have provided a great space in which to finish this book. Outside of Royal Holloway, many thanks also to Matt Hills for many well-argued intellectual debates.

Grateful thanks to all my friends – particularly Greg Woodward for introducing me to tele-fantasy, supplying me with a wealth of research material and providing invaluable and tireless help with the illustrations, Neil Grutchfield for making me always argue my case and Juanita Elias (and the other Cov girls) for making Coventry fun! Finally, thanks to Rob, not only for his insightful comments on the book, but also for everything else. This book is dedicated to my parents: Maria and Ron Haller-Williams, and Peter and Liz Johnson. They have supported me in so many ways over the years, always allowing me to be me, and providing me with a childhood full of books and ideas for which I'll be forever grateful.

An earlier version of Chapter 1 has been published as: 'Exploiting the Intimate Screen: *The Quatermass Experiment*, Fantasy and the Aesthetic Potential of Early Television Drama', in Janet Thumim (ed.), *Small Screens, Big Ideas: Television in the 1950s* (London: I. B.Tauris, 2002), pp. 181–94.

An earlier version of the section on *The X-Files* in Chapter 4 is due to be published as: 'Historicising *The X-Files* as "Quality/Cult" Television', in Michael Hammond and Lucy Mazdon (eds), *The Contemporary Television Series* (Edinburgh: Edinburgh University Press, 2005).

INTRODUCTION
Approaching Telefantasy

In October 1995, the US industry magazine *Broadcasting and Cable* reported on the rise of television series and serials dealing with 'Alien autopsies, strange occurrences, malevolent forces, mythical heroes, unexplained sightings, ghouls, ghosts and a whole collection of "things that go bump" on the tube' (Coe, 1995, p. 56). Programmes such as *The X-Files, Space: Above and Beyond, Star Trek: Voyager, American Gothic, Xena: Warrior Princess* and *Babylon 5* saturated network and syndicated television to an extent that Tony Jonas (President of Warner Bros. Television) claimed had not been seen since the 1960s (cited in Coe, 1995).[1] Britain was not immune from this trend. After the transmission of *The X-Files* on the BBC in the mid-1990s, a number of British fantasy dramas emerged such as *Neverwhere, The Last Train, Ultraviolet, Invasion Earth* and *The Visitor* (see Millar, 1998, p. 2). What were the reasons for the rise in the production of fantasy dramas in the US and UK television industries in the 1990s? What historical precedents were there for this trend?

Although there has been a considerable amount of academic attention given to television fantasy dramas, there has been surprisingly little consideration of the context within which these programmes have been produced. Much of the scholarship, on programmes from the 1990s such as *The X-Files* and *Buffy the Vampire Slayer*, and also on older programmes, such as *Star Trek, Dr Who, The Avengers* and *The Prisoner*, has approached these programmes as 'cult' texts, frequently exploring the fan cultures they have engendered.[2] In approaching these programmes as objects of fan attention, this scholarship has tended to separate television fantasy from 'normal' television and to understand such programmes as exceptional in television history. In fact, even within the scholarship not explicitly concerned with fandom, there has been a tendency to view these programmes as 'unique' in television history. This extends from older shows, such as the original *Star Trek* series, which Harrison *et al.* describe as a cultural phenomenon that 'is unique within the television world' (1996, p. 3), to more recent programmes, such as *The X-Files*, which Douglas Kellner claims is 'rather unique in the history of mainstream television' (1999, p. 164).

The starting-point for this book is to test this hypothesis. To what extent are these fantasy dramas 'unique' in the history of television? To answer this question, this book takes a dual approach. First, it brings together a range of fantasy drama series to explore the links between them and to ask how television fantasy drama might be constituted generically. Second, it asks how fantasy television drama might be understood historically, by asking what these 'exceptional' programmes offered to producers when they were originally created. Although there are some incisive production studies of programmes such as *Star Trek, Dr Who* and *The Avengers*,[3] and some excellent studies of the industrial changes in 1990s US television,[4] no comparative studies exist that look at the production of an historical range of television fantasy dramas.[5] The intention of this book is to redress this by bringing together a range of television fantasy series and serials, and by asking what debates recur around their production across different historical periods. To do this case studies are used from the UK and the US, and from two different historical periods: the 1950s/60s and the 1990s/2000s. From the 1950s/60s this book examines the *Quatermass* serials, *The Prisoner* and *Star Trek*, and from the 1990s/2000s it analyses *The X-Files*, *Buffy the Vampire Slayer*, and a remake of *Randall and Hopkirk (Deceased)*. The rest of this introduction explores the difficulties that television fantasy drama raises for genre theory and proposes a theorisation of 'telefantasy' as a way of understanding these programmes generically and historically.

What is Telefantasy?

While there remains little academic scholarship that brings together television fantasy dramas for analysis, within fan circles the word 'telefantasy' is commonly used as a broad generic category to describe a wide range of fantasy, science-fiction and horror television programmes. The term appears in fan magazines such as *Starburst* from the 1970s onwards, and is also used in popular surveys of television such as Cornell, Day and Topping's *The Guinness Book of Classic British Television* (1993). While I have borrowed this term from fan discourse for this book, there remain a number of problems in transferring the term to an academic context. The term telefantasy refers in fan discourses to a very wide range of texts – from *Dr Who* to *The Avengers*, from *Robin of Sherwood* to *The X-Files* – texts that are disparate enough to pose problems for a clearly defined generic classification. In addition, unlike genres such as science fiction and horror, telefantasy is not a term used by the industry or by general audiences, and therefore does not function – as with many film and literary genres – as a form of social contract between producers and audiences. As a term primarily used by fans, it is rather a way of separating out those texts that are of interest or could be included within a canon of sorts constructed by a specific set of viewers.

Although telefantasy is a term borrowed from fans, the association of telefantasy with cult television is both important and problematic. It is the case that a significant number of television fantasy dramas (as well as films, comics and novels) have gained fan followings. Indeed, Matt Hills convincingly argues that fantasy texts have a particular propensity to become media cults because the representation of the fantastic enables the maintenance of two textual attributes that are central to the cult text. These attributes he terms 'perpetuated hermeneutic' (a central mystery that repeats familiar characteristics but whose resolution is endlessly deferred) and 'hyper-diegesis' (an internally logical, stable, yet 'unfinished' fictional world) (2002, pp. 117–43). The 'perpetuated hermeneutic' is typically focused around a question or set of questions which drives the deferred narrative, for example in *The Prisoner*'s posing of the questions 'Who is Number 6? Where is the Village?' (Hills, 2002, p. 134), which leaves the space open for further speculation beyond the bounds of the original text. The 'hyper-diegetic' world of cult texts similarly leaves space open for 'creative speculation' (Hills, 2002, p. 138). For example, the fictional world of *Star Trek*, although internally logical and dense, is only partially revealed in the original series' seventy-nine episodes. As a consequence, there are many worlds, civilisations, organisations and societies referred to (or implied) within the diegesis of the programme which are never fully explored and allow scope, not only for a range of spin-off films and series, but also for fan creativity. The representation of the fantastic tends towards the creation of texts based on a perpetuated hermeneutic, in that the questions upon which they are premised are never fully resolved (what is the future of humankind in space?). Furthermore, the fantastic also invites the creation of a hyper-diegetic fictional world. In creating story-worlds based on the 'unreal', the fantastic invites the construction of fictional worlds which while internally logical and dense are only partially glimpsed, enabling speculation and imagination beyond the text itself.

However, while these textual attributes may be shared by all media cults, the presence of a 'perpetuated hermeneutic' and 'hyper-diegesis' within a text will not automatically make it a cult text. Producers may attempt to create a media cult, but it is only through the activities of audiences that a television programme can become a cult text. Consequently, cult television programmes can only finally be defined through their mode of reception, rather than textually or through their mode of production. Therefore, in order to understand historically the production context and textual attributes of television fantasy drama it is necessary to differentiate telefantasy from cult television. However, the origin of the term 'telefantasy' within fan cultures does highlight the discursive association of fantasy with cult media. While, as discussed, this association has shaped the scholarship surrounding television fantasy drama, I want to go on to argue that it has also had an impact on the production of telefantasy. First, however, I want to explore how to overcome the problems raised by a generic theorisation of telefantasy.

Telefantasy and Genre

While it is possible, as fans have done through their use of the term telefantasy, to identify an historical range of television dramas that represent fantastic events and characters, the fantastic is a generically unstable category. The boundaries between fantasy, science fiction and horror have consistently problematised explorations of these genres.[6] Furthermore, representations of the fantastic are frequently incorporated into a wide range of other genres. *Ally McBeal* and *The X-Files* both represent fantastic events, but does this mean that they can be usefully understood to occupy the same generic category? Over and above this, the tendency towards generic hybridity within television programmes has proved problematic for the study of television genre.[7] For example, *The X-Files* can be categorised as a science-fiction series (thematically concerned with alien invasion and the dangers of science, and replete with the iconography of spaceships and aliens) and as a detective series (following its detective protagonists through narratives of investigation).[8] The series is also frequently horrific in its representation of serial killers and murders, laced with ironic comedy in its treatment of social and genetic difference, and embedded in the action-adventure form common to series television in the US. *The Prisoner* can be categorised as a spy series (following its spy protagonist as he attempts to escape from his kidnappers) and as a science-fiction series (thematically concerned with technological developments to induce mind control and alter perception). The series also uses the narrative form of the action-adventure series and frequently adopts surreal representational strategies. While the fantastic is central to both series, in *The X-Files* this is represented through a thematically and visually dark aesthetic that *suggests* the presence of aliens, genetic hybrids and spacecrafts (see Chapter 4), while in *The Prisoner* this is represented through a surreal, colourful landscape that combines old-world charm with unexplained futuristic technology (see Chapter 2).

Despite these differences, both programmes contain significant representations of 'fantastic' events and objects that confound culturally accepted notions of what is believed to be real. As such, both programmes can be understood to engage with regimes of 'non-verisimilitude'. Steve Neale, writing about film genre, argues that the systems of expectation that spectators bring to the cinema, and which interact with the films they view, 'involve a knowledge of, indeed they partly embody, various regimes of verisimilitude – various systems and forms of plausibility, motivation and belief' (2000, p. 32). He argues for two types of verisimilitude. Generic verisimilitude corresponds to what is accepted as plausible or likely within the expectations of a particular genre. For example, it is accepted for a character to burst into song in a musical, or for an alien to land on Earth in a science-fiction film, while these events would seem implausible in a gangster film. Generic verisimilitude is constructed through the relationship between producer, text and viewer, and between texts that employ conventions of that genre, and therefore does not refer to a static set of expectations, but can change over time as new examples of the genre emerge. Socio-cultural verisimilitude does not equate directly with truth or reality, but with broader culturally constructed and generally accepted notions of what is believed to be true, and as such is also historically contingent. Hence, while some believe in alien abductions, there is a broader cultural consensus that aliens do not visit Earth.

Neale notes that within all genres there exists a tension between generic and socio-cultural verisimilitude. However, he goes on to argue that in certain 'non-verisimilitudinous genres [such as horror, science fiction and fantasy] these relations can be particularly complex' (2000, p. 37). These genres construct fictional worlds that do not correspond to the norms, rules and laws of everyday knowledge. While the depiction of an alien landing on Earth may be plausible in a science-fiction film (because it corresponds to the generic verisimilitude of the genre), it is also potentially implausible because is goes against broader culturally accepted belief systems about what is 'real' (socio-cultural verisimilitude). What is plausible within a science-fiction film (and other non-verisimilitudinous genres) therefore conflicts with accepted notions of 'reality'. As such, all texts that represent the fantastic ask questions that push the boundaries of socio-cultural verisimilitude. It may be socially accepted that aliens/vampires/demons and so on do not exist, but what if they did? Or, we cannot know with any certainty what will happen in the future, but what might space travel look like in the twenty-third century? However, this does not mean that these genres do not depend on socio-cultural verisimilitude to make their fictional worlds plausible or believable. Indeed, socio-cultural verisimilitude is a particularly important device in such genres. For example, when depicting an alien landing on Earth, socio-cultural verisimilitude is essential to make the Earth seem plausible and believable despite the presence of an alien being. While these genres may represent fictional worlds that challenge culturally accepted notions of 'reality', they are also crucially engaged with explaining the rules that govern their particular fictional world, a process that is only possible through generic and socio-cultural verisimilitude (Neale, 2000, p. 38).

Although Neale goes on to argue for maintaining a distinction between horror and science fiction (2000, p. 92), his linking of science fiction, horror and fantasy as 'non-verisimilitudinous genres' is useful as it suggests a theorisation of 'fantasy' that resolves the problems of delineating the boundaries between fantasy, science fiction and horror. Such an approach, while formed by Neale in relation to cinema, is particularly valuable in television studies, which has struggled to apply cinematic theories of genre. Jane Feuer has argued that the dominant characteristics of television as a medium make the applicability of theories of film genre to television problematic, pointing out that television programmes 'do not operate as discrete texts to the same extent as movies; the property of "flow" blends one program unit into another and programs are regularly "interrupted" by ads and promos' (1992, p. 157). While genre has been understood as central to the production and marketing of movies, the flow of television programmes may make genre a less significant factor than scheduling in television production and in the selection of programmes by viewers.

The difficulties raised when applying genre theory to television are particularly pronounced in relation to television series and serials, whose narrative structures are constructed precisely around the notions of flow and interruption. Unlike the contained narrative of a movie, a series is made up of a sequence of discrete yet linked episodes that must share a narrative and visual format while also developing and extending that format over time. Graeme Turner maintains that within the television industry the term 'format' is much more common than genre as a way of describing television programmes.

> Formats can be original and thus copyright, franchised under licence, and traded as a commercial property. Genres, by definition, are not original. Format is a production category with relatively rigid boundaries that are difficult to transgress without coming up with a new format. (2001b, p. 7)

Turner's description of format as a dominant category in television production suggests that format may be a more useful concept in approaching television programmes than genre. The notion of the format allows an analysis of the ways in which a range of different generic expectations may be combined within one format to create a set of expectations that are specific to a particular series. However, formats describe a set of expectations that are specific to *one* series, and that can be used to distinguish that series from other television programmes. Therefore, the term 'format' operates quite differently from genre, functioning primarily as a way in which programmes can be distinguished from each other, rather than as a set of expectations and conventions that can be shared by a range of programmes.

I want to suggest a number of ways to overcome these problems with a generic approach to television. Rather than attempting to construct theoretical television genres against which historical instances can be measured, it is possible to explore the development of historical genres by isolating specific examples. However, such an approach still depends on the identification of a series of texts that can be situated within a particular genre through the recognition that they share a set of similar characteristics. Neale tackles this by arguing that multiple generic participation is a characteristic of all texts, claiming that '*Friends* could be said to participate in the genres "television programme", "television series", "fictional narrative", "comedy", "situation comedy" and so on' (2001, p. 4). Furthermore, each of these genres carries its own sets of expectations, which a series such as *Friends* engages with. Rather than adopting a generic approach to television that attempts to construct a singular generic category, what Neale's analysis suggests is that it is possible to explore the ways in which texts participate in different genres, by exploring the ways in which they utilise a range of generic expectations. The notion of generic participation is particularly useful in approaching television genre as it enables an analysis of the ways in which television programmes often participate in a number of different genres, allowing an exploration of generic hybridity to be opened up rather than closed down.

However, the different categories within which Neale situates *Friends* are not of the same order and do not function in the same way. The expectations and conventions associated with a broad category such as 'television programme' are quite different to those associated with a more specific generic category such as 'situation comedy'. Deborah Thomas (2000) has argued in relation to cinema that a distinction should be retained between genres whose structural characteristics are relatively easy to define (such as the Western), and the other kinds of inflections and tendencies that might be shared by a range of films across a number of different genres. As such, she argues that there are broader narrative modes that can be identified across and within fiction films that go beyond genre, namely the melodramatic, the romantic and the comedic. These broad modes describe the tone or mood of films. For example, Thomas argues that comedic films create a spontaneous and safe world for the exploration of reciprocal desire (2000, p. 21). Furthermore, Thomas argues that the boundaries between these categories are not fixed, as a film might shift from the comedic to the melodramatic over the course of its narrative. Thomas's categories of the melodramatic, comedic and romantic are of a different order to the definition of telefantasy that I want to develop here. What telefantasy shares with Thomas's categories is that it refers to a set of representational strategies that go beyond genre. That is, any attempt to represent the fantastic leads to the use of similar strategies that are beyond, and transgress across, the expectations and conventions of specific genres such as science fiction and horror. As I will go on to argue, these strategies arise from the shared concern within fantasy programmes to solve the problem of how to represent that which 'doesn't exist', which confounds socio-cultural verisimilitude. These representational strategies are not specifically generic (as these programmes draw on a range of different generic conventions that are not all shared). Neither are they defined by Thomas's notion of tone, particularly as the tone of these programmes would be shared by programmes that do not represent the fantastic. Yet between the specific generic conventions and the tone of each programme, are shared concerns with representation, with the stability of the fictional world, with the role of seeing, and with the image that arise specifically through the representation of the fantastic and that link these programmes together as telefantasy. These concerns will be explored in this book as 'production' and 'textual' strategies. 'Production strategies' refer to the strategies put in place at the point of production, such as the decision to use colour in *Star Trek* to distinguish its fictional world as futuristic, or the development of a dark visual style in *The X-Files* to hide the fantastic in shadows. These are strategies that can only be understood in relation to the context of production, and enable us to understand how that context shaped the ways these programmes look and the kinds of stories they tell. 'Textual strategies' are essentially the implementation of the production strategies and as such refer to the particular ways in which colour is used in *Star Trek* or the use of darkness and contrast in *The X-Files*. By approaching these programmes as telefantasy, this book will look beyond the differences in genre between these programmes to argue that the representation of the fantastic itself invites the use of certain strategies, which, while they may be worked through in different ways in each context, are shared across these different instances.[9]

The Subversive Potential of Fantasy?

One of the characteristics of studies of non-verisimilitudinous genres is that fantasy is seen to have subversive potential because it represents the 'unreal'. For example, Rosemary Jackson, in her analysis of the fantastic in literature, argues that fantasy 'has to do with inverting elements of this world, re-combining its constitutive features in new relations to produce something strange, unfamiliar and *apparently* "new", absolutely "other" and different.' (1981, pp. 7–8). Like Neale, therefore, Jackson argues that the representation of the fantastic does not constitute an escape from 'reality', but rather an engagement with and dislocation from culturally constructed notions of what is perceived as reality. Jackson claims that the literary fantastic can be understood as a subversive literature that by 'eroding and scrutinizing the "real", constitutes, in Hélène Cixous's phrase, "a subtle invitation to transgression"' (1981, p. 180).

The understanding of fantasy's disruption of socio-cultural verisimilitude as a potentially subversive textual strategy is also apparent in studies of television fantasy. Analyses such as Lynn Spigel's (2001) examination of the 1960s US 'fantastic sitcom' and Elyce Rae Helford's (1996) exploration of masculinity in *Star Trek*, argue that by disrupting socio-cultural and generic verisimilitude through their representation of the fantastic, these series invite the viewer to question, not the fantastic aspects themselves, but the normative conventions of the everyday. Helford argues that the use of fantastic devices in *Star Trek*, which allow Kirk's personality to be displaced (into a woman's body in 'Turnabout Intruder') or divided (into two separate characters in 'The Enemy Within'), complicates a reading of his masculinity as stereotypically aggressive and dominant. Spigel (drawing on Todorov (1975), whose theorisation of the fantastic forms the basis of Jackson's study) argues that the introduction of fantasy into the conventions of the US sitcom in series such as *Bewitched*, 'presented critical views of contemporary suburban life by using tropes of science fiction to make the familial strange' (2001, p. 122).

For Helford and Spigel, an analysis of the fantastic as offering a challenge to dominant ideologies enables serious criticism of programmes that have been dismissed as 'escapist fantasy'. As Lynn Spigel argues of the 1960s fantastic sitcom,

> These programs have received little critical attention, most certainly because they seem to represent the 'lower depths' of television's primetime past. Typically in this vein, critics tend to view such shows within the logic of cultural hierarchies, seeing their value in negative terms – that is, as the opposite of high art. Rather than leading to knowledge, these programs are said to constitute an escape from reason. (2001, p. 108)

Spigel here raises issues central to the study of fantasy, which has been characterised as a 'low' form of culture.[10]

Jackson, Helford and Spigel's theorisations of fantasy therefore stem from an attempt to redeem fantasy from its dismissal as 'low culture'. They are arguing against a notion that the representation of the fantastic constitutes an escape from reality, at best, providing distraction for its audiences or, at worst, duping them into an ideological complicity which serves to reinforce structures of power. To do this, they argue that the fantastic, far from being removed from reality, can only be represented through reference to culturally constructed notions of reality. By both evoking and disturbing socio-cultural verisimilitude, the fantastic therefore is understood to offer new (and potentially subversive) perspectives on society. These debates surrounding the cultural value of fantasy are apparent in the production discourses and critical debates surrounding the programmes studied in this book. However, I want to argue that, to understand fully these debates, it is necessary to move beyond textual studies to examine the ways in which these arguments have been taken up within audience studies.

Theorising the Producer–Text–Audience Relationship

These debates about the subversive potential of cultural forms are not specific to fantasy, but have been central to the study of popular culture and television, both of which have (at times) been characterised as 'low' forms of mass culture that function to maintain structures of power. In television studies, these textual debates about the dismissal or redemption of popular culture have been increasingly explored in relation to how audiences 'read' texts. These studies examine whether the subversive potential identified by academics within popular culture texts have offered spaces within which actual audiences found resistance to dominant ideologies (see Brunsdon, 1990). In relation to telefantasy, most of this work has focused on the study of fans, whose engagement with and re-articulation of television texts have been understood as a form of 'active' spectatorship through which they resist dominant ideology and find spaces for social transformation (see Jenkins, 1992).

As Shaun Moores argues, the turn to the audience is concerned with engaging with long-running concerns in social theory with questions of agency and structure.

> Some theorists, then, have stressed the capacity of consumers to actively appropriate commodities and put them to creative use in the construction of everyday cultures. Others have tended to give more weight to the structural constraints that impose themselves on consumers – the limited economic and cultural resources available to those creative agents as a consequence of their social positionings. ... Alongside this pairing of agency/structure, or creativity/constraint, another key opposition is that between the forces of social transformation and the pressures of social reproduction (resistance versus domination). (1993, p. 117)

These oppositions, between agency and structure, creativity and constraint, resistance and domination, have shaped fan studies, with scholars arguing that fandom either replicates and reinforces dominant structures, or reworks them to offer spaces for resistance.[11] In contrast,

Matt Hills' (2002) theorisation of fan culture attempts to move away from such binary oppositions as a way of understanding the relationship between texts and audiences. Hills argues
that fan culture is inherently contradictory. Rather than attempting to close down these contradictions (as earlier scholarship has done), Hills posits a theorisation of fandom as a 'dialectic
of value'. For example, rather than seeing fandom as either embedded in consumer culture
or resistant to it, he examines the ways in which 'fans are both commodity-completists and
... express anti-commercial beliefs' (2002, p. 44). In doing this, Hills challenges a model in
which cultural power can be easily located in either media producers (who impose dominant
ideologies on audiences) or cult fans (who resist these dominant ideologies through 'active'
spectatorship).

Hills' arguments suggest a way to move beyond the dismissal/redemptive debate in two
ways. First, his study invites a reassessment of the subversive accounts of television texts. Early
fan studies grew out of textual studies that suggest, 'formal *textual* spaces which invite an
"active audience" process of working on the text' (Tulloch, 1995, p. 44). However, if fan
studies which have attempted to redeem fan culture as resistant to dominant ideologies have
failed to account fully for the contradictions in fan practices, to what extent have textual
studies that have redeemed fantasy as 'subversive' similarly failed to acknowledge the contradictions within these texts? Second, by challenging the construction of fans as 'active'
audiences, and suggesting that cultural power cannot purely be located in either the audience or producer, Hills' study invites a reconsideration of the producer–text relationship.
Georgina Born argues that the emphasis on agency within audience studies has led to a
monolithic model of production in television studies, claiming that,

> Implicit in the Television Studies romance of the audience is a psychic polarity in which
> production has been weighted negatively, associated with domination, ideology, state
> interests, capitalist accumulation or consumerism, leaving consumption to bear the burden of
> positivity as the sole potential moment of redemption. If production is theorized more
> adequately, including its potential for spaces for agency and redemption, both sides of the
> polarity are reweighted; it may even be possible to reconsider negative dimensions of
> consumption! (2000, p. 417)

While Born's call for an examination of agency in production studies is certainly a valuable
one, by situating this call within the oppositions of agency/structure, redemption/domination,
Born limits the potential scope of such an analysis. Rather than searching for spaces of 'agency
and redemption' within production discourses, this book explores whether it is possible (as
Hills suggests of audience studies) to go beyond these dichotomies and examine the ways in
which such struggles are actually articulated (often in contradictory ways) within discourses
of production.

Telefantasy series are particularly useful in undertaking such a study, because, as I have
argued, the discourses surrounding fantasy have been precisely negotiated around questions
of redemption and dismissal. The production studies undertaken by the Economic and Social
Research Council's Media Economics and Media Culture Research Programme in the UK (of
which Georgina Born's production study of the BBC was a part) suggest that questions of

cultural value are central to an understanding of television production (see Frith, 2000). Yet as Simon Frith argues, our knowledge of the judgments and negotiations of television production is relatively restricted:

> if decisions are being made all the time and at all levels about what is 'good' and what is 'bad' television, it is not at all clear on what sort of knowledge or judgements such decisions rest, whether they are consistent or coherent at different levels and in different sectors of the industry (independent producers consistently refer to commissioners' 'irrationality') or whether they in any way match or articulate accounts of good and bad television outside the industry. (2000, p. 39)

This book engages primarily with the last of these concerns, by exploring the production discourses around a range of telefantasy programmes. The representation of the fantastic has been understood to open up spaces for the disruption of conventional modes of representation and of the normative conventions of the everyday, yet is equally associated with low forms of popular entertainment. How much are these textual possibilities and discursive frameworks apparent in the discourses of production surrounding telefantasy programmes and what effect do they have on the final text? What can this analysis add to our understanding of the discourses of value that Frith and Born suggest are central to understanding television production?

Telefantasy, Television and Aesthetics

As well as raising questions about our understanding of television production and of the subversive potential of the fantastic, the discourses surrounding telefantasy also problematise the aesthetic paradigms dominant in television studies. As these paradigms have shaped the writing of much television history, this may indicate why these programmes have been characterised as 'exceptional' and 'unique' texts in the history of television. Mark Siegel's analysis of television science fiction indicates the difficulties that the representation of the fantastic raises for an understanding of television aesthetics. Writing in 1984, Siegel claimed that television science fiction had historically replicated cinematic science fiction's emphasis on spectacle, action and 'gimmick-laden space-opera' and preoccupation 'with juvenilia and with marvels and wonders rather than solid characterization or intellectually stimulating themes' (1984, p. 65). Siegel argued that the presence of such 'cinematic' elements in television science fiction was unsuccessful because it was unsuited to television's small screen and domestic setting. Adopting Horace Newcomb's (1974) construction of television's basic attributes, Siegel argued that the intimacy, continuity and immediacy of television as a medium was more suited to the intelligent illumination of contemporary social anxieties characteristic of science-fiction literature than the spectacular display of science-fiction cinema.

Siegel's analysis of television science fiction reflects a general tendency to understand television as inherently visually inferior to its cinematic counterpart. This stems from an historical model of the aesthetics of television and cinema that, as Martin McLoone points out, 'opposes the extremes, rather than the characteristics, of the two media – television at its least "adventurous" (aesthetically) and cinema in its big picture, "event" mode' (1997, p. 81). Noël Carroll argues that such attempts to differentiate cinema from television stem from a perceived need to

> show that TV was not just an ersatz form of cinema. TV, it was claimed, had its own unique features, features distinct from those of cinema, which, at least in principle, opened up the possibility of an autonomous art of TV. (2003, p. 266)

The delineation of these specific features of television tends to stem from an identification of the technological differences between the two media, leading to a privileging of television's small screen, capacity for live broadcast and domestic setting, which has led to the assumptions that:

> TV has an impoverished image (marked by low resolution and small scale) versus film's informationally dense imagery; the TV image is less detailed, whereas the film image is elaborate; in TV talk is dominant, while in film the image is dominant; TV elicits the glance, but film engenders the gaze; TV is in the present tense, whereas film is in the past tense; TV narration is segmented and serial, but film narration is uninterrupted and closed; and, given the previous distinction, the object of attention in TV is the flow of programming, while the object of attention in film is the individual, integrated, closed story (the freestanding feature film). (Carroll, 2003, p. 270)

However, as Carroll argues, while these differences may have some basis in fact (in relation to certain kinds of programmes or historical developments), these are not essential or ontological differences between television and cinema, but arise 'from a tendency to overgeneralize from period-specific or genre-specific properties of some TV (and some film) to claims about all TV (and all film)' (2003, p. 278).[12]

The dominance of these different discursive registers for defining the ontology of cinema and television has shaped the development of television studies. The opposition of television as a medium of dialogue/talk against the visual spectacle of the cinema reflects what John Caughie argues as a general omission in television studies of the analysis of style and narrative (1991b, p. 137). Accordingly, textual studies of the representation of the fantastic in television drama have largely concentrated on theme, or have argued, as Siegel does, that television is unsuited to spectacle. Contrastingly in cinema such genres have proved particularly fertile sites for an examination of the use of style, image and spectacle.[13] This suggests, therefore, that telefantasy could be a useful site from which to address the relative lack of analysis of style in television studies, and to explore the adequacy of the dominant paradigms of intimacy, continuity and immediacy for an understanding of the aesthetics of television.

The dominant understanding of television as unsuited to spectacle and visual display has been matched by a theorisation of television viewing as distracted. John Ellis (1982) argues that because of television's location within the domestic sphere and integration into the routines of everyday life, television is primarily 'glanced' at, rather than watched attentively.

Although Ellis is not making an argument about the aesthetics of television, 'glance theory' *implies* an understanding of television as ephemeral (fleetingly glimpsed rather than actively and repeatedly viewed), aural (something to be listened to and glanced at rather than watched), and lacking in intrinsic aesthetic value (not worthy of attentive viewing). Fan theory has countered 'glance theory' as a way of understanding television spectatorship by arguing that fans can be differentiated from regular viewers by their 'active' engagement with media texts (see Jenkins, 1992). However, such an argument leaves the notion of glance as the dominant mode of spectatorship intact in order to differentiate fans from 'regular' audiences. While fan studies imply that engaged spectatorship is the practice of a particular kind of 'fan' audience, to what extent does the visual representation of the fantastic in telefantasy encourage or even demand attentive viewing, and how might this challenge the adequacy of glance theory for understanding television spectatorship more generally?

Writing the History of Telefantasy through Case Studies

The history of telefantasy offered in this book is shaped by the debates around genre, production and aesthetics that have been outlined in this introduction. I have argued that telefantasy raises particular problems for genre study and that to attempt to construct telefantasy as a singular generic category would be a reductive (if not impossible) task. I have also argued that the existing debates surrounding fantasy make telefantasy a useful site to explore the discourses of value in television production, and to re-examine the dominant paradigms for understanding the aesthetics of television. Finally, I have suggested that it may be because of the challenge that telefantasy programmes pose to dominant notions of the aesthetics of television, that these programmes tend to be understood as exceptional in television history. In order to examine fully the issues raised by telefantasy, this book offers a small number of specific case studies from two historically distinct periods in the history of television, rather than attempting to offer a comprehensive history of telefantasy. These two periods have been selected because they correspond to historical shifts which have had a particular impact on the industrial history of television *and* on the histories of telefantasy. These particular programmes have been chosen because they have been understood as in some ways exceptional, unusual or unique in television history. As such, this book is offering a revisionist account of these programmes that, by bringing them together for analysis, asks whether this characterisation stands, and whether any links can be found between them. Perhaps the exception to this is the final chapter examining the 2000 to 2001 remake of *Randall and Hopkirk (Deceased)*. As I will argue in Chapter 5, the difficulty in examining contemporary British telefantasy, is that these programmes have failed to have the cultural impact of their US counterparts. However, *Randall and Hopkirk (Deceased)* stands as a useful example because it shares with the other programmes examined a fan following (mainly arising out of fans of the programme's stars, Vic Reeves and Bob Mortimer). As a remake of a programme from the 1960s, it also brings into relief, at the end of the book, the differences between the two historical periods that this book examines.

Chapters 1, 2, and 3 explore programmes produced in the 1950s and the 1960s. Chapter 1 looks at an early example of telefantasy by examining the *Quatermass* serials, to ask what fantasy offered television producers in a period when there was much debate about what was suitable as television drama. Chapters 2 and 3 examine *The Prisoner* and *Star Trek* respectively, two programmes produced in the 1960s when telefantasy developed as a particularly successful form of programming in the UK and the US. The 1950s and 1960s is a period of television's history that John Ellis has termed the 'era of scarcity' (2000, pp. 39–60). At this time national stations (such as the US networks and the UK terrestrial channels) were the primary providers of television, transmitting a small number of programmes to large national audiences. During this period when television provided 'the nation's private life' (Ellis, 2000, p. 46), the notion of 'cult television' was relatively unexplored. This is not to imply that, in the 1950s and the 1960s, audiences did not develop affectionate and loyal relationships with television texts. Rather, it is to argue that the notion of the television fan only emerged as a culturally prominent and broadly accepted idea over the 1970s. While programmes from the 1950s and the 1960s have attracted fan audiences and become media cults, in the industrial context within which they were produced the television 'fan' and the 'cult' television text were not culturally dominant concepts at the time. The three programmes examined in Chapters 1 to 3 have all gained fan followings, yet they were produced at a time when television offered universal provision to broadly defined consensus audiences.[14] These chapters therefore explore the discourses of production surrounding telefantasy in a period before 'cult' television was a dominant notion, and when television was primarily transmitting to 'national' audiences.

Over the 1970s and the 1980s, television fandom gradually became more culturally prominent with the increasing visibility of fan communities around programmes such as *Star Trek* and *Dr Who*. In the same period television industries underwent dramatic changes as the dominant position of the national broadcasters was challenged by the growth of satellite, cable, and later, digital television. The shift over the late 1970s and the 1980s towards what Ellis has termed the 'era of availability' has created a fragmented global economy in which television 'is at once more global and more highly individualised' (2000, p. 69). Ellis argues that as a consequence television has,

> Reconstructed itself to incorporate increasing choice, and to cater for the increasingly diverse demands of its viewers. ... Once more than three or four channels exist, more nuanced notions of the audience begin to develop. The audience is conceived as much more a loose assemblage of minorities to be brought into various kinds of coalition, or even to be addressed singly. (2000, p. 71)

Within this fragmented media economy, Matt Hills (1999) argues that the cult fan has begun to be recognised as an ideal audience segment in television production. Chapters 4 and 5 examine programmes from the 1990s and early 2000s, a period in which cult television and telefantasy became important parts of the mainstream primetime television schedules. Chapter 4 explores *The X-Files* and *Buffy the Vampire Slayer*, two series that are indicative of the rise of telefantasy in US primetime network television in this period. Chapter 5 examines telefantasy in the UK at the same time by looking at the scheduling of *Buffy the Vampire Slayer* (and to a lesser extent *The X-Files* and *Angel*). It then goes on to examine *Randall and Hopkirk (Deceased)*, a British remake of a series from the 1960s, and asks how UK terrestrial television has responded to the changes in the television industry and the rise of telefantasy over this period.

The programmes explored in this book, as well as coming from two different historical periods, also come from two different national contexts: the United States of America and the United Kingdom. While John Ellis's historical model of television's development from an era of scarcity to an era of availability is useful, an exploration of the development of tele- fantasy suggests that this history may be more nationally contingent than Ellis implies. The resurgence of telefantasy in the 1990s stems primarily from the US. This suggests that the notion of the fan viewer as an ideal audience in contemporary television production may be less applicable to the UK than the US, and that the shift from 'scarcity' to 'availability' may have very different consequences within different national contexts. The nationally com- parative approach taken in this book enables these differences to come to the surface and be thrown into relief. Furthermore, by concentrating on the changes to US *network* and UK *terrestrial* television, this book focuses particular attention on the ways in which these national broadcasters have changed in response to the fragmentation and diversification of the tele- vision economy since the late 1970s.

The nationally comparative approach taken in this book also enables an address to the transnational nature of television production and consumption. All of the programmes explored in this book that were produced and initially transmitted on US network television have since aired on UK terrestrial television. *Star Trek* has been a regular part of the UK ter- restrial schedules since it was first transmitted in the UK in 1969, and both *The X-Files* and *Buffy the Vampire Slayer* were transmitted on British terrestrial television (see Chapter 5). Fur- thermore, although not all of the British programmes examined here have been transmitted in the US, the relationship between the UK and US industries is an important factor in under- standing the production of each of these series. The *Quatermass* serials were not transmitted in the US, being produced at a time when the international export of television programmes from the UK was relatively rare, largely because most television production at this time was still live. However, when the *Quatermass* serials were adapted for cinema, the US market was particularly important.[15] *The Prisoner* was sold to the US network CBS as part of a strategy by the British company ITC to infiltrate the US television market (see Chapter 2), and although at the time of writing *Randall and Hopkirk (Deceased)* had not yet been transmitted in the US, thirteen episodes of the series were produced with the notion that this would improve its chances of being sold to US television.[16] The export of US programmes to the UK and vice versa, is not an equal exchange, with US television programmes making up a far more sig- nificant part of the British schedules than UK programmes do in the US. Despite this, US television has traditionally been evoked as a marker of what British television must avoid – an indication of the perils of over-commercialisation. Yet it is myopic to presume that British television can only be understood as those programmes produced within the British television industry. By adopting a transnational approach, this book offers a comparative analysis of the production of telefantasy in relation to the historical shifts in the UK terrestrial and US net- work television industries, and explores the ways in which the international export of programmes between the UK and the US has influenced indigenous television production. Such a comparative approach avoids an overly parochial view of television and addresses the complexity of the medium as at once a nationally specific industry and a collection of national and international texts.

Finally, this book focuses in particular on series or serials, rather than single dramas or plays. There are two reasons for this. First, this book offers a revisionist account of specific television fantasy dramas, and as such, it focuses on programmes that have received significant academic attention. These programmes have primarily been long-running series and serials, particularly because it is such series and serials that have tended to gain fan followings. Second, the series/serial form is quite different from the narrative structure of the one-off play and raises specific issues at the point of production and at the stage of textual analysis. This book explores the specific discourses that arise around the production of series/serial dramas which extend over a number of weeks (sometimes over a number of years) and also examines the complex ways in which genres and formats function within the series/serial structure.

Methodologically, although this book situates these texts within their industrial contexts of production, it differs from the tradition of production research undertaken by D'Acci (1994) and Born (2000). These studies are concerned with examining the experience of producing television programmes by interviewing those involved in the production and, if possible, directly observing the production process. By contrast, this book is less concerned with the actual *process* of production than with the broader *discourses* within which this process takes place. It is less interested in 'how' these series were produced than with understanding how different sets of expectations (associated with the discourses surrounding telefantasy) were negotiated in the broader debates surrounding the production of these programmes and the impact that these had on the text. As one of the principal objectives of this book is to question the extent to which our current understanding of these programmes as 'unique' cult texts has shaped the scholarship surrounding them, this book uses archive research rather than interviews to examine the context of production. While interviews are necessarily shaped by the present, archive documents from the period of production provide access to the discourses of production unmediated by the later construction of these programmes as cult texts. Sources such as articles, advertisements and interviews in magazines, newspapers and trade journals do not offer access to the processes of production, but are particularly valuable for examining the discourses within which a programme's production is negotiated.

Rather than attempting to write *the* history of telefantasy therefore, this book offers a series of case studies of television drama series and serials that contain representations of the fantastic. Each case study explores the questions raised in this introduction within a particular moment in the history of television through a production and textual analysis of one or two programmes. One of the problems with the case study approach is that it may lead to the canonisation of certain programmes, particularly in a revisionist study such as this where most of the programmes examined have already received significant academic attention. In addition, case studies have been criticised for fetishising detail at the expense of the general. However, such an approach, as Lynn Spigel has argued, need not constitute a rejection of the general and actually works against a notion of popular culture as homogenous and repetitive (2001, pp. 13–14).

From this point of view, individual case studies are not a set of fetish facts or mere anecdotal flourish with no relation to more abstract thought and generalization. Instead, the individual example becomes the ground for a theorization of language and culture that is capable of understanding things that do not fit into reigning epistemologies or social practices (as well as things that do). (2001, p. 14)

The value of the case study therefore, lies in its ability to raise questions that can then be applied to other cases and other programmes. Furthermore, while it is problematic to generalise too freely from a small number of case studies, the case study approach enables a combination of the synchronic and the diachronic, and a recognition of detail and the complexity of the historical moment that is balanced by a thorough discussion of the theoretical and historiographic consequences of those details. As such, case studies offer a useful counter to the totalising tendencies of grand theory, and open up history and theory to new questions and new lines of enquiry.

In bringing together a range of historical case studies, this book asks what recurring discourses arise across these instances and what an analysis of these discourses and their textual articulation can add to our understanding of television history, television fantasy and the aesthetics of television. By exploring programmes which appear to go against the dominant paradigms of television – as an intimate medium that privileges the spoken word over the image, and that offers a continuous flow of programmes glanced at by a distracted viewer engaged in everyday domestic routines – it asks how these specific historical instances might offer a starting-point from which to re-theorise the dominant paradigms within which the aesthetics of television have been understood. While each case study explores these debates in relation to a specific historical context, in the conclusion I will return to the broader theoretical and historiographic debates raised here about television genre, television aesthetics and television history.

Notes

1. The 1960s produced anthology series of strange tales, such as *The Twilight Zone* and *The Outer Limits*, family-orientated fantasy, such as *Voyage to the Bottom of the Sea* and *Captain Scarlet*, spy/fantasy series such as *The Prisoner* and *The Avengers*, fantasy sitcoms such as *Bewitched* and *I Dream of Jeannie*, and futuristic space dramas, such as *Star Trek* and *Lost in Space* (see Chapters 2 and 3).
2. See for example, Jenkins (1992), Bacon-Smith (1992), and Lewis (1992).
3. For *Star Trek* see Bernardi (1998) and Pounds (1999), for *Dr Who* see Tulloch and Alvarado (1983), for *The Avengers* see Chapman (2002).
4. Mark Jancovich and James Lyons' edited collection (2003) offers a fascinating account of the rise of 'quality popular television' as a consequence of the industrial changes in the US in the 1990s, that includes analyses of *Star Trek: The Next Generation* and *Buffy the Vampire Slayer*. However, they do not offer a sustained analysis of why fantasy television flourishes in this particular historical context.
5. M. Keith Booker's study of *Strange TV* (2002) does bring together an historical range of series that represent the fantastic (*The Twilight Zone*, *The Prisoner*, *Twin Peaks* and

The X-Files), although he does not specifically explore their context of production. Furthermore, rather than exploring these programmes as 'fantasy' television, he characterises them as a particularly valuable form of post-modern television that produces cognitive estrangement in its audience. As a consequence he retains a notion of these programmes as unusual in the history of television, as programmes that 'have a richness of style and content that places them well above ordinary television fare' (2002, p. 2).

6. For example, while Amis argues that the scientific realism of science-fiction literature makes it a separate genre from the 'anti-realistic' form of fantasy (1961, p. 31), Aldiss (1973) understands science-fiction literature as a subgenre of fantasy which can be traced back to the Gothic novel. Early studies of science-fiction cinema argued that these films could be more usefully understood as 'horror films with a veneer of scientific justification' (Scholes and Rabkin, 1977, p. 102), or as 'disaster' films (Sontag, 1966). While Paul Wells argues that because horror is characterised by a 'playful engagement with its own conventions', it has no clearly defined generic boundaries (2000, p. 7).

7. See Feuer (1992), Neale (2001) and Turner (2001a).

8. Indeed Bellon (1999) refutes *The X-Files*' classification as a science-fiction series and argues that it can be more usefully understood as a detective series.

9. While this book examines a relatively small number of case studies, as will be argued below, the cast study approach offers a theorisation of telefantasy that can be tested through the further analysis of other television fantasy dramas.

10. Neale also discusses the association of non-verisimilitudinous genres with 'low' forms of escapist culture, which he sees as a consequence of the cultural predominance of ideologies of realism (2000, p. 35).

11. See, for example, two of the case studies (E. Graham McKinley's study of fans of *Beverly Hills 90210* and Henry Jenkins's study of *Star Trek* fans) that John Tulloch (2000) examines in the conclusion to his survey of audience studies in television.

12. While Carroll argues against the tendency within film and television studies to emphasise the differences between cinema and television, he does acknowledge that 'the features of TV that are often cited as its essential features, especially in contrast to film, have some basis in fact' (2003, p. 278). Indeed, one of the problems with theorisations of the essential differences between these two media is that they fail to acknowledge the extent to which such differences are historically contingent and open to change. Furthermore, the historically changing theorisation of 'what television is' as a medium has been a central discursive factor which has shaped the production of programmes over the history of television.

13. See, for example, Buckland (1999) and Pierson (1999).

14. While *The Prisoner* and *Star Trek* have organised and international fan communities, the fan following for the *Quatermass* serials is much smaller, in part because of the difficulty in accessing the original serials.

15. The correspondence in the BBC Written Archive Centre suggests that Hammer pursued its interest in purchasing the rights to *The Quatermass Experiment* because of the

interest of their US partners in adapting the television series into a film (BBC Written Archives Centre, Caversham, UK, WAC, R126/401/1).

16. Indeed Charlie Higson (who adapted the 2000 version of *Randall and Hopkirk (Deceased)*) has argued that in order to enhance the series' attractiveness to the US market the series was constructed to play 'on American tourist ideas of what England was like' (cited in Lane, 2001, pp. 26–7).

1

SPECTACLE AND INTIMACY

The *Quatermass* Serials and British Television in the 1950s

Introduction: Post-war British Television

On 7 June 1946, the television service resumed in Britain after a seven-year gap in transmission during World War II. The resumed service had much in common with the limited service offered in the pre-war period. There was just one television channel, run by the BBC within their public service broadcasting remit. In 1946, there was only one transmitter capable of relaying the television signal in Britain, effectively limiting the service to the London region. In terms of technical resources, television production was based at Alexandra Palace, with only two studios and limited facilities. Despite this, the post-war television service was to differ significantly from the pre-war service. This was the period when, in the words of Val Gielgud (Head of Television Drama between 1949 and 1951), British television was 'just beginning to advance from what may be called the embryonic into the experimental and expanding stage',[1] and by the early 1950s, television broadcasting in Britain had entered into a period of maturation that would continue over the decade.

On 2 July 1953, the Postmaster General announced the extension of television broadcasting, with proposals for new transmitters in Aberdeen, Belfast, the Isle of Wight, Plymouth and Durham, and new stations to serve the Channel Islands and the Isle of Man. These planned developments would make television available to 90 per cent of the population in eighteen months.[2] Concurrent with the increased reach of the television signal was a gradual increase in ownership of television receivers in the UK, which rose from one million to five million between 1951 and 1955 (Briggs, 1979, p. 428). This growth in ownership exceeded the BBC's expectations, with combined sound and television licences reaching 2,142,452 in 1953, well above the BBC's estimated figure of 1,200,000 (Briggs, 1979, p. 241).[3] At the same time, the BBC's production facilities were under development. The BBC acquired the White City site in 1949 for a planned Television Centre to open in 1960, while television production moved from Alexandra Palace to the superior facilities of the Rank Studios at Lime Grove over the early 1950s.[4] In 1954, the government passed a Television Act, which broke the BBC's monopoly on television broadcasting and in September 1955, a second commercial television channel, ITV, began broadcasting under the auspices of the Independent Television Authority.

The *Quatermass* Serials: Intimate Spectacle

It was during this period of change and expansion that the BBC produced three telefantasy serials concerning the attempts of scientist Professor Bernard Quatermass to save the world from alien invasion, written by Nigel Kneale and produced by Rudolph Cartier.[5] The first serial, *The Quatermass Experiment* (BBC, 1953) explored the potentially horrific consequences of man's foray into space sixteen years before Neil Armstrong's first walk on the moon enthralled television viewers across the globe. This was followed two years later by *Quatermass II* (BBC, 1955), which tackled concerns about secret government installations, and then towards the end of the decade by *Quatermass and the Pit* (BBC, 1958–9), in which an unearthed alien pod suggested that man's origins may not be entirely of this world. All three serials were adapted into films by Hammer over the 1950s and 1960s and in the 1970s *Quatermass* was revived as a drama that was produced simultaneously as a film and a four-part television series.[6]

The *Quatermass* serials had a strong cultural resonance with audiences in the 1950s. By the third serial in 1958, the *Quatermass* programmes had become a cultural event with *Variety* reporting 'a motion at one local council that business shouldn't start until after the *Quatermass* transmission had ended', adding that 'cinema exhibs testify to the pull of the program by saying that they had one of the worst evening's biz in a long, long time'.[7] They have also been regarded as key texts in the historical development of British television. Charles Barr describes *The Quatermass Experiment* as 'a landmark both in BBC policy, as a commissioned original TV drama, and in intensity of audience response' (1986, p. 215). Yet as Lez Cooke points out, there is a danger of over-emphasising the significance of the *Quatermass* serials at this time (2003, p. 22). Produced at a time when most television was live, and when telerecording[8] was relatively limited, *The Quatermass Experiment* is one of the few dramas from the early 1950s for which we have an audiovisual record. It is difficult therefore, to judge comparatively whether the *Quatermass* serials were as stylistically ground-breaking as has been suggested. However, it is possible to look at the debates surrounding the production of the serials and to combine this with textual analysis, in order to examine whether the serials used any stylistic strategies that were discursively understood as unusual or innovative at their time of production.

Indeed, the files held on the *Quatermass* serials at the BBC's Written Archive Centre suggest that these dramas were particularly significant to the BBC's response to the arrival of competition. Although a second commercial channel did not arrive in the UK until September 1955, the development of a new channel had been widely debated in the early 1950s. The passing of the Television Act in 1954 ended the BBC's monopoly, and the Corporation had to consider how it would respond to the immanent impact of competition in television broadcasting from a commercial broadcaster.[9] In a memo written in 1954, Cecil McGivern (Controller of Television Programmes) argued that in the face of competition, the BBC must expand the Television Script Unit responsible for filtering and adapting scripts in order to improve the quality of television drama. McGivern here makes reference to *The Quatermass Experiment* as an illustration of the kinds of television drama that the BBC should be producing with the arrival of competition.

> H.D.Tel. [Head of Television Drama, Michael Barry] took on a young writer [Nigel Kneale] at
> £5,5.0 a week. ... Soon after that he gave us the serial, *The Quatermass Experiment*. Had
> competitive television been in existence then, we would have killed it every Saturday night
> while that serial lasted. We are going to need *many* more 'Quatermass Experiment'
> programmes.[10]

The powerful endorsement that McGivern gives to *The Quatermass Experiment* and to Kneale
suggests that this serial was considered to be exemplary of the potential for BBC television
drama with the arrival of competition. Whether or not these serials marked an innovative stylistic shift in British television, they were certainly significant products for the BBC during this
transformative period.

The aim of this chapter is to explore the role that the representation of the fantastic may
have in any understanding of the significance of these serials to television history. The *Quatermass* serials were certainly not the first fantasy dramas to be produced on British television.
The BBC had transmitted previous adaptations of literary science fiction, such as a thirty-five-
minute performance of Karel Capek's *R.U.R.* in 1938 and an hour long adaptation of H. G.
Wells' *The Time Machine* in 1949. In 1951 the children's programme *Whirligig* featured a
fortnightly insert of *Stranger from Space*, written specifically for television by Hazel Adair and
Ronald Marriott, about a young boy who discovers a Martian who has crash-landed on Earth.
Furthermore, in the post-war period the BBC produced a number of 'horror' plays, largely
thrillers and murder mysteries, such as *The Two Mrs Carrolls* (1947) about a man's plans to
murder his wife, and *Markeim* (1952) a visually eerie adaptation of R. L. Stevenson's short
story (see Vahimagi, 1996). As Jason Jacobs discusses, these horror plays were seen in part
as a means of extending the scope of the service's drama output by exploring new dramatic
terrain which offered opportunities for stylistic experimentation. However, there was also
concern that this material was unsuitable for transmission in the home, particularly as the
audience began to expand at the end of the 1940s and into the 1950s (Jacobs, 2000,
pp. 97–100). The notion, therefore, of fantastic tales offering a means of experimenting with
the formal and narrative possibilities of television is a current one before *The Quatermass
Experiment* in 1953, and part of the history within which these serials can be situated.

Considering that horror and fantasy plays were seen to offer the potential for stylistic innovation and to present a challenge to existing notions of what was suitable as television drama,
it is unsurprising that Nigel Kneale should turn to the fantastic when writing his first original
serial for television. Having published *Tomato Cain* in 1949, a collection of short stories that had
won the Somerset Maugham prize, Nigel Kneale gained casual work at the BBC in 1951 as a
reader/adapter for the newly formed Television Script Unit. In seeking employment at the BBC
he claimed that he wanted to 'know much more about the medium, to try and exploit it' and
went on to express the desire to be involved in a project 'breaking new ground'.[11] His work at
the Script Unit concerned reading scripts to filter out those that were unsuitable for television,
and adapting submitted scripts, novels and theatre plays for television. Yet at this time, the question of what was possible, appropriate and suitable as *television* drama was a central point of
debate and there was no clear consensus as to the criteria under which such judgments should
be made. As Kneale said of his work for the Script Unit, '[I was] mostly trying to make stage

plays a little more like "television", although nobody really knew what that was' (cited in Wells, 1999, p. 49). *The Quatermass Experiment* was Kneale's first opportunity to write an original drama script for television, a chance that he described as 'an opportunity to do something different – an adventure yarn, or something that wasn't people talking in drawing rooms' (Kneale cited in Wells, 1999, p. 50). Similarly, when Rudolph Cartier (an émigré film director from Austria) arrived at the BBC in 1952, he felt that British television drama was 'terrible ... the BBC needed new scripts, a new approach, a whole new spirit, rather than endlessly televising classics like Dickens or familiar London stage plays' (cited in Myles and Petley, 1990, p. 126).

Kneale and Cartier's rhetoric here may be imbued by the cultural status that the *Quatermass* serials have gone on to acquire. However, their comments indicate the particular kinds of aesthetic debates that were current in the early 1950s about the state of British television drama. Jason Jacobs has suggested that 'it is possible to identify two tendencies in the production of early television drama in Britain by the 1950s: the intimate and the expansive' (2000, p. 117). Within the intimate model, a suitable television drama was defined as one that emphasised the relay of a continuous live performance through the close-up lens of the studio camera. These intimate and penetrating images were transmitted directly into the familiar domestic location of the living room, where the small 405-line receivers, regarded as unsuitable for long shots because of the lack of definition, could reveal in close-up all the range and sensitivity of an actor's performance. Michael Barry (Head of Television Drama) exemplified this position in a 1953 article in *New Chronicle* entitled 'TV Is Creating It's Own Drama'. He wrote:

> There is no particular mystery in writing for television. But there are certain rules to follow. The television screen is very small, and so it is desirable to have as few characters as possible. ... The television camera is very penetrating. It shows what is going on in people's minds. Sincerity is, therefore, the most important quality required of both writers and actors. ... A great deal of television work is done in close-up. Thus, elaborate sets are often wasted.[12]

At a time when television was struggling to define itself as a form of broadcasting separate and distinct from radio, Barry was keen to stress the new stylistic and narrative possibilities of the medium (see Jacobs, 2000, pp. 95–6). Yet here, Barry defines the aesthetic possibilities of television drama through critical assumptions about the medium's technical and aesthetic limitations. This intimate model places a particular emphasis on the 'liveness' and simultaneity of television, which can relay the immediacy of a live performance *as it happens*. Unsuitable for crowd scenes or complex sets because of its small screen and low quality images, television's value is located here in its ability to relay the intimacy and sincerity of an actor's live performance into the viewer's home.

In a period when television drama was largely produced and transmitted live, television is here understood as a medium ideally suited to the mediation of a continuous dramatic performance.[13] In this 'intimate' model of television drama, the emphasis is placed on *what* is relayed through the television, rather than on the *process* of mediation. Here the technology of television, as John Caughie suggests, is seen to be at the *service* of the performance, rather than contributing to the *creation* of the performance:

Early television drama was a continual attempt to resolve the overwhelming contradiction between a rather cumbersome technology of mediation (however 'immediate') and an aesthetic of live performance. Some of the uncertainty of aim ... lay in the assumption that the technology was there simply to serve the aesthetic rather than to produce it. (1991a, p. 29)

Jason Jacobs argues that it was the arrival of Nigel Kneale and Rudolph Cartier at the BBC 'that challenged the intimate drama directly' (2000, p. 130). In talking about their early work, Kneale and Cartier placed a particular emphasis on television's potential as a *visual* medium with a closer affinity to cinema than radio. Talking about the influence of the cinema on his work, Kneale stated,

In the early years I went to the cinema about twice a week and was really influenced. I wanted to make my work more visual: less making points in verbal terms and more paying off through images, which you tended not to get then. Most of the stuff was designed for actors to make big points with a big verbal display in a speech instead of what one would try to do in a decent screenplay, which was to let the camera tell the story. (Cited in Wells, 1999, p. 49)

Kneale's rhetoric here, which opposes the visual to the verbal, relates directly to the 'intimacy' debate. Television is a visual medium. Kneale's desire to make his work 'more visual', needs to be understood specifically in relation to the *kind* of visuality against which he is fighting. He is arguing for a style where the drama and action are not to be found simply in the close-up relay of a sensitive, live performance by an actor, but in the construction of a story through images as they are framed and relayed by the camera. Here he argues against the 'intimate' notion of television as a technology that can unobtrusively relay an actor's performance, and instead emphasises the camera's role in visually constructing the drama.

In the tradition in which television horror thrillers are associated with stylistic experimentation, Kneale and Cartier used the fantastic premise of the three 1950s *Quatermass* serials to move away from locating the action in 'a big verbal display', towards exploring the potential for the story to be constructed visually through the camera. In each serial the narrative progresses towards the moment(s) in which a 'fantastic' event or object which confounds socio-cultural verisimilitude is *displayed* through a visual set piece. The penultimate episode of *The Quatermass Experiment* culminates with a huge plant-like alien (a mutation of the surviving astronaut of the first manned space flight) being spectacularly revealed overwhelming Poet's Corner in Westminster Abbey.[14] The final episode of *Quatermass II* depicts Quatermass and his colleague Dr Pugh travelling into space and destroying a large alien organism living on a meteor circling Earth. In the final episode of *Quatermass and the Pit*, a large, devil-like image is projected into the sky by an unearthed alien ship causing a wave of riots and telekinetic activity across London. In each serial there is an escalation of the drama, leading to the climactic moment in which the alien entity is *spectacularly revealed* to the audience (and the characters) in a *visual* set piece where the image plays a central signifying role.

To examine this further, I want to take *The Quatermass Experiment* as an example. Although there are no existing prints of the last four episodes of *The Quatermass Experiment* the camera script gives an indication of the shape and tone of the climax to the penultimate episode, which depicts a BBC outside broadcast from Poet's Corner in Westminster Abbey.[15] The action cuts between the interior of the Abbey and the interior of the scanner van where the director, his secretary and a television engineer prepare for the broadcast and give instructions to the crew within the Abbey. From within the van the secretary suddenly half rises and cries 'Look!' as she stares at the monitor transmitting images from the camera within the Abbey. The engineer also sees something on the monitor and exclaims 'Up above Poet's Corner – there's something moving'. The action remains within the scanner van for a moment as the director, secretary and engineer stare at the monitor before finally cutting to a model shot from within the Abbey of the alien descending down Poet's Corner. Here the fantastic element of the story is told in visual rather than verbal terms. The scant dialogue does not serve to describe the alien being but functions rather to emphasise the sheer spectacle of *seeing* the alien monster visually displayed.

In constructing a serial that climaxes with the depiction of a giant alien creature in a large historic British building, Kneale and Cartier are challenging an understanding of television as an intimate medium incapable of crowd scenes or complex sets. However, the technical limitations of early television production restricted the extent to which it could be used to create such visually spectacular set pieces. These scenes of the creature in Westminster Abbey were shot live in Studio A of Alexandra Palace with four bulky cameras that had been in use since the television service first began regular transmissions in 1936.[16] At a time when there was no special effects department for television production, Kneale describes the primitive techniques they used to create the model shots of the monster, 'I had a still picture of the Poet's Corner blown up to 4ft, cut a section out and put my hands through. They were covered with rubber gloves, wire, and wash leather. They looked like evil tendrils 40ft long'.[17]

The climatic conclusion in episode six of *The Quatermass Experiment*, where Quatermass enters the Abbey and appeals to the remnants of humanity in the creature, exemplifies the particular way in which Cartier and Kneale manipulated the technical limitations of television production through visual storytelling. The sequence is shot live in the studio almost entirely in close-ups, cutting between Quatermass and model shots of the monster, overlaid by sound effects of the creature's rustling tendrils. This suggests that Quatermass and the monster inhabit the same physical location without the need to create a life-sized model of the creature in the studio. Occasionally Quatermass and the monster are depicted in the same shot, but the use of close-ups allows this to be achieved through the creation of one or two 'life-sized' tendrils that can be operated from out of shot. For example, as Quatermass plays an audio tape of the moment when the astronauts were initially attacked by the creature in space, the alien becomes increasingly agitated. The camera script describes how this was achieved by remaining on a close-up of Quatermass as 'Tendrils sway into shot near Quatermass and quickly away'. These techniques allow Cartier and Kneale to provide a visually spectacular climax in which the monster is revealed while still functioning within the limitations of live television production. Furthermore, the use of close-ups to suggest that Quatermass and the monster are in the same physical setting also enables the mon-

In episode one of *The Quatermass Experiment*, Professor Quatermass confronts the one surviving astronaut, Victor Caroon, as he steps out of the first manned space craft that has crash-landed on Earth

ster to suddenly invade Quatermass's space, heightening the intensity and danger of the scene.

Cartier has argued that the close-up is a particularly powerful tool in television production. He claimed that within the dark and intimate environment of the living room, 'where close-ups appear life-size or even bigger' (Cartier, 1958, p. 10), the television close-up was capable of bringing the audience much closer to the action than they could be in the cinema. For Cartier, the intimacy afforded by the close-up in television was not restricted to an increased closeness between viewer and character/actor, as Michael Barry suggested. It provided a specific dramatic tool which, when coupled with the domestic location of television, could be exploited to increase tension and suspense.

Cartier's deployment of the close-up to evoke fear and horror is particularly evident in the cliff-hangers at the end of each episode. The first episode of *The Quatermass Experiment* is concerned with the return of the missing rocket ship after it disappears while orbiting Earth. When it crash-lands on Wimbledon Common, onlookers and reporters arrive to see the rocket, while the scientists wait for the hull to cool enough to release the astronauts. This scene is shot predominantly in mid-shots and is steadily paced to suggest the gradual passage of time. When the rocket is finally opened, Quatermass realises that Victor Carroon is the only one of the three astronauts to have returned and marches out to confront him. Carroon is centred in the frame and picked out by a key light while Quatermass stands on the left shaking him angrily. As Quatermass lets go of Carroon he falls directly towards the camera so that his face momentarily fills the screen, revealing a mere glimpse of the terror in his expression before the image dissolves into a blur and fades to the end credits.

Here again, Cartier uses the technical limitations of studio production and the fantasy/ horror story to his advantage. The bulky studio cameras used to shoot *The Quatermass Experiment* were not very mobile and had fixed lenses which made zooming or fast tracking impossible. Cartier overcomes this technical difficulty by keeping the camera still and moving the actor. The effect of this movement is heightened through the slow smooth choreography of the preceding scenes. After the careful build-up to the expected return of the heroic astronauts, the sudden and rapid close-up of Carroon's terrified face is a particularly shocking and potent device. Carroon falls into the camera, literally invading and occupying the entire space of the screen in the corner of the viewer's living room.

For Cartier, television as a medium was particularly suited to such 'horrific' scenes because of its domestic reception. He argued that the viewer at home, away from the distractions and reassurances of the communal viewing experience of cinema, was more easily frightened and ready to accept the fantastic as plausible. He compared the film and television versions of *The Quatermass Experiment* to make his point:

> When the viewer was watching these 'horrific' TV productions of mine, he was – I like to think – completely in my power, and accepted the somewhat far-fetched implications of the plot (such as the man who turned into a vegetable) without a murmur, while in the cinema, there was usually a titter or false laugh whenever one of these scenes came up. (1958, p. 10)

Cartier's comments about the reaction to the *Quatermass* serials presuppose a particular form of domestic television reception (the isolated viewer in a darkened living room) at a time when much television viewing was a communal activity structured around special events and fail to take into account the differences between the television and film versions of the stories. However, they do suggest that in constructing the horrific scenes in *The Quatermass Experiment*, Cartier developed a visual style that took advantage of the intimacy associated with the medium in order to engage and horrify the audience.

John Caughie has argued that the large number of 'demonstration' programmes in early British television 'gives a sense of the homeliness of television's early notion of the domestic and the delicacy with which the BBC intruded into the home' (2000, p. 32). As Jeffrey Sconce has demonstrated, the introduction of television as a domestic technology was accompanied by anxiety about the 'electronic presence' of this new medium that combined sound and moving images.

> The ability of this box in the living room to 'talk' and 'see' ... made the medium something more than merely an inanimate technology. Television exuded a powerful presence in the household, serving in the active imagination as a fantastic portal to other worlds or even as a sentient entity brooding in the corner of the living room. Early television owners recognized that this medium had a qualitative 'presence' that distinguished it from radio, a presence that made the medium even more fantastic and perhaps more sinister as well. (2000, p. 131)

Cartier played with this sense of unease about the alien presence of this seemingly sentient new medium within the domestic space of the home. Inverting the cosy domesticity with which the BBC traditionally addressed the viewer, he used the intimacy afforded by the tele-visual close-up to bring the viewer suddenly and unexpectedly face to face with the horrific.[18]

Although the *Quatermass* serials offered Cartier and Kneale a means of creating spec-tacular sequences that *expanded* the possibilities of television's 'intimate' screen, such moments of spectacle are equally constructed to *exploit* the intimacy of early television's small screen and domestic reception. As Jacobs (2000) has argued in relation to Kneale and Cartier's adaptation of Orwell's *1984* (BBC, 1954), their challenge to the intimate tendency in 1950s television was not a rejection of the notion of television as an intimate, domestic medium, but rather a rejection of the notion that these attributes negate the aesthetic poten-tial of television itself.

Representing the Fantastic: Narratives and Characters

While the representation of the fantastic in the *Quatermass* serials offered Kneale and Cartier the opportunity to experiment with the aesthetic potential of television drama in the 1950s, this occurred not just in relation to visual style, but also in relation to the construction of nar-ratives and characters. As discussed in the introduction, the representation of the fantastic involves certain regimes of expectation. As Steve Neale (2000) has argued, all genre texts combine generic and socio-cultural verisimilitude. However, this is further complicated in fan-tasy narratives, which are concerned in part with representing non-verisimilitudinous events or objects. That is, objects that confound the socio-cultural verisimilitude of the text itself and of the viewer's lived reality. Within each *Quatermass* story there are regimes of generic and socio-cultural verisimilitude that combine to represent the non-verisimilitudinous 'fantastic' events and/or objects. The serials make use of the generic iconography of science fiction, such as the space rockets in *Quatermass II* and *The Quatermass Experiment*, and the curved metal alien spaceship in *Quatermass and the Pit*. They depict scientific advancements beyond their time of production, such as manned space flight in *The Quatermass Experiment* and the pro-duction of synthetic food in *Quatermass II*. In these serials the viewer is encouraged to read these generically coded 'fantastic' elements *as* 'real'. While giant vegetable aliens and space-craft confound the socio-cultural verisimilitude of the 1950s viewer, the serials work hard narratively and stylistically to reinforce the plausibility and believability of such fantastic elements. These are depicted as being as 'real' as the socio-culturally verisimilitudinous rep-resentations of elements, such as Wimbledon Common and the streets of London.

The serials use a number of strategies to reinforce the plausibility of their fantastic narra-tives. Each serial is situated within a fictional world that is written and shot to resemble 1950s Britain. All three serials use contemporary 1950s costumes and sets, with visual and narrative references to current events, such as the extension to London's underground system, which was taking place in 1958 and forms the setting for *Quatermass and the Pit*. This is further enhanced through the use of filmed sequences within all three serials. The use of filmed inserts in television drama was relatively limited in the early 1950s, and was often reserved for establishing location shots, or to give the actors a chance to change costume or location. Jacobs argues that the ways in which Cartier *integrated* filmed inserts into the studio footage can be understood as part of his attempt to expand television drama out of the intimacy of the television studio (2000, pp.130–2). Cartier was particularly skilled at overcoming the difficulties of matching the filmed inserts to the studio footage, as the two different types of material were visually quite distinct. However, this integrated use of filmed footage in the *Quatermass* serials can also be understood to situate these narratives within a fictional world that is visually grounded in the socio-cultural verisimilitude of the 'real' world of the 1950s viewer. In *The Quatermass Experiment*, a filmed sequence of St James's Park in London is combined with studio sets of the park to reveal the devastation left by an almost fully mutated Carroon. In *Quatermass II*, filmed inserts of the Shell Haven refinery in Essex are mixed in with studio sets to represent the experimental plant overtaken by alien invaders. *Quatermass and the Pit* begins with the filmed sequence of a construction site for the extension of the underground in London's Knightsbridge before cutting to a studio set of the dig in which an alien spaceship is unearthed. The relative lack of such filmed location material in live studio television drama, combined with the skill with which Cartier overcame the difficulty of matching the filmed inserts to the studio footage, heightens the sense of contemporaneity and plausibility in these serials by combining fantastic images with recognisable locations.

This contemporaneity is further reinforced by a narrative emphasis on the impact of the alien invasions on the everyday lives of ordinary people. In *The Quatermass Experiment* an elderly woman's home is destroyed by the returning space rocket and the infected Carroon brutally kills an innocent chemist. Sequences such as armed guards killing a working-class family picnicking next to the secret installation in *Quatermass II* emphasise the threat of the fantastic events to ordinary people and their everyday pleasures. In the climax of *Quatermass and the Pit*, the unearthed alien craft triggers a repressed memory in humans that results in a violent riot that sweeps across London. The action cuts from the disturbed site of the alien craft to a local pub and depicts the rapid descent of the customers from communal camaraderie to violent destruction.

As Peter Hutchings argues, such sequences evidence the ways in which these tales of alien invasion engage with the social anxieties of post-war Britain, both in their ambivalent attitude towards science, and in their deconstruction of the pervasive wartime concept of the national collective (1999, pp. 40–1). For Kneale, science-fiction and horror narratives offered an opportunity to develop challenging material that tackled issues of contemporary social importance at a time when television was a relatively open arena for the exploration of new material. He wrote in 1959:

> that is the attraction of television at the present time – its readiness to tackle subjects that the film industry might balk at. Minority-appeal pieces, or what later turn out to be majority-appeal pieces but which at first are new and frightening to the delicate senses of impresarios. TV is more receptive simply because its programme space has to be filled somehow, and costs are relatively low. (1959, p. 88)

Kneale implies that, in this period of growth and experimentation, television provided him with a forum to experiment with the narrative (as well as visual) possibilities of popular fictional forms that were not readily available in British cinema.

The production processes of television in the 1950s made it particularly suited to the exploration of socially relevant subject matter. The time from commissioning to transmission in television was relatively short. Indeed, the final episodes of *The Quatermass Experiment* were being written while the first episodes were being transmitted (Pixley, 1998, p. 41). This enabled television to address contemporary issues with an immediacy that was not possible in the cinema. In the foreword to the published script of *Quatermass II*, Kneale explains how the fantastic premise of the drama dealt with social anxieties which were relevant to its specific period of production and transmission in 1955.

> It was 1955, an unconfident time. There was much public concern about a new brand of
> bureaucracy, which manifested itself in the form of secret establishments: giant radars
> reputed to endanger human life and concealed in huge plastic pods; germ-warfare
> establishments behind barbed wire; atom-proof shelters for chosen administrators. Imagine,
> then, a huge plant that looks something like an oil refinery with some inexplicable additions,
> set up ostensibly to produce synthetic foodstuffs, which indeed it does make but not for
> human consumption ... and the menace is firmly established on Earth before its real nature
> can be known. (1979, p. 6)

Hence, while the representation of the fantastic enabled the metaphorical treatment of social anxieties, the immediacy of television production allowed these serials to deal with issues that were particularly resonant to their contemporary audiences.

The emphasis on socio-cultural verisimilitude in the series' representation of the fantastic is reinforced through narrative explanation, primarily in the form of scientific discourse, which functions to reassert the plausibility of the fantastic events portrayed. As a leading scientific innovator, Quatermass is invested with scientific and moral authority. Over the three serials, this authority is tested and undermined. Quatermass's rocket in *The Quatermass Experiment* is the catalyst for the ensuing alien invasion. In *Quatermass II*, Quatermass struggles to overcome the technical difficulties in sending another rocket into space, and in *Quatermass and the Pit* he is forced to fight for the integrity and control of his scientific plans for further space missions against interference from the military. Despite this, the narrative structure of all three serials works to reinforce the authority invested in Quatermass and in science. Although scientific enterprise is responsible for disastrous consequences in the first two *Quatermass* serials, it is only through science that the alien invasions are overcome. Here the character of Quatermass is central. First, he is the primary protagonist and the only character to recur in all three serials. Second, he is invested with the narrative authority to understand and *explain* the fantastic events depicted.

These two elements function through the structure of the television serial to assert Quatermass's narrative authority. Each *Quatermass* serial is a self-contained story consisting of six thirty- to thirty-five-minute episodes. The primary narrative thrust of each serial is towards uncovering, understanding and overcoming the alien threat to Earth. As such, while the serials are more commonly associated with science fiction and horror, their basic narrative premises are much like that of the detective story in which the viewer acquires clues with the 'detective' (Quatermass), who is able to showcase his skills by piecing them together to solve

the mystery. As a consequence, the threat is overcome and the story is brought to a clear resolution.[19] Franco Moretti argues that, 'Detective fiction, through the detective, celebrates the
man who gives the world a meaning' (1988, p. 155). In the finale of each *Quatermass* serial, it is Quatermass who, through his scientific investigations, is able to explain the events
of the narrative and, through his knowledge, avert catastrophe and bring about narrative
resolution.

However, in these serials the acquisition of 'clues' through scientific analysis has a second
powerful function. With each piece of information and each act of deduction the extent of
the alien threat is further revealed. Hence while the acquisition of knowledge by Quatermass
eventually leads to the destruction of the alien threat, it equally corresponds to the increase
in tension, fear and danger over each serial. This gradual increase of tension is exacerbated
by the narrative structure of these serial dramas, which places an emphasis on disruption,
suspense and uncertainty through the use of cliff-hangers at the end of each episode. The
cliff-hangers therefore have two related functions: the revelation of a discovery (often scientific) that extends our knowledge of the alien threat; and the increase in fear and suspense
as the danger becomes more palpable. For example, the narrative thrust of *Quatermass II*
concerns the attempts by Quatermass and his colleagues to investigate the appearance of
unusual objects on Earth and their link to an experimental government project to develop
synthetic food. In episode four Quatermass goes to the plant where synthetic food is being
pioneered. His suspicions that the plant is a cover for an alien invasion are confirmed in the
final shot of the episode. As he inspects a vast chamber that should contain synthetic food,
a point-of-view shot depicts a writhing alien monster living within. This shot both reveals the
alien and offers visual proof of the alien threat to Quatermass and to the audience, combining narrative development and spectacular display in a single moment.

Furthermore, while the domestic location of these television serials may have intensified
the creation of horror and fear (as Cartier (1958) argued), when combined with the use of
extended serial narratives, it equally functions to create intimacy between the viewer and the
recurring characters. The structure of the serial form functions to balance narrative/character
development with the repetition of familiar pleasures. Hence, while each episode of *The
Quatermass Experiment* introduces new narrative twists, at the same time it must correspond
to the expectations established in the opening episodes, in terms of tone, setting, characters
and so on. Furthermore, as Martin McLoone argues in relation to the 1950s television Western series, because of the domestic location of television, extended television narratives
become intimately integrated into the weekly routines of viewers:

> intimacy results from the context of viewing – the home, most commonly imagined as the
> family home. But intimacy also comes from the continuity of the television series or serial, the
> recurring characters, locales and situations that become part of the habituated viewer's
> domestic experience. (1997, p. 89)

The kinds of Western series that McLoone discusses have a different narrative structure to
the *Quatermass* serials as each episode presents a self-contained story based around a recurring setting and group of characters. Yet, the intimacy and familiarity to which he refers is

also apparent in the *Quatermass* serials. As I have argued, the exploitation of the close-up in the creation of a horrific cliff-hanger functions precisely in relation to the intimate and domestic location of television. Furthermore, for the regular viewer, these moments are integrated into an ongoing narrative that, for the six weeks of transmission of each serial, would become part of their weekly routine, offering a particular kind of intimacy and familiarity between the viewer and the recurring characters. This 'domestication' places an important emphasis on the construction of the characters. Indeed, moments of visual display function as much to create an intimate relationship between character and viewer, as to create shock, awe or fear. When Carroon falls into the camera at the end of the first episode of *The Quatermass Experiment* the viewer is intimately drawn into his personal anguish, while the revelation of an alien organism in the synthetic food plant in episode four's cliff-hanger in *Quatermass II* reinforces the narrative authority invested in Quatermass.

This domestication in the *Quatermass* serials takes place within each serial and across the three serials as a whole. The two sequels to *The Quatermass Experiment were* produced within the context of the success of the original serial, at a time when the *Quatermass* format was known to viewers and programme-makers, and within a new era of competition for the BBC following the introduction of ITV in September 1955. Jacobs notes that the introduction of competition necessitated the differentiation of BBC programming from ITV, leading to the routinisation of the schedules and an increase in the production of serial drama (2000, p. 115). The organisation of the schedules into regular patterns was already occurring in the early 1950s, as television began to establish a place in the daily lives and routines of its viewers. On a typical Saturday in 1953, the BBC transmitted sport during the day, two hours of children's programmes during the early evening (5.00–7.00pm), and a drama serial, a selection of variety programmes and news in the evening (7.00–11.00pm). *The Quatermass Experiment* was produced to fill a gap in this schedule, and although the transmission time for this first serial varied, its half-hour episodes were consistently aired between 8.15pm and 9.30pm over six consecutive Saturdays, in a slot that was regularly used to screen thirty-minute serial drama.[20]

The scheduling for *Quatermass II* and *Quatermass and the Pit* was further formalised with each episode transmitted at the same time every week. The standardisation of the scheduling of serial drama becomes particularly important in a competitive environment as it situates each episode in a regular slot in the schedules. As Jacobs argues:

> Until this point, scheduling of Saturday night serials had been variable, with episodes of the same serial shown perhaps half an hour later or earlier from one week to the next. Now that the BBC schedule was in competition with ITV this inconsistent approach to transmission times was inappropriate: *Quatermass II* was always shown and repeated at the same times. (2000, p. 115)

The increase in the production of serial dramas after 1955 and the development of regular scheduling patterns reflected the value of serial production to the BBC as a form of drama which was both cheaper to produce than the single play and which ensured a regular audience over a number of weeks. The BBC's viewing figures for the three *Quatermass* serials all indicate a similar viewing pattern in which the audience numbers remain largely consistent, though with a gradual increase for the final instalments.[21] In BBC research conducted on sample audiences, over 75 per cent of the viewers watched at least five episodes of *The Quatermass Experiment*, while this grew to 90 per cent for *Quatermass II* and 79 per cent for *Quatermass and the Pit*. What these figures indicate is the potential for serial drama to attract regular audiences over an extended period of time. The serials' cliff-hanger narratives contribute to this, enticing viewers to watch the following week's instalment.

As a sequel produced in a newly competitive environment at a time when the television audience had grown by over 50 per cent,[22] *Quatermass II* needed to maintain the appeal of the original serial while not alienating new viewers. This problem is further complicated for a serial whose appeal lay largely in its originality. In an article in *Radio Times* to promote *Quatermass II*, Kneale said of *The Quatermass Experiment*, 'Part of the impression it made was perhaps due simply to being the first of its kind' (Kneale, 1955, p. 7). Yet Kneale was at pains to assert that *Quatermass II* 'has no direct connection with its predecessor' (ibid.).[23] In a memo to Cecil McGivern defending the quality of the script for *Quatermass II*, Kneale asserted

> I have tried to make this serial as effective as its predecessor, but in quite a different way: a logical extension. Given the publicly-expected components of the dogged professor, rocketry and things from space, in terms of (substantially) live production, the possibilities are not infinite; but I eventually worked out a story that seemed more than mere repetition.[24]

This suggests that for the second and third serial, the public expectations associated with the repeated elements of the *Quatermass* 'format', such as 'the dogged professor, rocketry and things from space' were as significant as the expectations associated with science fiction and horror as genres. While this notion of a serial format differs from Cawelti's notion of formulas as 'universal story archetypes' (1976, p. 6), it retains a similar relationship to audience expectation. Cawelti argues that formulas create their own field of reference and are judged by audiences in relation to previous examples of the type itself. Formulas therefore function by 'intensifying an expected experience' (Cawelti, 1976, p. 10). Here Kneale is situating his construction of *Quatermass II* precisely in relation to this need to fulfil and intensify audience expectations of the *Quatermass* format, formed either from direct viewing or from hearing about the original series. This sense of expectation is further enhanced for the production of the third serial. According to the BBC viewer research report for the first episode of this serial,

> even those viewers who were a trifle lacklustre about the first part of *Quatermass and the Pit* wanted to see further episodes, some supporting a manager's point that this was 'not primarily because of today's instalment but because of previous serials' (which were remembered with pleasure).[25]

The expectation encompassed in the *Quatermass* format shifts the terms by which the function of spectacle and narrative within these serials can be understood, as the original *Quatermass* serial itself (and the public discourses surrounding it) became part of the generic verisimilitude through which the sequels were viewed. One of the primary ways in which spectacle is created in *The Quatermass Experiment* and the intimate address of television expanded, is through the representation of images and techniques not common to television production in 1953. For example, the use of model shots to represent the mutated astronaut inside Westminster Abbey, and the careful integration of filmed inserts with live studio transmission. At this time, television's capacity for visual spectacle and expansive drama was limited by the technological restrictions in television production and the low definition of the receivers. By 1955, BBC television production had moved to the superior facilities at Lime Grove, and television budgets had begun to increase.[26] The most striking difference between *The Quatermass Experiment* and its sequels is the increase in location shooting and crowd scenes, which responds in part to the technological improvements in television production and receivers,[27] and the need for 'something different in atmosphere and story' (Kneale, 1955, p. 7). The emphasis on these two developments enables the sequels to display the expansion of the scope of television drama that *The Quatermass Experiment* had been particularly noted for, staying within the expectations for the serial while offering drama that is still stylistically exciting and unusual. For example, in episode five of *Quatermass II*, a filmed sequence depicts the workers at the plant under investigation mounting a riotous attack against their employers. This dynamic sequence combines close-ups of individual characters with long shots of the crowd of workers as they engage in an armed fight with the plant's guards. While part of the impact of this scene comes from the representation of such a violent, working-class uprising, this is reinforced by the use of a rapidly edited filmed sequence that displays television's ability to represent spectacular crowd scenes without compromising its intimacy.

The combination of spectacle and intimacy is evident in episode four of *Quatermass and the Pit* in which a workman unleashes a wave of telekinetic activity causing lamps and cables to move of their own volition

The sequence cuts from close-ups of the workman's terrified face to long shots, such as this one depicting cables lashing around him as he tries to escape, which display the series' special effects

The use of spectacle to display television's propensity as a visual medium is further exploited through the increasing presence of special effects in *Quatermass and the Pit*, where the unearthed spaceship unleashes a wave of paranormal occurrences which recur over the serial. By this time, the BBC had a special effects team who were responsible for dealing with the effects' requirements within all television dramas, and supervised the creation of all the effects for *Quatermass and the Pit*. Episode four ends with an extended sequence in which a workman causes a frenzy of telekinetic activity. While this scene (transmitted live from the studio) focuses on the workman, frequently cutting to close-ups of his anguished face, it combines this with a series of spectacular special effects in which planks of wood and cups and saucers fly independently through the air and cables violently lash of their own volition. These sequences both fulfil and intensify the expectations for the aesthetic and technical experimentation of *The Quatermass Experiment*, as well as the generic and narrative expectations for exciting cliff-hangers and a suspenseful narrative.

Representing Cinema and Television in the *Quatermass* Serials

Finally, the complex regime of expectations at work in the *Quatermass* serials needs to be understood in relation to the broader generic expectations associated with both science fiction and television in the 1950s. Despite the use of iconic and narrative conventions associated *with* science fiction within all three serials, Nigel Kneale was anxious to avoid labelling them *as* 'science fiction'.[28] In 1959 he wrote, 'I don't like the term "science-fiction" ... The form is appropriate, if taken seriously. And that is the way I do take it. I try to give those stories some relevance to what is round about us today' (1959, p. 88). Kneale's resistance to the term science fiction stems from the dominant associations of science fiction with US cinema in Britain in the early 1950s. Indeed, the primary competition for *The Quatermass Experiment* was seen to come from science-fiction cinema, and in 1953 this was primarily in the form of films from the US.[29]

Despite the production of British horror thrillers on film and television in the post-war period, there was relatively little British science fiction in cinema or television in the early 1950s. When Kneale was writing *The Quatermass Experiment* in 1953, the most visible form of audiovisual fantasy narratives in the UK came from US cinematic science fiction, which had begun to develop as a popular film genre after the release of *Destination Moon* in 1950 (see Sobchack, 1987, p. 12; and Biskind, 1983, p. 102). It was not until the release of Hammer's film adaptation of *The Quatermass Experiment* in 1955 that British science-fiction/horror cinema emerged as a popular film genre. Indeed, the distinct blend of horror and science fiction that would go on to characterise the British cycle of the film genre over the 1950s and 1960s has been attributed to the innovations of the television version of *The Quatermass Experiment* (see Petley, 1986; and Hunter, 1999).

Therefore, despite his desire to make his television dramas more 'cinematic', Kneale was keen to differentiate the *Quatermass* serials from the expectations associated with US science-fiction cinema of the early 1950s. Looking back on writing the first serial in 1953 he claimed:

At that time most science-fiction films were terrible, nearly always American, full of flag-waving sentiments and crude, dreadful dialogue, made with a singular lack of imagination and a total lack of interest in human characters. I wanted to get away from all that, plant it very firmly on the characters because there was no other choice, you simply couldn't launch into a load of special effects because there weren't any. (Cited in Petley, 1984/5, p. 23)

Kneale's rhetoric here seems to oppose his earlier description of the *Quatermass* serials as offering a means to move away from a form of drama that focused on character dialogue towards a more visual form of storytelling. Yet this is only the case if character and spectacle are viewed as being in opposition. As has been argued, throughout each of the *Quatermass* serials an emphasis on character works hand in hand with the build-up towards spectacular display in order simultaneously to make the alien threat both plausible and horrific. This use of character to enhance the visual and narrative impact of the spectacle works within the specific demands of the structure of serial television. Kneale's differentiation of *The Quatermass Experiment* from similar generic cinema points to the specific possibilities that he associated with *television* fantasy. Unable to create a vast number of sophisticated special effects, Kneale stresses the need for *television* fantasy to place an emphasis on character complexity and development. Yet for Kneale, the emphasis on character was not simply an inevitable consequence of the technical limitations of television, but a particular possibility that could be exploited through the specific aesthetic attributes of television as a medium.

Kneale is not only at pains to differentiate the *The Quatermass Experiment* from science-fiction cinema in interviews, but also through his representation of cinema and television within the fictional diegesis of the serial itself.[30] In episode four of *The Quatermass Experiment*, the astronaut Victor Carroon begins to mutate physically into an alien entity and goes on the run, hiding out in a cinema screening a 3-D US science-fiction film, *Planet of the Dragons*. The sequence in the cinema mixes filmed inserts of the movie, in which a Space-Girl and a Space-Lieutenant find love in the face of terrible danger from space dragons, with studio shots of an audience of middle-aged women watching the matinée screening while eating and talking noisily. The use of 3-D film here is a reference to the technological developments in Hollywood in the early 1950s designed to entice declining audiences back to the cinema. According to the camera script, the 3-D effect was created by double-printing the filmed sequences from *Planet of the Dragons*. As a consequence, far from looking visually spectacular, in this scene the 3-D effect would have made the sequences from *Planet of the Dragons* appear visually inferior to the clarity of the rest of the televised action. The irritated comments of one audience member within the diegesis, who exclaims of the 3-D spectacle, 'I dunno which is worse – with them on or with them off. Get a 'eadache or be driven loopy tryin' to watch it –', further denigrates the cinematic experience in favour of the experience of the television viewer watching comfortably at home. Furthermore, within *Planet of the Dragons*, moments of action take place off-screen. The monsters are heard, but never represented. This lack of spectacle is in direct contrast to the narrative of *The Quatermass Experiment*, which depicts Carroon's gradual transformation and finally reveals his monstrous alien form.

Science-fiction cinema is further denigrated within the diegesis through the comparisons drawn between the treatment of similar thematic material in *Planet of the Dragons* and *The Quatermass Experiment*. As the Space-Lieutenant begins a characteristically corny monologue, a slide is projected onto the screen displaying a photograph of Carroon and a caption 'Have you seen this man?'. The dialogue of the movie continues over these images as the Space-Lieutenant proclaims:

> There's a new world waiting to be built right here, Julie. Some day, maybe, on this very
> planet of the Dragons, kids'll be able to sit down in a corner drugstore, same as home.
> There'll be roads and schools and movies – same as back home. We'll build that new world,
> Julie … you and me … and a lot of ordinary people like us.

The juxtaposition of this monologue over the police notice to locate Carroon makes ironic reference to the treatment of the theme of alien invasion within both narratives. In the movie, it is the humans who are colonising an alien planet, recreating the landscape and ideology of the United States through the destruction of its indigenous inhabitants. In the television drama, it is Earth that is threatened with colonisation by alien invaders and humanity that stands to be destroyed. The film's cavalier treatment of the themes of invasion and colonisation, in which the Space-Lieutenant's commitment to the invasion of the alien planet is the catalyst for the Space-Girl's declaration of love for him, is contrasted with the television drama's more complex treatment of the consequences of alien invasion. The narrative of *The Quatermass Experiment* warns of the dangers of space exploration and of complacency towards man's position in the cosmos. It depicts Carroon's suffering as he struggles to resist the invading alien entity, and the fear and bravery of ordinary people in the face of potential destruction. The insertion of this film within the fictional diegesis therefore draws a contrast between the serious treatment of the themes of invasion, colonisation and scientific experimentation within the television narrative and the trivial treatment of similar generic terrain in US science-fiction cinema.[31]

In setting up a dichotomy between the simplistic, crude US science-fiction cinema and its own complex and serious narrative concerns, *The Quatermass Experiment* asserts the relevance and value of its fantastic narratives. This dichotomy is further emphasised by the representation of television within the fictional diegesis of *The Quatermass Experiment* itself. The moment in which the alien is revealed at the end of episode five, not only places an emphasis on *seeing* the alien creature, it also comments on television as a means of witnessing the world. Once the Abbey is evacuated at the start of episode six, the abandoned camera transmitting to the scanner van through which the alien was first viewed, becomes the only means by which information can be gained of the creature's activities.

It is particularly significant that the alien is depicted in Westminster Abbey, the site of Queen Elizabeth II's coronation just a month before. The televising of this historic occasion indicated the full potential of the new medium, as outside broadcast cameras transmitted the event live to receivers across the country, watched by over half the nation.[32] Peter Hutchings sees the use of this location in the climax of *The Quatermass Experiment* as 'a kind of iconoclasm . . . a furtive pleasure in seeing the Queen supplanted by a deadly alien monster about to reproduce' (1999, p. 38). However, there is also a commentary being made here on the relative roles and pleasures of television. While the coronation of Elizabeth II may have demonstrated the potential for television as a realistic medium capable of the live relay of significant events, the climax of *The Quatermass Experiment* suggests its capacity for a different kind of spectacle – the visual representation of fantastic events within an exciting and dramatic narrative.

There is a self-consciousness apparent in this use of the Abbey, which is further reiterated in the scenes depicting the technical and organisational background of live television. At the end of episode five, as the producer, his secretary and a television engineer prepare for the live outside broadcast from the Abbey, they discuss the potential difficulties of the programme and rehearse various camera movements. Finally they go on air, and as they do so, the action moves between the producer selecting camera shots within the van and the actual broadcast. In doing so, this sequence reiterates the aesthetic of 'liveness' that pervaded early television when the majority of television was broadcast live. As this sequence deconstructs the production processes of live television just moments before the monster is revealed within the Abbey (to both the fictional characters and the actual audience), it offers a powerful reminder that the spectacular images witnessed by the viewer are being relayed live from a television studio. By emphasising the sense of co-presence created by the liveness of early television drama, this sequence heightens the sense of realism. The viewer is seeing an image that actually exists at the moment of transmission, albeit in a different location. However, by drawing attention to the technical processes of television production, this sequence also heightens the sense of spectacle. The viewer is invited to marvel at the technical sophistication of the production of *The Quatermass Experiment* itself. The fictional representation of television within *The Quatermass Experiment*, therefore, has a dual function. First, in high-lighting television's role in relaying significant events live to the public it heightens plausibility and grounds the fantastic events depicted in a strong sense of socio-cultural verisimilitude. Second, through inviting comparison with the recent televising of the coronation, it draws attention to the new and daring nature of what is being represented within the serial, and in doing so displays the potential for television's fictional dramatic forms to depict images of an exciting and spectacular nature.

The self-consciousness with which *The Quatermass Experiment* represents both cinema and television within its fiction emphasises its production at a time when there was no con-sensus as to the precise nature and role of television as a medium. These aesthetic debates find particular currency in Kneale and Cartier's differentiation of television from film within the diegesis of *The Quatermass Experiment*, and in their discussion of the production of all three serials. Kneale and Cartier use the fantastic premise of the *Quatermass* serials, to explore the potential of television in a particular way. In attempting to challenge a conception of tele-vision as a medium whose value lies in the relay of adaptations of pre-existing high cultural forms or live events of historic significance, they use the propensity for spectacle in fantasy narratives to display television's potential to deliver visually exciting forms of popular fiction. However, in producing the *Quatermass* serials, Kneale and Cartier were not simply attempt-ing to create more expansive and spectacular drama. As Jacobs (2000) has argued, their desire to expand television's intimate screen involved a recognition of the particular formal features of early television – live production, domestic reception, small screen, serial narrative – as exemplifying the possibilities, rather than the limitations, of the medium. What is particularly striking about Cartier and Kneale's approach to creating the *Quatermass* serials is that they attempt to expand the scope of television drama into the action and spectacle afforded by fantasy narratives, while simultaneously recognising and exploiting the continuity, immediacy and intimacy created through the transmission of the extended narrative of the television serial into the viewer's domestic space.

Kneale and Cartier's desire to expand *and* exploit the aesthetics of early television drama is facilitated by the particular demands of the representation of the fantastic. The central premise of each serial relies on the representation of non-verisimilitudinous creatures, that is, beings that confound culturally constructed notions of what is believed to be true, such as the alien form that can transform humans into a large plant-like organism in *The Quatermass Experiment*. Yet, for this non-verisimilitudinous creature to be intelligible as such, it must be constructed in relation to generic and socio-cultural verisimilitude. In *The Quatermass Exper-iment* this occurs through: the placement of generic elements, such as space rockets, within a fictional world that corresponds to the social reality of the viewer; the denigration of sci-ence-fiction cinema to emphasise the complexity and plausibility of the television narrative; the investment of authority in a scientific discourse that provides narrative explanation; the exploitation of the 'liveness' aesthetic of early television; and the metaphorical treatment of contemporary anxieties. These generic and aesthetic elements function in relation to viewer expectation to construct a story which is recognisable and interpretable as both 'fantastic' (in that the events depicted go against socially constructed notions of reality) and 'real' (in that these fantastic events are made plausible and relevant to the contemporary viewer).

Conclusion

In exploring the representation of the fantastic in the *Quatermass* serials, it is apparent that Kneale and Cartier used the particular possibilities offered by the fantastic in relation to the specific demands of television production at this time. For Kneale and Cartier, these fantastic stories had two primary (and related) functions: to explore the stylistic possibilities of television drama; and to expand the thematic range of television drama by metaphorically addressing contemporary anxieties through new generic forms. The thematic concern with exploring contemporary anxieties in these serials functions with the formal concern of exploring contemporary television aesthetics to create drama that is *both* expansive and intimate, spectacular and character-driven, suspenseful and familiar, fantastic and socially relevant.

The *Quatermass* serials exemplify Jason Jacobs' claims that fantasy offered Kneale and Cartier 'a faster tempo and a broader thematic canvas ... in order to get out of the dominant stylistic trend of television intimacy' (2000, p. 134). However, the representation of the fantastic did not only demand new formal and stylistic innovations. In order to assert the plausibility and relevance of their fantastic tales, the *Quatermass* serials rely on the dominant aesthetic of liveness and intimacy in early television. As a consequence, in telling their fantastic tales, the *Quatermass* serials use familiar narrative and visual conventions, while equally challenging the dominant representational strategies of 1950s television production. What the next chapter goes on to explore is whether the same production and textual strategies recur in the representation of the fantastic in *The Prisoner*, and how they are negotiated within this different historical context of production.

Notes

1. WAC, T16/62/1, 9 August 1951.
2. Announced in the *Radio Times*, 10 July 1953, p. 3.
3. In 1953 sound-only licences fell below eleven million for the first time in five years, and they continued to fall as the number of combined sound and television licences grew (Briggs, 1979, p. 240).
4. The first new studio at Lime Grove was opened in May 1950, but it was not until 1954 that television broadcasting at Alexandra Palace was officially closed (Briggs, 1979, p. 238).
5. Cartier was credited as 'producer' of the serials, however, as Jason Jacobs points out, it was not until the middle of the decade that the differentiation between producer and director began to be established (2000, p. 111).
6. The film rights to *The Quatermass Experiment* were bought by Exclusive Films Ltd (who owned Hammer) in 1954, and in 1955 they released a film version entitled *The Quatermass Xperiment*. The title change was a marketing strategy used to highlight its classification under the X certificate which had been introduced for films with an adult content in 1951. Further film adaptations by Hammer of *Quatermass II* and *Quatermass and the Pit* followed in 1957 and 1967 respectively. In 1979, Thames transmitted a four-part television series entitled *Quatermass*, which was simultaneously produced as a film (entitled *The Quatermass Conclusion*) by Euston Films (see Newman,

1989; and Petley, 1984/5). See Appendix A for transmission details for the three *Quatermass* serials produced in the 1950s.

7. Cited in WAC, T5/2, 306/1, 13 March 1959.

8. Telerecording (known in the US as kinescope) made it possible to record live television transmissions on to film, and was used by the BBC from 1949 onwards, primarily to enable repeats of broadcasts of public events. From the early 1950s, telerecording was also occasionally used to record drama transmissions. However, repeats usually consisted of a second live performance rather than the transmission of the telerecording due to the higher visual quality of direct transmission and the contractual problems of transmitting a recorded repeat (see Barr, 1997, pp. 60–1). It was not until the mid-1950s that the repeat of the telerecording became more common, as in the repeats of *Quatermass II* (Jacobs, 2000, pp. 113–15).

9. It is worth stressing that although ITV was a commercial broadcaster funded by the sale of advertising, rather than by a licence fee, it was also regulated under a public service broadcasting remit (see Scannell, 2000, p. 51).

10. WAC, T31/141/1, 10 November 1954.

11. WAC, T28/124, 16 July 1951.

12. WAC, P655, 5 January 1953.

13. In July 1954, the first filmed serial, *I Am the Law*, imported from the US, was transmitted by the BBC and in November of that year, the BBC transmitted their first filmed series, *Fabian of the Yard*. However, at this time the majority of dramas (including the three *Quatermass* serials) were transmitted live.

14. The significance of Westminster Abbey as the site for this finale will be discussed below.

15. Telerecordings of the first two episodes of *The Quatermass Experiment* are held at the National Film and Television Archive in London, while the camera script for the entire series is held at the BBC Written Archives Centre.

16. WAC, Script for *The Quatermass Experiment*, Films 53/54. Also see Holliss (1983, p. 40).

17. WAC, P667, 12 November 1955.

18. Jason Jacobs argues that the representation of the telescreen in Kneale and Cartier's famous adaptation of George Orwell's *1984* (BBC, 1954) also challenged the 'cosy' address of BBC television by offering a representation of television which functions as a 'figurative reconstruction of the less "cosy" ideas of nearness, observation, visibility, and control' (2000, p. 153).

19. *Quatermass II* could be considered an exception to this as, although Quatermass destroys the alien, the final shot of him returning to Earth in his experimental rocket was ambiguous enough to cause a number of viewers to write to the BBC anxiously enquiring after the fate of their hero (WAC, T5/2, 540/1).

20. Jason Jacobs briefly discusses the development of the Saturday-night serial in relation to the consolidation of the television schedule in the early 1950s (2000, pp. 111–12).

21. The listening and viewing barometer produced by the BBC used a sample of viewers to estimate the percentage of the adult civilian population in the UK which watched each

programme (see Sydney-Smith for a useful overview of the BBC's audience research, 2002, pp. 15–19). For *The Quatermass Experiment* the audience percentage rose from 9.4 per cent for episode one, to 13.6 per cent for episode six (WAC, R9/35/2). When *Quatermass II* was transmitted the increase was less significant, probably due to the known quality of the serial, rising from 21 per cent to 24 per cent between the first and final instalments (WAC, R9/35/4). The viewing percentage for *Quatermass and the Pit* rose from 20 per cent for episode one to 29 per cent for episode six (WAC, R9/35/7).

22. Between 1953 and 1955 the number of combined sound and vision licences grew from 2,142,452 to 4,503,766 (Briggs, 1979, p. 240).

23. The desire to disassociate *Quatermass II* from *The Quatermass Experiment* in this publicity stems partly from Kneale's disappointment with the film version of the original serial, which was released almost simultaneously with the television transmission of *Quatermass II* in October 1955 (see Kneale, 1955, p. 7).

24. WAC, T5/2, 540/1, 5 November 1955.

25. WAC, T5/2, 302/1, 7 January 1959.

26. *Quatermass II* cost £7,308 to produce, £1,908 over its allocated budget of £5,500, and £3,308 more than the £4,000 budget allocated to *The Quatermass Experiment*. *Quatermass and the Pit* was allocated a budget of £15,000.

27. The size of television receivers gradually increased over the 1950s. In 1949 the largest television receivers had twelve-inch screens. Over the 1950s this gradually increased with the introduction of receivers with screens of fourteen to nineteen inches.

28. In fact the *Radio Times* listed *The Quatermass Experiment* as a 'thriller' (10 July 1953, p. 46).

29. A memo from the BBC's publicity officer to Lime Grove's television publicity officer specifically requests secrecy about the content of *The Quatermass Experiment* due to 'strong competition with films in science fiction of this kind' (WAC, T5/418, 17 June 1953).

30. A similar representation of television is found in *Quatermass and the Pit*, where the disastrous consequences of the military's attempts to enter the unearthed alien pod are captured by an outside broadcast unit televising the incident across the nation. However, neither *Quatermass II* nor *Quatermass and the Pit* contain representations of the cinema, largely because the expectations associated with the 'fantastic' elements of the *Quatermass* serials themselves had come to replace the expectations associated with US science-fiction cinema.

31. This sequence, while denigrating science-fiction cinema in favour of the television experience, is also offering a typically negative comment on the 'Americanisation' of popular culture in the post-war era.

32. The BBC's research indicated that 53 per cent of the adult population of Britain watched the procession to Westminster Abbey on television, while 56 per cent viewed the actual service (Briggs, 1979, p. 458).

2

SERIOUS ENTERTAINMENT

The Prisoner and British Television in the 1960s

Introduction

Over the 1960s, British television continued to expand, with the consolidation of the commercial television network at the beginning of the decade, and the introduction of a second BBC channel, BBC2, in 1964. This chapter will explore the use of fantasy as a production and a textual strategy in this different historical context, focusing on a case study of *The Prisoner* (ITV, 1967–8), a seventeen-part series produced for the commercial British independent television network (ITV). In *The Prisoner*, a man (known only as Number Six) is kidnapped and taken to a bizarre location termed 'the Village'. Unable to escape, Number Six (Patrick McGoohan) is subjected to a series of increasingly surreal physical and mental tests to uncover the information that he conceals. From a comparison of this description of the basic narrative of *The Prisoner* with the narratives of the *Quatermass* serials, the difficulties of dealing generically with fantasy are immediately apparent. If genre were understood as a form of classification, then *The Prisoner*'s tales of kidnap and interrogation would seem to be quite different from the *Quatermass* serials' stories of alien invasion. However, both of these programmes are premised upon the representation of 'fantastic' events that go against culturally received notions of 'reality'. By moving away from approaching fantasy in terms of what kinds of stories are told, to exploring how these stories are told, it is possible to ask whether these programmes share any production and/or textual strategies in the representation of the fantastic.

The Prisoner was produced in an industrial environment in which the impact of commercial television on the UK television industry was pivotal. This was a period in which the commercial imperative of independent television came under frequent criticism as anathema to the moral and cultural responsibilities of public service broadcasting. Criticisms of the increasing trivialisation of television broadcasting with the introduction of competition were bound up with concerns about the social effects of television, as the medium became increasingly integrated into everyday life. What impact did these debates have on the use of fantasy as a production and a textual strategy in *The Prisoner*? What does this analysis add to our understanding of telefantasy and television aesthetics?

Competing Television: ITV, Commercialisation and the US Market

Although established within a public service model regulated by the Independent Television Authority (ITA), independent television introduced competition into British television broadcasting for the first time. Initially ITV struggled to compete with the BBC, in part because of the technical restrictions on the new service.[1] At the end of 1955, only 30.8 per cent of television-owning homes (12.5 per cent of all homes) were capable of receiving ITV programming. However, the ITV network expanded rapidly with the installation of new transmitters and, by the end of 1965, this figure had grown to 94.4 per cent of television-owning homes and 82 per cent of all homes.[2] Despite the restrictions on the reach of the new network, as early as 1957 ITV's audience share in those homes capable of receiving both services was around 70 per cent, with the BBC audience share only 30 per cent.[3] The apparent popularity of the new ITV service over the BBC that these statistics suggested raised problems for the justification of the BBC's licence fee. Huw Weldon (Managing Director of BBC Television, 1968–75) suggested that in the late 1950s the 'seriously diminishing audiences put the very financial foundation of the BBC at risk' (Weldon, 1971b, p. 4). The BBC's position was further problematised by the sharp increase in the operating expenditure for television, from £7,033,044 in 1955–6 to £13,988,812 in 1958–9.[4] The Corporation responded by shifting its programming practices. The BBC rationalised its schedules, creating certain weekly 'landmarks', such as the Tuesday documentary, *The Wednesday Play*, and the Saturday-night variety show, to provide viewers with recognisable and high-profile BBC programmes at regular points throughout the week (see Fox, 1969, p. 8). The BBC also adopted a more competitive scheduling practice, placing similar programmes against those being shown by ITV. These competitive strategies were further enabled with the arrival of a second BBC channel, BBC2, in 1964. With a remit to offer minority-interest programming, BBC2 provided a site within which to schedule programmes with a more specialised appeal, as well as to offer alternatives to the programmes provided by both BBC1 and ITV.[5] By 1968, ITV had lost its ratings domination over the BBC and the audience ratio for BBC1 and ITV stabilised at around 50:50 (Fox, 1969, p. 9).

In television drama, the 1960s also saw a shift in production practices and an increasing dependence on the commercial foreign export market to offset the growing expense of television production in the UK. Technologically, the introduction of Ampex magnetic recording in 1959–60 led to the decline of live studio drama as television images could now be recorded onto videotape. There was also an increase in the amount of filmed drama, both in terms of filmed inserts in studio productions, and in terms of dramas originated on film itself (see Barr, 1997). These technological developments increased the costs of television production but also facilitated the export of television programmes abroad, creating an additional market where programme costs could be recouped. In 1961, BBC Television Enterprises was established as a commercial wing of the BBC's Television Service, and was largely responsible for the sale of BBC television programmes abroad. In 1966, BBC Television Enterprises exported 11,492 programmes, mainly to the Commonwealth.[6] As early as 1962–3, ITV exported around 14,000 programmes overseas, primarily drama series and light entertainment.[7]

At this time, the US television industry was becoming increasingly important for British television. While the US imported more television programmes to the UK than any other foreign country, for the UK broadcasters the US market offered a potentially lucrative site for British television exports. Lew Grade (managing director of the ITV programme company Associated Television (ATV)),[8] was particularly keen to infiltrate the US market.

My whole effort, as far as I'm concerned, is in television, production of television programmes and sales of programmes overseas, because what I found when I really went into the selling business was nobody knew that British television existed. And everybody looked upon America as *the* country in television. I said 'This is going to stop. We're going to sell all there is.' (Grade, in Bakewell and Garnham, 1970, p. 275)

Grade's television production company, the Incorporated Television Company (ITC), co-produced *The Adventures of Robin Hood* (ITV, 1955–9, CBS, 1955–8) with the US company Sapphire Films. The series was sold to the US network CBS in 1955, and ITC went on to find similar success in the US with *The Buccaneers* (CBS, 1956) and *The Adventures of Sir Lancelot* (NBC, 1957). In 1958, ITC was taken over by ATV, and in 1961, the company purchased the British National Studios (renamed Elstree Studios) for the production of television series (see Osgerby, Gough-Yates and Wells, 2001, pp. 18–19). Over the 1960s, ATV developed an increasingly successful export strategy, recognised in 1967 by the Queen's Award to Industry for outstanding achievements in the field of exports. The company focused on exporting to the lucrative US market through the production of filmed drama series. Drama series originated on film were the primary form of television programme imported from the US to the UK and also made up the largest part of the US networks' primetime schedules.

Although British broadcasters restricted the amount of foreign television imported into the UK (to around 15 per cent of programmes aired),[9] the presence of US dramas in the UK schedules affected both the production and scheduling of British television. The US television programmes imported to the UK were primarily filmed series whose episodes were either twenty-five or fifty minutes long, the standard timings required in the US to fit programmes into thirty-minute and one-hour scheduling slots with the addition of advertisements. These timings were gradually replicated in the BBC and ITV schedules, to accommodate both US programmes and British programmes produced for the UK and US markets. As Paul Fox states of the rationale for planning the BBC1 schedules in the late 1960s, 'we usually work in 25- and 50-minute segments . . . that is a key requirement: these are the only acceptable lengths for export; they are also the running time of programmes we import from the United States' (Fox, 1969, p. 7). The US television industry also favoured the production of long-running series produced in 'seasons' of around twenty-six episodes which were transmitted between September and June with repeats scheduled over the summer months. As the US market became increasingly attractive to British television producers, larger numbers of British television dramas were produced in this series format, and British television schedules began to adopt a similar pattern of 'seasons'. As Paul Fox explained in relation to scheduling on BBC1

The season – a term we are using more and more – runs from September to the beginning of June. The remaining three months are the summer season: this is the time when audiences are on holiday, artists are in summer shows, and television programmes feature repeats. (1969, p. 6)

This is not to suggest that, during the 1960s, British television simply adopted the scheduling and programming practices of US television. Over this period, British television continued to function within a public service remit, with a mixed schedule of programming and a strong commitment to the social and cultural responsibilities of public broadcasting. However, it is to argue that the presence of foreign, particularly US, programmes in British television schedules, combined with the increasing practice of exporting British programmes to the lucrative US market, had a direct effect on the organisation of British television schedules and on the types of programmes produced and transmitted. In the area of drama, this was most apparent in the development of filmed television series structured in seasons and running over a number of months. While the drama serial had been present on British television from 1938,[10] there was an increase in the development of British filmed series that adopted the form and genres of the imported US filmed series. ITC was at the forefront of this move, producing filmed action-adventure series such as *Danger Man* (1960–1, 1964–7), *The Saint* (1962–9), *The Prisoner* (1967–8) and *The Champions* (1968–9). While drama serials develop one overarching narrative that runs across all the episodes, these are all series that broadly adopt the action-adventure format of the US filmed series, with a narrative formula that enabled the depiction of recurring characters in a different perilous situation each week with little or no continuous narrative over the series as a whole.

Until the mid- to late 1990s, such action-adventure series had been largely omitted from histories of British television, which tended to focus on institutions and/or on programmes which fitted into a dominant notion of British television as primarily 'social realist' in style. In particular, studies of 1960s television had been shaped by an understanding of this period as a 'Golden Age' of British television drama that was characterised by social realist single-authored plays. Over the late 1990s, a body of work began to develop which attempted to redress this historical imbalance by reinstating other forms of drama (such as the action-adventure series and the police series) as an important part of the development of British television drama.[11] Despite this, scholarship on the history of British television drama in the 1960s is in danger of developing into two apparently separate and unconnected strands: one that explores the 'serious', difficult and controversial social realist dramas; and a second that explores the apparently commercial, popular and entertaining action-adventure series. The value judgments inherent in this choice of adjectives are deliberately provocative here. I do not want to suggest that the action-adventure series of the 1960s are never controversial (indeed, *The Prisoner* was particularly controversial). Nor do I want to suggest that the social realist dramas of the 1960s, such as 'Cathy Come Home' (BBC, 1966) were not popular or entertaining. What I do want to suggest is that these programmes tend to be discussed within different registers, and ones that spring from the existing notions of the differences between the authored, politically interventionist and socially relevant single play, and the formulaic, repetitive and playful drama series. These differences are further exacerbated when one considers that the majority of the 1960s dramas considered as 'serious' (to borrow from John Caughie's term (2000)) were transmitted by the BBC, and the majority of the action-adventure series were transmitted by ITV.[12] Hence we have a set of binary oppositions:

'Serious' Drama	*'Popular' Drama*
Social realist	Action-adventure/Generic
Deals with social concerns	Stylish and playful
Challenging and controversial	Entertaining and popular
Politically motivated	Commercially motivated
Primarily BBC	Primarily ITV

These oppositions are not necessarily misleading in relation to particular programmes or con-texts of production. Indeed, a recognition of the range and multiplicity of histories (in terms of form, production context and so on) in television is important if we are to fully account for the complexity of the medium's history. However, a failure to think across and beyond these binary oppositions can limit our understanding of the historical development of British television, and in particular our understanding of television in the 1960s. Indeed, by going on to explore the debates that arose around the production of *The Prisoner*, this chapter will argue that in the 1960s it is often around the very definition of and boundaries between the 'popular' and the 'serious' that the debates surrounding the production of television were enacted.

Producing *The Prisoner*

In many ways *The Prisoner* is exemplary of the 'popular' ITV drama of the 1960s. The series was central to the ITC's commercial success in the UK and the US in the late 1960s. Despite its early success in the mid-1950s with *The Adventures of Robin Hood*, *The Buccaneers* and *The Adventures of Sir Lancelot*, ITC struggled to successfully export British series to the US in the early 1960s. In 1961, the US network CBS transmitted ITC's spy drama *Danger Man* for a short six-month run,[13] but it was not until ITC reworked *Danger Man* specifically for the US market in 1965 (under the new title *Secret Agent*), extending its half-hour episodes to fifty minutes and shooting in colour film, that the company made a significant impact on the US market. *Secret Agent* was transmitted by CBS for two seasons between 1965 and 1966, while also running on the ITV network in the UK under its original title. In 1965, *Secret Agent*, and *The Saint*, were singled out by *Variety* as British series that 'firmly nailed a once-predominant notion that British production values are too sluggish for the US "big-league" broadcaster' (cited in Miller, 2000, p. 42).

The success of *Secret Agent* and *The Saint* facilitated the export of a number of other British action-adventure series to the US networks, such as *The Baron* (1966) and *Court-Martial* (1965). *Secret Agent* also made a star of its lead actor Patrick McGoohan both in the US and the UK, and by 1967 McGoohan was the highest paid actor on British television, reportedly earning over £2,000 a week (Davis, 1967, p. 30). It was primarily in response to McGoohan's success as the spy John Drake in *Secret Agent* that CBS purchased his next series *The Prisoner*.[14] As with the other ITC productions of this period, *The Prisoner* was a com-mercial project produced simultaneously for the UK domestic and the US export markets. The series was expensive to produce, with each episode costing around £75,000 and was shot at the MGM Studios in Borehamwood on 35mm colour film.

The decision to shoot the series on colour film is particularly indicative of the importance of the US market to the ITC at this time. When *The Prisoner* was first transmitted in the UK in October 1967, it was in black and white. By contrast, the series was transmitted in colour on the US network CBS. Although the first colour television transmissions occurred in Britain in 1967, these were restricted to BBC2, and it was not until 15 November 1969 that BBC1 and ITV followed suit (see Briggs, 1995, pp. 858–60). In the US, colour-television transmissions occurred as early as 1954, although it was not until the mid-1960s that the price of colour receivers had fallen enough to make them commercially attractive to viewers and the US networks began to heavily invest in the promotion of colour-television broadcasting. The increasing importance of colour broadcasting in the US led to the production of a number of British series, such as *The Prisoner*, that were shot on colour film and transmitted in colour in the US while being aired in black and white in the UK.[15] As the *ITA: Annual Report and Accounts 1966–67* suggested

> Filmed drama series are being produced increasingly in colour. In part this is in preparation for Independent Television's own colour service, in part it is an inevitable result of rising costs within the industry. It is increasingly difficult to recover the costs of a major filmed series within the United Kingdom: but at the same time the most important overseas markets demand colour. (1967, p. 13)

At this time, therefore, the filmed series offered a double bind to television producers in the UK, at once offering the possibility of increased revenue from overseas sales, while simultaneously increasing costs in order to meet the demands of the export market.

Despite the importance of overseas sales to the production of *The Prisoner*, the series was also a significant production for the ITV network. In the UK, *The Prisoner* was competitively scheduled across the ITV network on Sunday nights at 7.25pm,[16] a key slot in British television schedules. Audience research in the 1960s indicated that '50 to 60 per cent of the audience for most programmes come from the programme immediately before on the same network' (Fox, 1969, p. 11). Dubbed the 'inheritance factor', this research suggested the 7.30pm slot as a pivotal point for attracting an audience that would be likely to remain for the rest of the evening's viewing (see Weldon, 1971b, p. 6).[17] Therefore, the placement of *The Prisoner* at this point in the schedules suggests that the series was produced as part of a competitive *domestic* strategy to draw a large audience for the rest of the evening's programming on ITV, as well as being produced to appeal to the international (and specifically US) export market.

As with *The Prisoner*, the majority of the action-adventure series in the 1960s were produced for commercial television and many were successfully exported abroad. As such *The Prisoner* would seem to exemplify an increasing dominance of commercial imperatives in British television production in the 1960s. Yet in Britain the demands on commercial television in the 1960s were not simply financial. In 1962, the *Report on the Committee of Broadcasting 1960* (commonly referred to as the Pilkington Report after the chairman of the committee Sir Harry Pilkington) heavily criticised British commercial television for failing to fulfil its public service remit. The Report argued that the responsibilities of a public service broadcaster could not be reconciled with the profit motive upon which independent television had been established in the UK.

> The [Independent Television] Authority's task is to reconcile the two objects for which independent television is constituted and organised: two objects which do not coincide and which are, in a greater or lesser degree, opposed to one another. Because the incidental object – the sale of advertising time – is the commercial interest and duty of the companies, the natural inclination will be to pursue it as the main purpose. Their commercial product is desirable advertising time. As commercial organisations they exist to create and sell that product; it is their interest and duty as commercial undertakings to do so as successfully as they can …. This private objective does not coincide with the primary and essential public objective, the best possible service of broadcasting. (1962, pp. 168–9)

Having established a dichotomy between the commercial incentive of independent television (a *private* objective) and the quality of provision expected of a *public* service broadcaster, the Report went on to cast its primary criticisms against ITV, which was criticised for failing to recognise the full effect of television on its viewers, and for not providing a fair and reflective balance of programmes.

ITV was also criticised for the 'triviality' of its programming, a term which is used in the Report to refer less to the subject matter itself than to 'the way a subject matter is approached and the manner in which it is presented'.[18] The Report opposes 'triviality' to 'serious' programming. In the late 1950s, the BBC Secretariat had established a definition of 'serious' television as a programme 'whose primary intention is informational, educational or critical' (Fox, 1971, p. 20), a category that excluded all television drama. In the first year of commercial television in the UK, ITV came under attack in the press for the 'retreat from culture' in its programming, although it was gaining a larger audience share than the BBC in homes capable of receiving both services.[19] For the BBC, 'serious' television was an important term by which the Corporation could justify its audience loss to ITV through recourse to the public service emphasis on the value of intellectually edifying programming over audience ratings. The Pilkington Report largely adopts this view, examining the percentage of peak viewing hours devoted to 'serious' programmes (excluding drama) by ITV and BBC and concluding from the greater percentage on BBC that a higher quality of service was provided by that broadcaster.

By using the criterion of 'serious' programming as one of the ways in which the provision of broadcasting is evaluated, the Report dismisses audience ratings as an assessment of the value of a broadcasting service. This is reiterated in the rhetoric by which it explores the 'dissatisfaction' expressed in the submissions received by the committee.

> The themes common to nearly all those submissions which expressed dissatisfaction was that programme items were far too often devised with the object of seeking, at whatever cost in quality or variety, the largest possible audience; and that, to attain this object, the items

nearly always appealed to a low level of public taste. This was not, of course, to say that all items which attracted large audiences were poor. But in far too many the effect was to produce a passively acquiescent or even indifferent audience rather than an actively interested one. There was a lack of variety and originality, an adherence to what was 'safe'; and an unwillingness to try challenging, demanding and, still less, uncomfortable subject matter.[20]

While not dismissing the possibility of producing 'quality' programming that attracted a large audience, the Pilkington Report criticises a broadcasting ethos based primarily (and above all other considerations) on seeking 'the largest possible audience'. In doing so, the Report makes a series of value judgments: that seeking a large audience often leads to an appeal to 'a low level of public taste'; that in doing so, such programmes produce a passive and indifferent, rather than an active, viewer; and that this ethos leads to undemanding, unchallenging and comfortable programming. As such, the Report casts the responsibilities of the public service broadcaster in terms reminiscent of the political avant-garde, advocating a television service that creates an active, critical and engaged viewer through the production of challenging and experimental programming. As John Caughie argues,

> [The Pilkington Report] echoed in liberal form the appeal of the political avant-garde in theory and practice for Brecht's 'active spectator' who had not left his brain with his hat at the door. For Pilkington, this imperative was tied to the moral responsibilities of citizenship, of a citizen who has the rights of choice but also the responsibilities of judgement. (2000, p. 83)

Caughie goes on to argue that the discursive rhetoric of the Pilkington Report gave the broadcasters a 'licence to controversy' (2000, p. 86) that facilitated the rise of a 'Golden Age' of British television. For Caughie, this Golden Age of British television can be situated directly in relation to the developments in European modernist theatre, literature and cinema over the 1950s and 1960s, and was epitomised by the politically motivated and formally experimental drama documentaries of Ken Loach and Tony Garnett. In the plays that they produced for the BBC's *The Wednesday Play* strand, Tony Garnett and Ken Loach challenged the dominant form and subject matter of television drama at the time. They shot on film and made extensive use of location shooting, while plays such as 'Up the Junction' used both actors and real people in its fictional portrayal of working-class life in Clapham Junction. These plays have been placed at the centre of a 'Golden Age' of television, in which the aesthetic and social responsibilities of television broadcasting were united through dramas intended to 'rivet the audience with disturbing truths, reflect a society in crisis, shatter form and redefine content' (MacMurraugh-Kavanagh, 1997, p. 375). This is what Caughie terms 'serious' television drama,[21] legitimated by and responding to Pilkington's call for an aesthetically and socially responsible form of television broadcasting in the UK.

Yet little has been explored about the effects of the Pilkington Report on commercial television. If the Report legitimised the potential for television to be controversial and formally and politically challenging, then how did this manifest itself on commercial television, and how did the commercial programme companies respond to the Report's criticisms? First, it is

important to note that the recommendations in the Pilkington Report for the restructuring of
ITV were largely rejected in the subsequent 1963 Television Act (see Sendall, 1983). The primary impact of the Pilkington Report therefore was to set the tone of the debate about
broadcasting for the next decade. The ITA responded to the criticisms of the Pilkington Report
by adopting its evaluative criteria of 'serious' television, and between 1961–2 and 1965–6
the *ITA: Annual Report and Accounts* included a section devoted to 'The Development of
Serious Programmes' across the ITV network.[22] However, although the ITA conformed to the
definition of 'serious' programmes in the Pilkington Report, at the same time the *ITA: Annual
Report and Accounts 1961–62* criticised the validity of the term and in particular the exclu-
sion of drama from the classification of 'serious' television.

> The classification of television programmes into 'informative' and 'entertaining', or 'serious'
> and 'light', presents its difficulties, and the terms certainly cannot be taken to correspond
> with 'valuable' and 'worthless'. A play is 'entertainment', but it may have a purpose more
> serious and a value more significant than, for instance, a poor political discussion. (1962,
> p. 13)

Here the ITA Report is engaging precisely with the relationship set up in the Pilkington Report
between 'serious' television and aesthetic and social value. Using television drama as an
indicative example, the ITA challenges the tendency within the Pilkington Report to equate
'entertainment' with worthless or trivial programming.

The ITA's simultaneous adoption of and challenge to the criteria of 'serious' programming
points to the conflicting position occupied by the ITV broadcasters in aligning their commercial imperatives with their social responsibilities as public service broadcasters. An attempt to
negotiate this conflicting position is apparent in the *ITA: Annual Report and Accounts 1967–68*.
In defending its drama provision (particularly its series and serials) for the year it stated:

> it became increasingly obvious, too, that the distinction made in the past between 'plays' (to
> which great prestige attaches) and series and serials (which are thought of as the bread-and-
> butter of television) is often unrealistic. The 'single play' may present one of the greatest
> challenges to the writer, the producer, and the director, but it is by no means clear that the
> audience derives the greatest satisfaction from it. Three of the most interesting ventures of
> the year fell outside the ambit of the conventional play. Rediffusion's *A Man of Our Times*
> showed that there is no inherent conflict between the drama of ideas and character, and the
> serial form. In *Inheritance* Granada married skill in creating historical atmosphere to a
> technique that enabled television cameras to capture the sweeping horizons of the Yorkshire
> moors. ATV's *The Prisoner* provoked more critical controversy than is usual for a genre series
> of this kind: both devotees and critics were united in praise of the production, and it is
> regrettable that it had to be shown here in monochrome, rather than in the original colour in
> which it was made. (1968, p. 23)

The ITA here attempts to validate the position of commercial television within the terms of
value adopted by the Pilkington Report. Yet in doing so, the ITA complicates these very cri-

teria by challenging the aesthetic distinction between plays and series, and valuing the 'sat-isfaction' of the viewer over the challenge presented to the producer. In the case of *The Prisoner*, the aesthetic value placed in the 'critical controversy' provoked by the series (which implies that the series challenged viewers), is seen to be in conflict with its identification as a 'genre series'. The need to distinguish *The Prisoner* from other 'genre series of this kind' in order to assert its aesthetic value is indicative of the difficult position that the independent broadcasters were attempting to negotiate at this time. As both a 'genre series' and a criti-cally controversial drama, *The Prisoner* straddled the conflicting aesthetic and commercial demands on independent television, and in doing so, occupied a position that could not be easily reconciled within traditional criteria of aesthetic value.

Marketing *The Prisoner*

The Prisoner was therefore produced in an environment within which the social responsibil-ities of television broadcasters were cast in part in aesthetic terms through the call for programmes that were challenging and controversial in terms of both form and content. These debates had a particular resonance for independent television which had come under criticism for neglecting the powerful role of television and pandering to a 'mass' audience with 'trivial' programming. However, the difficulty remained for the ITV broadcasters, who relied on the sale of advertising (and increasingly the sale of programmes abroad) for their funding, to negotiate a position between the criticisms of the Pilkington Report and the financial viability of their television service. Television drama occupied a particular place within this problematic, suggesting one potential site in which the apparently conflicting attributes of 'entertaining' and 'serious' television could be united within one programme.

An attempt to negotiate the apparently conflicting demands on commercial television in Britain is apparent in the marketing for *The Prisoner*. ITC's promotional material for the series integrated an address to the 'active' viewer with the familiar and pleasurable expectations of the generic action-adventure series. It described *The Prisoner* as:

> the most challenging and unusual series ever filmed for television, devised by Patrick McGoohan himself. It is a series with depth, stories that will make viewers think, and, at the same time, will keep them on the edge of their seats in excitement as the Prisoner resists every physical and mental effort to break him. There is mounting suspense as each new dramatic story is unfolded ... stories of one man's tremendous, unflinching battle for survival as an individual in a macabre world in which every move is watched by electronic eyes and in which all his neighbours are suspect. Where is the Village? Who are his captors? Who are his fellow prisoners? What country is he in? Viewing appeal which is simultaneously electrifying, controversial and gripping. (Reproduced in Carrazé and Oswald, 1990, pp. 220–1)

This text is accompanied by images of McGoohan and of the unusual setting of the Vil-lage. Although McGoohan is primarily shown in action poses (running, turning, crouching) in all of these images his face displays resilience and thoughtful intelligence. As with the text, therefore, these images function to integrate the promise of action with a depth of meaning implicit in McGoohan's facial expressions. While *The Prisoner* offers excitement and adventure, it is clearly presented as 'serious' (rather than frivolous) in its address.[23] What is promoted here is a series that is both cerebral and emotional in its appeal, combining the 'excitement' of the action-adventure drama with 'stories that will make viewers think'.

The press publicity for *The Prisoner* displays a similar negotiation of 'seriousness' and 'entertainment'. The *TV Times* publicity for *The Prisoner* prior to its first week of transmission constructs it as an action-adventure series that also contains 'food for thought'.

> The Village is the ultimate in indoctrination and the subjection of the individual. The establishment has taken over entirely. Individual freedom is dead. People no longer want to think for themselves, even if they are capable of doing so. The Prisoner of the title is the one man who is resisting. And freedom of the individual, one feels, is what McGoohan is driving at. There is a second theme: the Prisoner's efforts to escape. This provides the suspense and excitement of a physical nature that one associates with a man like McGoohan.[24]

Both of these promotional articles equate the formal experimentation of the series with the individual creativity of McGoohan. *The Prisoner* was produced by McGoohan's production company Everyman Films Ltd for ITC,[25] and McGoohan gets a sole credit as Executive Producer, as well as starring in every episode and writing and directing a number of others.[26] At a time when single-authored plays were considered the aesthetic peak of television drama, the contributions of other writers, directors and producers to the series are overlooked in the promotion of *The Prisoner* as a 'single-authored series'. In a move typical of the publicity surrounding the series at the time of its transmission, the *TV Times* article clearly attributes the creativity of the series to the authorship of McGoohan:

> McGoohan believes that he is breaking into completely new television territory – in presentation and stories alike. The idea is his own. He is also the executive producer. He has taken over the direction of many of the sequences (but without giving himself a screen credit for this). He has buried himself in the cutting-rooms during the editing of the episodes. And he has worked on every script, irrespective of who may have written it.[27]

The construction of McGoohan as the single creative force behind *The Prisoner* is used to validate this commercially produced action-adventure series as 'the most challenging and unusual series ever filmed for television' (ITC promotional material). Crucially, aesthetic value is here utilised as a marketing strategy, rather than as a critical evaluation of the series. This suggests that the discourses of value apparent in the Pilkington Report are being used to *attract* viewers. Note the similarity in language, in the emphasis on the 'unusual' and the 'challenging' in the ITC's material. The use of this language in the marketing strategy suggests that such terms of aesthetic value were not anathema to a 'mass' audience and could actually be used to attract a larger audience to the series.

However, it is important to note that this appeal to aesthetic value works in tandem with a strong emphasis on the generic elements of *The Prisoner* as an action-adventure series and an exploitation of McGoohan's star persona. McGoohan came to fame through his performance as John Drake, the protagonist in *Danger Man*, who was a tough international spy with unwavering integrity. The combination of action and integrity is central to McGoohan's star persona. In an article about McGoohan in the *TV Times*, Anthony Davis wrote, 'He has declared his unwillingness to play TV parts he regards as immoral and barred gratuitous gun-play and brutality from his programmes because "children may be watching" ' (1967, p. 30). Here Davis is picking up on the anxieties at this time about the effects of television, particularly on the young.[28] The action-adventure series were central to these debates, frequently criticised for their amoral or irresponsible representation of violence.[29] By referencing McGoohan's professional integrity, Davis's article constructs McGoohan as an 'action' star who transcends the potential amorality of the action-adventure series by taking the effects of television seriously. This contributes to the marketing of *The Prisoner* as a form of 'serious entertainment'. It is through the integrated appeal to the generic elements of the action-adventure series with challenging and unusual material, constructed as authored by a creative and morally responsible star, that this marketing strategy attempts to negotiate the conflicting demands on ITV to produce commercially viable programming that fulfilled the social and aesthetic responsibilities of a public service broadcaster. In doing so, the marketing challenges the aesthetic dichotomies between 'popular' and 'serious' television.

Style, Narrative and Genre

If an attempt to straddle the conflicting demands on commercial television in Britain at this time is apparent in the marketing of *The Prisoner*, then how might the series' narrative and visual style be understood in relation to these debates? To answer this question, it is important to situate *The Prisoner* in relation to the debates about television, politics and popular culture in the 1960s which have been seen as central to understanding the 'serious' play, but which have been largely ignored in relation to the 'popular' action-adventure series. I want to begin with Troy Kennedy Martin's polemical article 'Nats Go Home: First Statement of a New Drama for Television', published in 1964.[30] In this article, Kennedy Martin advocated a new form of television drama that appears to respond to the Pilkington Report's call for television that challenges and actively engages its audience. Kennedy Martin focused his criticisms on what he saw as a prevalent and institutionalised naturalism in British television drama, characterised by the centrality of dialogue to storytelling, the use of natural time (in which studio time equates with drama time) and a visual style in which the close-up dominated (1964, p. 19).[31] For Kennedy Martin this is a naturalism that visually evolved from the techniques of classical Hollywood film-making and naturalist theatre, which absorbs the spectator into emotional identification with the characters. What Kennedy Martin argues for is a new drama in which the director exploits *mise en scène*, lighting, design and montage, and he is particularly aware of the potential for shooting television drama on film. Kennedy Martin is not opposed to audience involvement, but argues that television drama must 'stimulate mind and imagination' and 'directly disturb the senses' (1964, p. 23) and that to achieve this the director must exploit the possibilities of montage. Here Kennedy Martin is clearly influenced by the theories of montage developed by Soviet film-makers in the 1920s, which have historically had a significant pull for British film-makers (see Caughie, 2000). For Kennedy Martin, this new form of television drama would not just challenge what he saw as the dominant naturalistic style of British television drama, but would also challenge the position of the viewer by breaking their absorption with the interiority of the characters in order to achieve the kind of distanciation associated with Brecht's political avant-garde.[32] In this elaboration of what an 'experimental' television drama might look like, Kennedy Martin's concern for the impact of form on the subjectivity of the viewer picks up precisely on the debates raised by Pilkington about the relationship between the aesthetic and moral responsibilities of television broadcasters.

The visual style of *The Prisoner* is characterised by the expressive use of *mise en scène*, composition and montage described by Kennedy Martin. From the opening title sequence, the series showcases the narrative centrality of the montage of images and music. The rapidly edited opening condenses the narrative premise of the series into a three-minute sequence in which dialogue is all but absent, used only in voice-over once Number Six arrives at the Village. The sequence opens with a loud crack of thunder against the image of dark storm clouds, followed by a rapid cut to a long straight road. As an open-topped sports car drives towards the camera, the heavily syncopated title theme gradually fades in, creating an immediate association between sound and image. What follows is a rapidly edited sequence that draws attention to the composition of the shots and the movement of the camera. This montage of shots – a close-up of the driver's face, a low static shot as the car speeds past, a panning close-up from the front to the back of the car as the car continues to speed forward, a mid-shot from the road as the camera pans to follow the passing car – functions primarily to showcase the series' visual sophistication. The sequence goes on to depict Number Six resigning from an unnamed job and being gassed and taken to the strange location of the Village, continuously maintaining the rhythmic associations between image and music, the use of unusual camera angles, and rapid editing. From its opening sequence therefore, *The Prisoner* establishes a visual style in which composition and montage play a primary narrative function.

The opening sequence is indicative of the visual style of the series, which appears to fulfil Kennedy Martin's call for a drama in which the camera is freed from shooting dialogue and the structure is freed from natural time. The series uses this reliance on montage and visual storytelling to disrupt the conventions of television drama and hence to undermine the viewer's security in their point of view and their interpretative frameworks. This is because the Village is itself a site of overwhelming surveillance where hidden cameras survey every area, relaying the images to large screens in the Village control rooms. These screens by which the Village authorities monitor the activities of the prisoners are repeatedly equated with the television screen which the viewer is watching. As Chris Gregory suggests, 'the use of screens-within-screens represents a commentary on the relationship between the viewer and the television screen itself' (1997, p. 48). For example, in episode eleven, 'It's Your Funeral', the conventional shot-reverse-shot pattern as a woman enters Number Six's house is subverted as the camera zooms out to reveal the Supervisor and Number Two watching the image on a screen in the control room. After a rapid cut to a close-up of the Supervisor watching the woman, the scene reverts to the conventional shot-reverse-shot pattern until once again the camera zooms out to reveal the watchers. This blurring of the viewer's screen and the control room's screen implicates the viewer in the voyeuristic activities of the Village. Furthermore, this disruption of the shot-reverse-shot makes the conventions of film-making apparent and thus makes the audience aware of the construction of the sequence.

While this moment of disruption is contained within the narrative (shifting the subjective identification from the character being watched to the watcher), there are other moments throughout the series which completely undermine the conventions of audiovisual storytelling. For example, in the second episode, 'The Chimes of Big Ben', Number Six is depicted escaping from the Village. His journey back to Britain locked inside a large crate is conveyed by a montage of shots of the crate being loaded onto planes and boats, interspersed with shots of Number Six from within the crate. However, when Number Six arrives in what he believes to be Britain, it is revealed that he is still inside the Village. For the viewer this raises a number of questions: did Number Six ever leave the Village? If not, how are the images of his journey to be interpreted? The visual narrative, upon which the series relies so heavily for its storytelling, is drawn into question here as a potentially deceptive device. In doing this, the series challenges the conventional form of television drama which enables the viewer to construct meaning from a set of visual and narrative clues. In *The Prisoner* there are many clues, but the meaning behind them is deliberately offset. *The Prisoner* is formally constructed to disorientate the subjectivity of the viewer, robbing its audience of a stable 'objective' position from which the drama can be viewed. This draws attention to the conventions of the television series and invites the viewer to actively engage in a process of interpretation and deconstruction.

This is further apparent in the series' use (and disruption) of the conventions of the action-adventure and spy genres. In many ways, *The Prisoner* adopts the generic conventions of the 1960s television spy series, which had become increasingly prevalent in British and US television in the mid- to late 1960s with series such as *I Spy*, *The Man from U.N.C.L.E.*, *The Avengers* and *Callan*. These series pitted their spy protagonists against villainous individuals and organisations, combining elements of the detective and thriller genres in the use of intriguing narratives and action-packed denouements. As Cynthia W. Walker has argued, the television spy series is extremely difficult to categorise generically because of the fluid boundaries between the spy drama and other genres, particularly the detective and thriller genres (1997, p. 1563). However, she suggests that the television spy series of the 1960s tended to share three central characteristics: the presence of a government or quasi-government agency in the life of the protagonist; villains (often foreign) whose intentions are political or global; and an expansion of the plot beyond the local or national (ibid.).

In its first episode *The Prisoner* promises to fulfil all of these generic expectations. The opening credits depict Number Six driving into London, entering a building and resigning. The central London setting, the costuming of Number Six and the man to whom he resigns in traditional dark suits imply government civil service, while the subsequent shot of a vast underground filing system suggests a powerful and large organisation. The exotic location to which Number Six is kidnapped is also in keeping with the conventional use of foreign locations in spy series in the 1960s. This opening therefore fulfils Walker's three characteristics of the 1960s television spy series and functions alongside the associations of McGoohan with the spy drama (from his previous starring role in *Danger Man*) to suggest a particular narrative interpretation. Number Six is a British spy who resigns and is then kidnapped and taken to a mysterious location by a villainous organisation intent on gaining his government secrets.

However, although *The Prisoner* sets up these generic expectations, they are consistently undercut and unfulfilled. The identity of the organisation from which Number Six has resigned, and the position he held there, is never confirmed by the series. Furthermore, while the Village is certainly populated by people from a range of different countries, the speech, apparel and demeanour of its controllers replicates that of the established institutions of British society – the public school boy, the civil servant, the politician, even the spy. Essentially, all the references to the spy genre within the series are *implied* rather than asserted. The Village *may* be run by a villainous international organisation or by the British government itself. Number Six *may* be a spy concealing secret information. The Village *may* be set in a foreign location. Yet, at the same time, none of these readings is confirmed. It is never revealed who runs the Village, where it is located, why the Village authorities kidnapped Number Six, or what information they wanted from him. The answers to the questions that Number Six demands in the opening title sequence – 'Where am I? What do you want? Whose side are you on? Who are you? Who is Number One?' – are never offered to either the viewer or Number Six over the course of the series.[33]

Part of this stems from *The Prisoner*'s inversion of the conventions of the action-adventure series. *The Prisoner* adopts the typical form of the television series with each episode following the same narrative structure which can be repeated every week with little or no continuing storyline running across the episodes.[34] After the title sequence, the scenario that will face Number Six is introduced. As Number Six engages in the scenario a significant event occurs that pushes him towards an act of rebellion, either attempting to escape or to subvert the power of the Village, involving a number of physical action sequences. Regardless of his efforts, each episode ends with an act of reversion, returning Number Six to his original captive state in the Village. This narrative structure broadly follows the conventions of the action-adventure series of the 1960s. In each weekly episode, the status quo is disrupted allowing the hero to engage in a number of exciting action sequences. In order for the series to repeat its familiar narrative pattern every week, events must be fully resolved by the end of the episode, reverting to the status quo of the opening. What is unusual about *The Prisoner*'s format is that it inverts the basic premise of the traditional action-adventure series. In an inversion of the usual action-adventure narrative, the series begins not from a position of safety but with Number Six's entrapment, returning him to that state at the end of each episode. This inversion of the basic heroic principle of the action-adventure series particularly worried CBS executive Michael Dann who feared that the US public would not identify with a central character who failed each week (see Rakoff, 1998, p. 32). Therefore, although *The Prisoner* positions itself broadly within the narrative conventions of the action-adventure series – pitting its skilled hero, through a series of action sequences, against a powerful organisation run by apparently villainous individuals – each of these elements is undercut. While Number Six displays all the physical ability and mental ingenuity expected of an action hero, he never succeeds in his plans to escape or to uncover the identity of his captors.[35]

A further difference from the generic conventions of the spy and action-adventure series comes in the setting of the Village. The series was shot in Portmeirion in Wales, a town built by architect Clough Williams-Ellis as a 'living museum' (Williams-Ellis cited in Gray, 1967, p. 19) that brought together replicas and reconstructions of European architectural styles from a range of historical periods. This bricolage of historical and national cultural signifiers creates a surreal location that appears to transcend time and space. The spatial and temporal disorientation of this exterior setting is continued across the set and costume designs. Number Six's house in the Village is furnished in a traditional Georgian style, while the Village store is dressed as a typical English rural village shop. These signifiers of traditional British life are carried through into the costume designs. The Village authority figures dress in the traditional clothes of the British upper class (suits, school scarves, walking sticks, bowler hats and so on), while the villagers wear Victorian capes and costumes reminiscent of the uniforms of the British holiday camp (a reference solidified by the public announcements regularly transmitted through the Village tannoys). These signifiers of different elements of traditional British culture are combined with visual signifiers of 1960s pop culture, from the projected images of larva lamps and the spherical Aarnio 'globe' chairs in the Village control rooms, to the Mini-Moke that is used as transport around the Village. These emblematic designs of 1960s futurism are further combined with technological gadgetry within the Village which goes beyond the bounds of scientific knowledge in the 1960s: a 'mindswap' machine; a computer that controls through subliminal messages; a seemingly sentient spherical ball (named Rover) that prevents escape from the Village. No scientific explanation is offered for these technological devices. These objects are deliberately constructed as fantastic machines that defy the conventions of socio-

The Prisoner's exteriors are filmed in the village of Portmeirion, with its bricolage of architectural styles

The futuristic interior of the Village control room with its spherical Aarnio 'globe' chairs is combined with the costuming of Number Two (Guy Doleman) in the traditional attire of the British public school boy

cultural verisimilitude. The combination of these contrasting signifiers imbues the visual landscape of the series with a pervasive sense of temporal and spatial disorientation.

However, this combination of traditional and futuristic was not anathema to the 1960s spy series, and is particularly apparent in the technical gadgetry of the James Bond films and in the television series, *The Avengers*, which frequently combined signifiers of traditional British life with a fascination with technical and scientific experimentation. What differs in *The Prisoner* is the function of the fantastic elements. James Chapman has argued that the use of fantasy in *The Avengers* extended the basic concerns of the series' thriller narrative: '[*The Avengers'*] bizarre and fantastic plots represent in extreme form one of the underlying assumptions of the thriller genre: that chaos and anarchy may erupt at any moment from beneath the "thin protection of civilisation"' (2000, p. 43). For Chapman, therefore, rather than inverting the expectations of the thriller genre in its use of the fantastic, *The Avengers* pushed them to an extreme in order to heighten the underlying assumptions of the genre. In contrast, *The Prisoner* does not simply introduce the 'chaos and anarchy' of the fantastic into a stable and recognisable fictional world. Rather, it situates its very narratives within an already unstable fictional world in which the veneer of civilisation exists only as an effect. In doing so, *The Prisoner*'s use of the fantastic is akin to that described by Todorov in relation to the literary fantastic. Todorov argues that the creation of hesitation in the reader is central to the literary fantastic as a genre:

First, the text must oblige the reader to consider the world of the characters as a world of living persons and to hesitate between a natural and a supernatural explanation of the events described. Second, this hesitation may also be experienced by the character, and at the same time the hesitation is represented, it becomes one of the themes of the work ... Third, the reader must adopt a certain attitude with regard to the text: he will reject allegorical as well as 'poetic' interpretations. (1975, p. 33)

Todorov's three conditions of the literary fantastic can be usefully applied to *The Prisoner*. The series creates a fictional world of 'living persons' (we are not invited to interpret Number Six as being of another world) and does not offer the reassurance of either natural or supernatural explanations for the bizarre events depicted.[36] The hesitation is experienced both by Number Six and by the viewer and is established as the key narrative premise of the series as Number Six attempts to understand and escape from his environment. Finally, while, as Chris Gregory (1997) argues, *The Prisoner* can be understood allegorically, the series does not offer a clear basis upon which this narrative interpretation can be made. In its use and disruption of the generic conventions of the action-adventure spy series, its use of a visual style designed to disorientate the subjectivity of the viewer, its bricolage of signifiers in its location, set and costume designs and its lack of explanation for the fantastic elements represented, *The Prisoner* creates a fictional world that invites hesitation between supernatural, generic and allegorical explanations for the events depicted.

The Prisoner does seem to respond to Kennedy Martin's call for a television drama that disturbs traditional modes of representation in order to challenge and to actively engage the viewer. Yet, while it is possible to recognise a formal experimentation with montage, point of view and genre within *The Prisoner*, they serve quite a different function to the formal experimentation in the social realist plays of Loach and Garnett. Centrally, Loach and Garnett are concerned with exploring and exposing contemporary social issues and with representing subjects which had been previously absent in British television drama. The avant-garde strategies used within their plays have a clear political purpose in exposing the typicality of these social problems and refusing to provide the viewer with easy resolutions for them. In contrast, *The Prisoner* does not have an overt and direct socially relevant political message. Furthermore, while the series partly disrupts the conventions of the action-adventure spy series, equally its combination of 'avant-garde' strategies with the generic conventions of the spy thriller and action-adventure genre is often used to increase the effect of those generic conventions. For example, the use of jump-cuts when Number Six first arrives at the Village in episode one invites identification with the disorientation experienced by Number Six. Similarly, while the escape sequence in 'The Chimes of Big Ben' invites the audience's attention to the conventions of narrative storytelling, it equally functions to create narrative suspense and an emotional identification between viewer and protagonist. However, to argue that the series' formal experimentation works to reinforce its generic conventions is not to argue that any radical potential is lost within those conventions, or that the action-adventure series as a form is not at all political. Rather, I want to suggest that these elements work together in *The Prisoner* to create a series whose political purpose can be more closely associated with 1960s pop art than with an historical avant-garde linked to the modernism of Brechtian distanciation and Soviet montage.

Pop Art in the 1960s

Both the historical avant-garde and pop art have been understood as an attack on the autonomy of bourgeois art and an attempt to break down the barriers between high and low art (Huyssen, 1988). However, there are specific qualities that distinguish pop art from the avant-garde art of the first half of the twentieth century. Pop art emerged in the 1950s and 1960s from the rebellion of the younger generations against traditional forms of authority. In this period, the stress on individual pleasure and a freer choice of lifestyles came into conflict with existing traditional ideologies based on moral continence and social discipline. As such, pop art can be linked both to the rise of youth culture and to the accelerated consumer culture of the post-war era, in which products increasingly took on a use value related to the lifestyle they projected over and above the function they performed. The inherent contradiction within pop art lies in its links with counter-cultural movements on the one hand and consumer culture on the other. Hence, pop art can be linked to the counter-cultural movements of the 1950s and 1960s which developed as alternatives to traditional ways of life, thought and expression. Yet, by the same measure, pop was also incorporated into the production cycle of the 1960s with cultural industries creating new use values and encouraging rapid shifts in lifestyle, style and fashion. As a consequence, there is a tension as to whether pop art functions as an affirmation of affluent consumer society and mass production or as a criticism of bourgeois values and traditions. While pop artists such as Warhol brought everyday consumer products into the gallery as artefacts, television as a medium offered its own problems and possibilities for pop art. Television as a domestic technology epitomised the development of consumer culture in the 1950s and 1960s as the home became increasingly the site of new domestic and entertainment technologies. Furthermore, television made visible the increasing array of lifestyle choices, while commercial television advertised the fashionable products of consumer society.[37]

The narratives of *The Prisoner* clearly engage with the concerns of pop art. The series depicts an individual's struggle against an unnamed authority that is associated with traditional bourgeois institutions of power (the government, the judiciary, the public school and so on). Central to this struggle is the need for Number Six to retain his sense of individuality, which (the series suggests) is not possible within these traditional institutions. Hence Number Six's struggle to escape the Village becomes a struggle for self-expression that is not simply a private objective but necessitates conflict between the private self and bourgeois public institutions. David Buxton likens the Village to an existentialist hell, 'an old-fashioned modernity in which advanced technology is used to increase the possibilities of state control and repression rather than those of individual freedom' (1990, p. 95). Yet Buxton argues that the series suffers from,

> an ideological thinness, an obsessive concern with individual freedom in a setting which is
> too facile to allow the issue to be treated with the necessary complexity. The problem is thus
> insufficiently focused: in a political confusion peculiar to the 1960s, a 'radical'-minded anxiety
> over state interference in private life and the use of the media to manipulate citizens into a
> dull conformity spills over into a conservative attack on the welfare state itself, seen as
> effacing the individual personality into a mere number. (1990, p. 96)

Hence for Buxton, the series falls into the trap of much pop art, ultimately implicating itself within its own critique through the creation of a fictional world in which individualism could only be asserted through the (impossible) rejection of society itself.

However, Buxton's account of the series as pop art focuses primarily on its narratives and themes and fails to consider fully the series' stylistic project. The series' combination (and disruption) of conventional generic elements with more avant-garde stylistic practices can be understood in relation to a broader cultural shift concerned with exploring the boundaries of the popular, which was a central element of 1960s pop art. The series does not attempt to smuggle avant-garde strategies in 'through the back door' of a popular generic form, but rather to combine both to tell stories that articulate the conflict and contest between the boundaries of the traditional and the counter-cultural, the public and the private. After all, Number Six (as with most spy heroes) is a member of the traditional establishment. It is implied that he is a defected spy and he is certainly a well-educated, upper-middle-class white male, not a representative of the counter-culture. The series does not advocate 'alternative' lifestyles, yet it treats the traditional hierarchies of bourgeois society with great suspicion. To see the series as simply Number Six's attempt to assert his individuality is to fail to consider the full impact of the complex range of signification it offers. Rather, the series articulates Number Six's struggle to find his way through a world in which traditional signifiers are no longer reliable indicators of value and meaning. It is this sense of disorientation, of the loss of secure signifiers, which is particularly well articulated by the series' combination of formal experimentation and traditional generic conventions. This mix of the 'serious' and the 'popular' functions precisely to heighten the sense of hesitation, to create a world in which generic conventions cannot be relied upon as secure indicators of knowledge and expectation. The series does not suggest the rejection of society, rather it uses its critique of the bourgeois institutions of power and authority to explore the ambiguity and uncertainty of living in a society in which traditional signifiers no longer suffice. This is not the kind of direct social intervention offered by *The Wednesday Play* dramas such as 'Cathy Come Home' and the series certainly fails to offer any resolution for the social crisis it explores. Yet it is an attempt to work through a significant social shift that is particularly relevant to the late 1960s.

Narrative Structure, Familiarity and Repetition

However, the narrative structure of the action-adventure series to which *The Prisoner* adheres presents a further complicating factor. The series' narrative is based on the repetition of certain key elements: the basic narrative structure of action and resolution that prevents Number Six from escaping; the location of the Village; the themes of individualism versus authority; the use of narrative and style to disorientate the viewer and so on. However, these narrative and stylistic devices are repeated over the first twelve episodes of the series and, through repetition, become themselves conventions of the series' narrative. If part of the premise of the series itself was to disrupt conventional forms of storytelling in order to create hesitation and uncertainty in the viewer, then after twelve episodes this disruption becomes formalised as one of the conventional elements of the series itself, and those stylistic devices that had initially been disorientating become enjoyable aspects of the familiar pleasures offered by the series. In the last five episodes of the series, however, this format was gradually challenged as the series built to a surreal denouement that bore little resemblance to the format established in its early episodes. For example, the fourteenth episode, 'Living in Harmony', plays out the majority of the narrative within the setting of a Western, only reverting in the final scenes to the familiar setting of the Village. The following episode, 'The Girl Who Was Death' again takes Number Six out of the Village, and depicts him as a parody of his previous spy persona in *Danger Man*, although again returning him to the Village at the end of the episode. In both of these episodes, a narrative explanation is offered for the stylistic disruption. The Western setting is revealed to have been induced by hallucinogenic drugs, while the spy parody is the visual depiction of a story told by Number Six to the children of the Village.

It is in the final two episodes that the series most radically departs from its previously established narrative and stylistic format. In episode sixteen, 'Once Upon a Time', Number Six engages in a surreal battle against Number Two. This is a highly theatrical episode shot almost entirely on one set that is littered with props which are used to regress Number Six through the various stages of his life. The final episode, 'Fall Out', enacts a bizarre trial in which it is suggested that Number Six himself controls the Village. The episode includes a beat-style version of 'Dry Bones', and ends with a highly stylised violent uprising choreographed to The Beatles's 'All You Need Is Love'.

While the previous disruptions in *The Prisoner* were contained within a series format which inverted but still maintained the basic narrative structure of the action-adventure series, these closing episodes completely abandon the generic and narrative expectations established over the course of the series. The series' denouement caused critical controversy and a slew of complaints from disgruntled viewers who felt cheated by the lack of narrative resolution (Knight, 1968). Although audience reaction to the series as a whole was mixed – journalist Anthony Davis wrote just before the screening of the last episode, 'people have liked it. They have also been confused, baffled, bewildered and irritated' (1968a, p. 5) – it was the final episode that caused most controversy. While the *TV Times* recorded a range of positive and negative responses to the episode in its letters page,[38] press reaction was stronger. Peter Knight's review in the *Daily Telegraph* described 'Fall Out' as,

> as baffling as its predecessors with no solutions given to any of the problems ... despite all the production gloss, sophisticated writing and fine acting, the lasting impression was a heap of hokum carried off with the smoothness of a confidence trick. (1968, p. 13)

McGoohan reportedly left the country because of the negative response to the series. In a 1984 documentary on the series screened on Channel 4, he stated

> People may say 'Let's see something original' but basically people like a good story that ends up the way it should. This one didn't, of course. There was an outcry – I nearly got lynched and had to go into hiding. They thought they'd been cheated. (Cited in Rogers, 1989, p. 139).

Yet McGoohan's explanation for the controversy caused by the final episodes is perhaps too simplistic. Until its final five episodes, *The Prisoner* balanced the use of conventional generic expectations with stylistic and narrative devices which challenged the dominant forms of television drama. The maintenance of this balance depended upon a central ambiguity at the heart of the series – a hesitation about how to read the series – that allowed it to explore, rather than resolve conflict. The expectations of narrative closure cannot be reconciled within this dynamic. Although the format of *The Prisoner* denied the space for answers to the questions posed in the series' opening credits, there was a strong expectation that the final episode would provide some kind of narrative resolution. This expectation was created in part by the publicity surrounding the transmission of the final episode,[39] and in part by the series' use of the conventions of the action-adventure series, which is predicated upon offering its audience narrative solutions.

In order to offer narrative resolution, *The Prisoner* could either follow the generic path – essentially offering a realist account for Number Six's entrapment – or (as it does) a 'surreal' path – essentially offering an allegorical account for the series' narratives. While the generic path might have offered audiences the narrative solutions they sought, it might equally have left the series open to criticisms of pandering to a mass audience and of turning its back on its attempts to be challenging and controversial. On the other hand, the 'surreal' path allowed the series to maintain a sense of aesthetic integrity and authenticity. In doing so, however, it removed the hesitation that was central to the series by offering surreal answers to the questions posed (Number Six is Number One, the whole world is the Village, and so on) ultimately suggesting an allegorical reading.

This is not to suggest that the final episodes undermine the political import of the series, for it is in these two episodes that the series most overtly engages with the politics of the counter-cultural movements of the mid- to late 1960s. However, it is to draw attention to the fragility of the balancing act that the series was attempting to maintain. This fragility does not exist because conventional generic drama is not politically engaged or because commercial television could not deal with conflict and ambiguity, but because, despite all the challenges and conflicts of this period, the boundaries between the 'popular' and the 'serious' still remained as powerful discursive forces shaping the production and reception of texts. Ultimately the series' status as a genre text remained the central discursive framework against which it was evaluated and against which it was seen to have failed. Yet equally, despite the integration of avant-garde strategies into a generic action-adventure series, the final abandonment of the generic reflects a broader (and persistent) cultural sense that generic drama itself cannot be challenging. To fully understand the complex ways in which the series is working here, the shift in the final episodes should not overshadow the significance of the earlier episodes. When dealing with long-running series, it is important to recognise that series change and can be contradictory. Finally, the significance of *The Prisoner* lies not in its closing surreal episodes (although these remain highly unusual examples of serialised television drama) but in its particular combination of formally experimental and generically conventional strategies. Its radically surreal denouement, rather than pushing the series' creative experimentation to its full, actually abandons its most radical and creative element – its careful balancing of the 'serious' and the 'popular'.

Conclusion

The use of fantasy in *The Prisoner* is quite different to that examined in the *Quatermass* seri-als in Chapter 1. In the *Quatermass* serials, the fantastic is situated within a fictional world that corresponds to the socio-cultural reality of the 1950s viewer in order to explore metaphorically contemporary social issues. By contrast, *The Prisoner* creates a fictional world in which (until the final episodes) the viewer is invited to hesitate between natural or super-natural explanations of the events depicted. Yet, as with the *Quatermass* serials, the fantastic is used in *The Prisoner* to explore the dominant aesthetic model of television drama, although the form of this experimentation differs within this specific historical context. Partly because of its association with 'cult' television, and partly because of a reluctance within television studies to engage with aesthetics, historically *The Prisoner* has fallen outside discussions of the aesthetic. However, by situating *The Prisoner* in terms of the debates surrounding its production, it is apparent that the aesthetic is central to understanding the series.

The Prisoner is constructed to fulfil the conflicting commercial and public service demands on independent television in the 1960s. The combination of the formal experimentation of the avant-garde and the familiarity of the genre series in *The Prisoner* is used to promote it to a 'mass' audience and to assuage the criticisms of triviality in commercial television pro-gramming. In its experimentation with form and narrative, *The Prisoner* does not replicate the political project of the avant-garde or the conventions of the action-adventure/spy drama, yet it is clearly embedded in both. It is through the maintenance of this dialectic between generic familiarity and formally disruptive textual strategies that *The Prisoner* negotiates its conflicting position as 'serious entertainment'. In doing so, the series challenges the dichotomies apparent in the Pilkington Report, which set in opposition commercial television (associated with entertainment which appealed to a low level of public taste by offering fam-iliar pleasures) and public service broadcasting (associated with a responsibility to provide formally experimental material which challenged the viewer). The aesthetic judgments through which *The Prisoner* was produced are not singular but are precisely concerned with satisfying traditional criteria of aesthetic value (single authorship, creativity, challenging material) and appealing to a large enough audience to fulfil the commercial demands of tele-vision production.[40] In attempting to negotiate this position, *The Prisoner* is neither 'popular' nor 'serious' television, but occupies a seemingly contradictory position between the familiar pleasures of generic entertainment and the formally disruptive strategies of the avant-garde, a position that ultimately came into conflict in its final episodes.

Notes

1. In 1956–7, the BBC's television coverage reached over 96 per cent of all 15 million homes in Britain. ITV's television coverage extended to only 1 million homes in 1956, but expanded rapidly to 5.25 million in 1958 and 9.75 million in 1960 (Briggs, 1995, p. 30).
2. Figures obtained from *ITV 1967: A Guide to Independent Television* (ITA, 1967).
3. The ITA claim that at the end of 1955–6, the weekly audience in those homes capable of receiving ITV and BBC television divided 60:40 in ITV's favour (*ITA: Annual Report and Accounts 1955–56*, HMSO, 1956, p. 13). The 'Tamratings' (audience figures

produced for the ITA) reveal that as early as the week ending 7 October 1956, ITV was gaining an average of 71 per cent of the audience in homes capable of receiving both services.

4. The BBC's operating expenditure for television continued to rise steeply over the 1960s to £59,447,503 by 1969–70 (see Briggs, 1995, p. 1007).

5. See Curran, in Bakewell and Garnham (1970, p. 216), and Weldon (1971a, pp. 17–18).

6. *BBC Handbook 1967*, p. 33.

7. Out of the 14,000 programmes exported by ITV in 1962–3, around 5,000 were sold to the Commonwealth, around 3,000 to colonial territories or protectorates, nearly 2,300 to Latin-American countries and nearly 1,000 to the US (*ITA: Annual Report and Accounts 1962–63*, HMSO 1963, p. 11). By 1963–4, this figure had risen to almost 22,000 (*ITA: Annual Report and Accounts 1963–4*, HMSO 1964, p. 23).

8. Lew Grade was Deputy Managing Director of ATV from 1955 to 1962, when he became Managing Director.

9. The *BBC Handbook* for 1967 notes that over 85 per cent of BBC programmes are produced by the BBC, so that in nearly 100 hours of BBC television, only fifteen hours consist of programmes from the US or other foreign countries (1967, p. 25). In 1957–8, the ITA stipulated that the amount of foreign material should not exceed 14 per cent. Their discussion centres primarily on the inclusion of US programmes in the UK ITV schedules (*ITA: Annual Report and Accounts 1957–58*, HMSO 1958, p. 19).

10. The first television drama serial was *Ann and Harold* about the romantic lives of a London society couple (see Vahimagi, 1996, p. 9).

11. See, for example, Osgerby and Gough-Yates (2001) and Chapman (2002) on the action-adventure series, Wheatley (2002) on Gothic television, Cooke's (2003) history of British television drama, and Sydney-Smith (2002) on the police series.

12. An exception to this is the action-adventure series *Adam Adamant Lives!* (BBC, 1966–7), produced by the BBC as a replacement for the US action-adventure spy series *The Man from U.N.C.L.E.* (see Chapman, 2002).

13. *Danger Man* ran on CBS between 5 April 1961 and 13 September 1961.

14. See Rogers (1989, p. 132), and Carrazé and Oswald (1990, p. 210).

15. For example, *The Avengers* shifted to colour production for its fifth season in 1967 despite being transmitted in the UK in black and white, to facilitate the continued sale of the series to the US network ABC (see Chapman, 2000, p. 44), and *The Saint* moved to colour for its third season in 1966 before being picked up by the US network NBC (see Osgerby, 2001, p. 37).

16. *The Prisoner* consisted of seventeen fifty-minute episodes aired weekly between 1 October 1967 and 4 February 1968. On the Southern network, the series was screened at 7.25pm for the first twelve episodes and was then moved to a later slot of 10.05pm until the transmission of the final episode, which was once again at 7.25pm. In fact, the screening of the series was so varied across the ITV regions that it prompted Anthony Davis to comment in his 'Ad Lib' column for the *TV Times*, 'if all the regions decide to take a series – as they did with *The Prisoner* – it is difficult to see why they must not only show it at a different time on different days but in different weeks'

(1968b, p. 11). The problem for ITV's schedules lay in its regional structure, with different networks having responsibility for the production of a regional service.

17. The ITA's audience research indicated that the television audience grew from around 65 per cent between 6.00 and 8.00pm to around 80 per cent between 8.00 and 10.00pm (*ITA: Annual Report and Accounts 1961–62*, HMSO, 1962, p. 15). Therefore, although *The Prisoner* was scheduled to begin at 7.25pm, it offered a lead into the peak viewing time in the middle of the evening.

18. *Report of the Committee on Broadcasting 1960*, HMSO, 1962, p. 34.

19. See the *ITA: Annual Report and Accounts 1955–56* for an account of the ITA's response to these criticisms (1956, p. 13).

20. *Report of the Committee on Broadcasting 1960*, HMSO, 1962, p. 16.

21. Caughie's definition of 'serious' television differs from that discussed earlier in that it is a theoretically elaborated term that centres on television drama. However, in using the term, Caughie recognises its associations with a *legitimate* form of television within public culture (2000, p. 4).

22. The *ITA: Annual Report and Accounts 1965–66* notes an increase in the number of hours devoted to serious programmes from 19 per cent in October 1956 to 35 per cent in March 1966 (1966, p. 13).

23. This is a key distinction between *The Prisoner* and its contemporary action-adventure spy series, *The Avengers*, whose promotional material poses its smiling central characters in playful settings.

24. 'New on Southern This Week', *TV Times*, 30 September–6 October 1967, p. 4.

25. Everyman Films Ltd was formed in 1960 by McGoohan and David Tomblin (producer, writer and director on *The Prisoner*).

26. Patrick McGoohan was writer and director on the following episodes of *The Prisoner*: 'Free for All' (written under the pseudonym Paddy Fitz), 'Once Upon a Time' and 'Fall Out'. He also directed 'Many Happy Returns' and 'A Change of Mind' (both under the pseudonym Joseph Serf).

27. 'New on Southern This Week', *TV Times*, 30 September–6 October 1967, p. 4.

28. In 1958, the Nuffield Foundation published the results of the first major survey of the effects of television on children, which was followed by a joint BBC and ITV committee who published their findings in 1960. In 1964, the Television Research Committee's first working paper considered *The Effects of Mass Communications, with Special Reference to Television* (Halloran, 1964), and in 1966, Mary Whitehouse's pressure group, the National Viewers' and Listeners' Association, held their first convention (Whitehouse, 1967).

29. See, for example, Denis Harley's article in the *TV Times* in which a psychologist gave advice on the representation of 'acceptable' violence in television action-adventure series (1967, p. 14) and George Melly's review articles in *The Observer* which frequently expressed concern about the violence in television action-adventure series (1967, p. 25; 1968, p. 28).

30. See Caughie (2000) for an insightful discussion of Kennedy Martin's article in relation to 'serious' television drama in the 1960s.

31. As Jason Jacobs (2000) has discussed, Kennedy Martin's arguments evidence an amnesia about the history of television that ignores the work of television writers and directors like Nigel Kneale and Rudolph Cartier in the 1950s (see Chapter 1).

32. As John Caughie argues, the clear association made by Kennedy Martin between form and effect is problematic and has been widely debated within Cultural Studies (2000, pp. 106–8).

33. The final episode of the series, 'Fall Out', implies that the Village is actually run by Number Six himself. However, as I will discuss below, this is a highly surreal denouement that poses more questions than it answers.

34. The exceptions to this are the last five episodes whose disruption of *The Prisoner*'s format is discussed below.

35. Although Number Six does go on to subvert subtly the power of the Village in later episodes (such as 'Hammer into Anvil' in which Number Six forces Number Two to resign), this is a small victory compared to the aversion of evil regularly carried out by the protagonists in other contemporary action-adventure series.

36. As I will go on to explore, this hesitation breaks down in the final episodes of the series.

37. Rob Turnock (2003) theorises this as a 'new visibility' that emerges with the expansion of television broadcasting in the 1950s and 1960s.

38. These responses range from one viewer who argues that 'if the whole action was seen as an allegory on life it clicked into place' to another who complained that the final episode lacked any 'semblance of a story' ('Viewerpoint', *TV Times*, 17–23 February 1968, p. 16).

39. For example, Anthony Davis's article in the *TV Times* on the week in which 'Fall Out' aired, questioned McGoohan about the narrative resolution that would be offered in the series' final episode (1968a, p. 5).

40. As the analysis of the marketing of *The Prisoner* demonstrates, these two functions were not considered to be in opposition, but traditional criteria were actually used alongside generic expectations to promote the series to the viewer.

3

'REGULATED INNOVATION'

Star Trek and the Commercial Strategies of US Television in the 1960s

Introduction

So far this book has examined two series produced within the context of British public service broadcasting. In this chapter, the production of telefantasy within the different context of US network television will be explored, focusing on a case study of one of the most enduring telefantasy programmes ever produced, *Star Trek* (NBC, 1966–9).[1] *Star Trek* first aired in the US in 1966, the year before *The Prisoner* first aired in the UK. While *The Prisoner* was the product of a commercial broadcaster struggling to unite the conflicting demands on public service commercial television in the UK, *Star Trek* was the product of a competitive, profit-driven commercial industry. As with *The Prisoner*, it emerged at a time when telefantasy was becoming an increasingly prominent form of television drama. Yet *Star Trek* offers a different representation of the fantastic from both *The Prisoner* and the *Quatermass* serials. *Star Trek*'s depiction of the adventures of a spaceship and her crew in the twenty-third century extrapolates from current scientific knowledge to project humanity into an apparently 'plausible' future. Such a narrative emphasis on 'actual, extrapolative, or speculative science' (Sobchack, 1987, p. 63) has been seen as a central characteristic of science fiction in literature and cinema.[2]

Despite of, or perhaps because of, the apparent ease with which *Star Trek* can be generically categorised as science fiction, most academic analyses of the series have not been primarily concerned with exploring the series' use of genre, focusing instead on accounting for the intensity and longevity of the series' appeal.[3] Indeed, *Star Trek* has a significant place in the history of cult television and fan studies as one of the earliest television series to gain a long-standing international fan following. As a consequence, *Star Trek* was at the centre of the development of fan studies in the 1990s which challenged earlier theorisations of fans as infantile and pathological dupes. While I do not want to deny the cult status that *Star Trek* has come to occupy, or to downplay the significant and valuable role the series plays in the lives of its fans, my concern is to reinstate *Star Trek* into its historical context of production. Thus far the case studies of the *Quatermass* serials and *The Prisoner* have demonstrated how the representation of the fantastic opened up the possibility to explore the boundaries and expectations of television drama. This chapter asks to what extent this was also true of *Star Trek* at a moment in history when US television was dominated by a three-network oligopoly that has been understood to stifle creativity and innovation (see Brown, 1998). Asking what the representation of the fantastic offered in this particular context also complicates the generic categorisation of *Star Trek* as science fiction, tracing the generic lineage of the series in relation to telefantasy while equally valuing the series' links to the action-adventure, Western and crime series.

The US Television Industry in the 1950s and 1960s

National television broadcasting in the US developed out of the institutional structures of radio broadcasting as a commercial, profit-making business licensed to broadcast in the 'public interest, convenience or necessity'. Despite this apparently public service requirement (set down in the Radio Act of 1927 and the Communications Act of 1934), the situation was a far cry from the British model of public service broadcasting. The industry's regulatory body, the Federal Radio Commission (later the Federal Communications Commission, FCC) was primarily concerned with the allocation of licences and the organisational structures of broadcasting. The FCC did not have the power to determine what that public interest was, or to censor programme content (Barnouw, 1982, pp. 58–60) and programming decisions were determined by the financial considerations of profit-making networks and production companies. Despite this, the early days of live television production in the 1940s and 1950s have been characterised as a 'Golden Age' of US television in which creativity and innovation were actively courted by broadcasters in an attempt to attract audiences to this new medium. Central to the 'Golden Age' were anthology series, such as *Kraft Television Theater*, in which each episode was a self-contained and separate television 'play'. These anthology series often drew on recognised talent from the theatre, including rising acting and directing talent such as Paul Newman, Joanne Woodward and Arthur Penn (Barnouw, 1982, p. 156). As with early British television drama, these live plays frequently offered intimate, close-up access to an actor's live virtuoso performance. However, as Jacobs argues, 'there was also a tendency stylistically to emphasise a difference from the theatre, particularly in the excessive display of virtuoso camera movements, or staging the story in what seemed to be "impossible" situations for live studio production' (2000, p. 75). The decline of 'Golden Age' drama over the 1950s has been attributed to a number of institutional, regulatory and technological shifts which gave increased power to a small number of networks which were seen to stifle aesthetic ambition and creativity in pursuit of profits.

First, the decision by the FCC to allocate commercial television in the VHF band of the electromagnetic spectrum in the late 1940s, along with the FCC's suspension of licence approvals between 1948 and 1952, effectively led to the development of a network oligopoly. The FCC's policies at this time benefited those companies, such as NBC and CBS, who had already established businesses in broadcasting. The allocation policies of the FCC did not allow effective competition between more than three national networks and from 1955, network broadcasting in the US was dominated by NBC and CBS, with ABC making up the rest of the market.[4]

Second, funding for programme production gradually moved from the sponsors (who bought slots in the networks' schedules for their programmes) to the networks. As production budgets increased over the 1950s (partly as a consequence of the shift from live production to originating programmes on film), programme production became an increasingly risky investment for a sole sponsor. Television production shifted from a system of full sponsorship to the increasing practice of joint sponsorship (in which sponsors shared production costs with networks and/or production companies) and participation advertising (in which sponsors withdrew from direct programme production and bought airtime from within a network's schedules for their advertising). This reduced the financial risk for advertisers while providing the networks with more power over production and scheduling decisions.[5] Film also increased the potential revenue from one production as filmed programmes could be sold to syndication and abroad,[6] and saw the shift of television production from New York to Hollywood. By 1960, 40 per cent of network programmes were produced by the major Hollywood studios, 20th Century-Fox, MGM, Paramount, Warner Bros., MCA Universal and Columbia Screen Gems, with a number of Hollywood-based, independent production companies also contributing significant numbers of telefilms to the networks.[7]

By the early 1960s, US television programme production was centred in Hollywood, largely financed by the networks, and primarily originated on film. NBC, CBS and ABC had developed as powerful, vertically integrated companies with some involvement at each level of television production and distribution. Each network owned holdings in television stations in the most profitable markets and by 1960, the three networks had around 200 affiliated stations each, giving approximately 60 per cent of their airtime to network programmes (Brown, 1998, p. 147). In particular, the networks dominated primetime programming, between 7.00pm and 11.00pm when television gained its largest audience. Primetime was the most profitable time in the television schedules in terms of sales of advertising, and network programming occupied approximately 75 per cent of the available hours during primetime, frequently attracting 85–90 per cent of the available primetime audience. About half of the profits from television broadcasting in the US went to the three networks and their fifteen owned and operated VHF stations and by 1964, the three networks owned or had property rights in 93 per cent of all primetime network programming (MacDonald, 1990, p. 147).

The network schedules were constructed around the ability to sell airtime slots to advertisers based on existing and projected ratings provided (from 1949) by the A. C. Nielsen Corporation. These ratings were based on sample households and measured the number of viewers tuned to a particular programme at any one time. Ratings also affected the value of the television networks on the stock market. In the mid-1960s, Wall Street began correlating the stock values of the networks with the monthly Nielsen ratings reports. As a consequence the network that came top of the average ratings could make $20–30 million more than its closest competitor (Brown, 1998, p. 154). By the 1960s, television broadcasting was a successful and profitable commercial industry in the US, particularly for the networks. Between 1962 and 1968, the gross profits for the US television industry rose from $1.3 billion to $2.5 billion (MacDonald, 1990, p. 147).

Despite this economic profitability, the industry came under a number of attacks over the late 1950s and 1960s as a series of scandals raised questions about the viability of the regulatory and commercial structures of US television broadcasting. In 1957–8, the House of Representatives undertook a special investigation of the FCC following reports of misconduct in television licensing, leading to the resignation of one commissioner and the commission's chair. A year later, a New York grand jury began investigating allegations of irregularities in televised quizzes and the House of Representatives special sub-committee on legislative oversight began to call witnesses to investigate charges of fraud and other unethical practices in network television broadcasting.[8] In 1961, Newton Minow, the recently appointed chairman of the FCC under Kennedy's newly elected Democratic administration, launched a direct attack on the US television industry. Addressing the National Association of Broadcasters in his first public speech since taking up the position, Minow characterised US television broadcasting as a 'vast wasteland'.[9] Minow attacked both the violent content of programmes and the dominance of 'formulaic' genre shows. He argued that, although these programmes attracted high ratings, they did not necessarily represent an accurate reflection of public interest.

> Your obligations are not satisfied if you look only to popularity as a test of what to
> broadcast. You are not only in show business; you are free to communicate ideas as well as
> relaxation. You must provide a wider range of choices, more diversity, more alternatives. It is
> not enough to cater to the nation's whims – you must also serve the nation's needs.
> (Reprinted in Kahn, 1984, p. 286)

As with the Pilkington Report's criticisms of British commercial broadcasting a year later, Minow's speech reflected an anxiety about commercial television's ability to serve the needs of the public and evidenced a growing sense of the power and social significance of the medium. The restriction of choice caused by the network oligopoly and the reliance on ratings as a means of assessing whether the networks were fulfilling their responsibilities as broadcasters, is seen here to have led to an aesthetic decline in which the former quality dramas of the 'Golden Age' had been replaced by violent, formulaic series.

Yet, despite these criticisms, Minow was keen to emphasise his ideological opposition to government censorship. His speech reflects the paradoxical role of the FCC established in the Communications Act of 1934. Here the FCC's ability to enforce the requirement for broadcasters to operate 'in the public interest, convenience and necessity' was complicated by the First Amendment of the Constitution, safeguarding the right to free speech and thus limiting the regulation of programme content, scheduling and so on. Minow concluded by appealing to the broadcasters' integrity claiming, 'what the Commission asks of you is to make a conscientious good-faith effort to serve the public interest' (reprinted in Kahn, 1984, p. 213).

While the broadcasters argued that the profit incentive was not anathema to the provision of broadcasting in the public interest, the industry as a whole (and the programmes they scheduled in particular) continued to come under criticism in the 1960s. Extensive examples of this debate can be found in the first issues of *Television Quarterly*, a journal set up by the National Academy of Television Arts and Sciences in 1962 to take 'a serious look at television'.[10] For example, in 1962, Hubbell Robinson complained that 'it is in its almost total refusal to cope with themes of depth and significance that television entertainment reduces its audience to the ranks of the emotionally and mentally underprivileged' (1962, p. 36). The industry also came under pressure from public organisations, such as the Civil Rights groups, NAACP (National Association for the Advancement of Colored People) and CORE (Congress

on Racial Equality) who attempted to improve the employment opportunities and cultural representation of ethnic minorities in US television. Yet, while public criticism of US television
continued over the 1960s, the financial position of the three networks (and particularly NBC
and CBS) remained strong.

Star Trek and the Television Industry in the 1960s

This understanding of the US television industry in the 1960s as financially secure but aesthetically impoverished is a dominant one that pervades the first published account of *Star
Trek*'s production history written by Stephen Whitfield with Gene Roddenberry (the series'
creator) in 1968 while the series was still in production. Whitfield and Roddenberry characterised *Star Trek* as an unusual networked series that went against the dominant network
strategy of producing formulaic programmes designed to appeal to the lowest common
denominator.[11]

> *Star Trek* has proved that it really does matter to the viewer what he sees on television.
> Contrary to what the networks may believe, people *do* care about television programming.
> And they do not at all mind learning while being entertained. Learning implies believing.
> Learning also implies intelligence – the ability to see relationships, in a Vulcan, a Gorn, or a
> Horta. The response to *Star Trek*'s message is irrefutable proof of the totally inaccurate
> network concept of the viewer as a clod. (Whitfield and Roddenberry, 1991, p. 351)

The ability for *Star Trek* to go against the tide of 'formulaic and mindless' programming
on the US networks is attributed to Roddenberry's creative use of the science-fiction genre
to develop television drama that is intellectually stimulating and addresses social issues.

> Roddenberry was determined to break through television's censorship barrier and do tales
> about important and meaningful things. He was certain television's audience was not the
> collection of nitwits that the networks believed it to be. By using science-fiction yarns on far-
> off planets, he was certain he could disguise the fact that he was actually talking about
> politics, sex, economics, the stupidity of war, and half a hundred other vital subjects usually
> prohibited on television. (Whitfield and Roddenberry, 1991, p. 19)

Whitfield thus situated the idealistic Roddenberry against the constraints of the networks that
deliberately refrained from the intellectual treatment of meaningful contemporary issues. In
creating a network series with a social conscience, Whitfield argued that Roddenberry used
science fiction to disguise from the networks the fact that the series tackled contemporary
social issues.

The understanding of US television in the 1960s as a period of decline in the quality of
programming following the Golden Age of the 1950s is a pervasive one in histories of US
television. Typically, historians have argued that, as a consequence of the relatively unregu-
lated commercial domination of the television industry by the three-network oligopoly, US
television in the 1960s was characterised by repetitive, formulaic and homogenous programming. Les Brown claims that by the mid-1960s, 'scores of pilots for new series were

produced each year, and nearly all were mere variations on proven formulas' (1998, p. 154). He goes on to claim that the ratings war that ensued as the financing of production shifted from full sponsorship to participation advertising seriously stunted creative programming, so that 'networks lost virtually all ability to be boldly venturesome in programming' (ibid.).

However, a commercial network strategy that emphasises audience quantity with predictable schedules dominated by filmed genre series cannot necessarily be equated with formulaic and homogenous programming. Barry Litman argues that, in order to maintain an effective oligopoly, the three networks functioned in a '"spirit of cooperation", featuring common industry-wide pricing, with rivalry and individual firm success limited to how well one does in the nonpricing areas of product differentiation (that is, differences in product quality, advertising, and packaging)' (1990, p. 116). Litman here suggests that it was in the area of production that the competitive battles between the three networks were fought.

Mark Alvey argues that product differentiation is a particularly important commercial strategy during periods of great change and is therefore central to understanding television production in the 1960s.

> No industry is fraught with more such tensions than the television industry, and no period in the medium's history is more apt an example of such an environment than the late 1950s and early 1960s. As *Variety* reported in late 1959, networks and producers were busily seeking alternatives that would free them from the 'quiz-violence-western-hook'. In the prevailing climate of the television industry as the 1960s began, the calls for innovation could not be ignored. This atmosphere of change and differentiation established a tenor that would characterise the evolution of programming throughout the decade. (1997, p. 150)

Alvey goes on to argue that the independent studios were central to this period of change and innovation.[12] With the market for network programmes monopolised by the three networks, and the increasing prevalence of deficit financing as network policy (in which the networks projected the overall profitability of a series, including potential foreign and ancillary sales, and reduced their financial investment accordingly), the financial situation of the studios was particularly precarious. However, far from concluding that this led to stagnation in programming, Alvey argues that the studios, particularly the independents that lacked the financial infrastructure of the majors, turned to a strategy of 'regulated innovation' (1997, p. 154) in order to survive.

> The independent producer had to differentiate to survive, had to distinguish his production from the competition. Granting that independent production is an avowedly commercial enterprise, concerned with producing popular texts for a large audience, the evidence suggests that the independents were testing the limits of convention and expanding the horizons of popular television entertainment, albeit within fairly circumscribed formal limits. (1997, p. 152)

Rather than simply equating the economic security of the networks in the 1960s with the production of formulaic programming, Alvey and Litman offer a more complex understanding of the industry as one in which product differentiation was central to the networks and to the independent production companies who made many of their programmes. By situating *Star Trek* within this understanding of 1960s network television production as a period of 'regulated innovation', I want to move away from understanding the series as a uniquely innovative programme enabled by Roddenberry's ingenious use of science fiction. Rather, I want to ask how the production of the series responded to the needs of commercial US television at this time.

Alvey's concept of 'regulated innovation', in which the independent studios played a major part, is useful in approaching *Star Trek*, particularly as the series was produced by the independent studio Desilu. Founded by Lucille Ball and Desi Arnez, Desilu entered television production in 1951, four years before the first major motion-picture studios entered the industry in 1955. Desilu began by producing *I Love Lucy* (starring Ball and Arnez) on a rented sound stage for the CBS network. The series was hugely successful in the 1950s and consistently ranked in the top three of the Nielsen ratings between 1951 and 1957. In 1957, Desilu bought RKO's studio facilities where it continued to produce a number of successful television programmes for the networks. By the early 1960s, Desilu had become the top supplier of telefilms to the networks. However, after the divorce of Lucille Ball and Desi Arnez, the studio began to falter. It produced a number of unsuccessful pilots and by the mid-1960s was only surviving through the continued success of *The Lucy Show* and the rental of its studio facilities. CBS, who had established a long-standing relationship with Desilu through the success of *I Love Lucy* and *The Lucy Show*, intervened by creating a development fund for the studio to produce new series (see Solow and Justman, 1996, p. 5). The studio hired Oscar Katz (who had been Vice President of Network Programmes for CBS) to run Desilu, and Katz brought in Herb Solow (previously Director of Daytime Programmes for NBC) as Vice President with responsibility for the development of new programmes. Solow employed a number of writers to create pilots for filmed television series that could be sold to the networks. One of these writers was Gene Roddenberry, who had been working as a writer/producer of television series for the major Hollywood studio, MGM.

In the early 1950s, when most television production was live, Desilu pioneered the use of film in the production of *I Love Lucy*, by using a three-camera film set-up that allowed them to shoot in front of a live studio audience, but still be able to re-shoot and edit. However, within the context of the early 1960s, when the industry had almost exclusively moved to film for drama production, Desilu was in danger of lagging behind. Having made its reputation with three-camera, half-hour sitcoms, Desilu was keen to prove that it could move into the production of hour-long filmed drama series, the primary form of drama in the prime-time network schedules by the early 1960s. Desilu's intention to produce hour-long telefilms was a commercial strategy designed to move the studio into the most competitive and financially rewarding area of television drama production in the 1960s. It was as part of this commercial strategy to reinvigorate the declining presence of Desilu in the television production market that *Star Trek* was produced. As a struggling independent studio, Desilu certainly seems to fit Alvey's understanding of the context of production for the US television industry in the 1960s. Yet, to what extent can *Star Trek* be understood to offer 'regulated innovation' at this time?

Regulated Innovation and Genre

One way in which it is possible to assess whether a programme offered innovation, however regulated, is to look at its use of genre. Although Whitfield and Roddenberry (1991) claimed that *Star Trek*'s use of science fiction was innovative in itself, the series was certainly not the only science-fiction or fantasy series on US television at the time. In 1964, when Roddenberry produced the story outline to pitch *Star Trek* to the networks, there were already two types of series that could be broadly understood as science fiction or fantasy on US network television. First, there were episodic series aimed primarily at children and family audiences, such as Irwin Allen's *Voyage to the Bottom of the Sea* (ABC, 1964–8), Gerry Anderson's puppet series *Fireball XL-5* (NBC, 1963–5), which was imported from the UK to NBC in 1963, and sitcoms such as *My Favorite Martian* (CBS, 1963–6). Second, there were anthology series, such as *The Twilight Zone* (CBS, 1959–62, 1963–4) and *The Outer Limits* (ABC, 1963–5), which offered unusual tales of the macabre and tended to deal with more adult themes or contain stronger references to horror. In the early 1960s, these anthology series were the main site for adult-orientated, primetime fantasy drama.

The series outline that Roddenberry produced to pitch *Star Trek* to the networks in 1964 situated the series in relation to existing science-fiction and fantasy television drama, offering 'regulated innovation' by associating it with and differentiating it from other television science fiction.

> *Star Trek* will be a television 'first' ... A one-hour science-fiction series *with continuing characters*. Combining the most varied in drama-action-adventure with complete production practicality. And with almost limitless story potential. *Star Trek* is a new kind of television science fiction *with all the advantages of an anthology, but none of the limitations*. (Cited in Whitfield and Roddenberry, 1991, p. 20)

Roddenberry attempted to sell *Star Trek* by differentiating it from existing science fiction television, as a series with the story latitude of the anthology series, but with the audience identification of the continuing series. *Star Trek* provided product differentiation by offering a type of television drama that had not been done before, a continuing science-fiction series with the audience appeal and story latitude of the anthology series.[13]

The terms within which Roddenberry differentiated *Star Trek* from existing television science fiction are particularly significant here. The most valuable series for the US networks at this time were those which ran over 100 episodes, the minimum number of episodes for a series to be considered viable for sale to syndication. A long-running series that could be sold to syndication was likely to be significantly more profitable for both the network and the studio producing the programme. Roddenberry pitched *Star Trek* as a series which overcame the potential barriers to creating a long-running primetime science-fiction series. In differentiating *Star Trek* from extant television science fiction, he stressed its potential to fulfil the three primary criteria in producing a long-running network series: production practicality, audience identification and story latitude. It is these three elements, rather than the series' generic associations with science fiction, which are emphasised in this outline, and they are central to the debates surrounding the production of the series. Indeed, as I will go on to argue, the generic categorisation of *Star Trek* as science fiction was particularly problematic for the network.

Roddenberry pitched *Star Trek* to NBC and CBS, and in May 1964, the NBC network provided Desilu with money to develop three story outlines for *Star Trek* and then chose one story to be developed into a pilot episode.[14] After a mixed response when testing the first pilot with audiences, NBC commissioned a second pilot of the series. Stephen Whitfield argues that the reasons for this highly unusual step stemmed from the first pilot's 'cerebral' treatment of intellectual issues, stating that

> The overall reason given for the rejection [by NBC] was that the pilot was just 'too cerebral'. NBC felt the show would go over the heads of most of the viewers, that it required too much thought on the part of the viewer in order to understand it. (Whitfield and Roddenberry, 1991, pp. 107–8).

However, Whitfield's account of NBC's opposition to the more 'cerebral' aspects of the first pilot (which reiterated the dominant conception of 1960s network television as conventional and unintelligent) does not fully explain why the network commissioned a second pilot instead of rejecting the series outright. Oscar Katz has argued that the network's difficulty stemmed from the initial choice of episode to be developed into a pilot. He claims that NBC had selected a story outline for development into the first pilot that would test the production practicality of the series. According to Katz, NBC commissioned the most technically complex story for development into a pilot to verify Desilu's capabilities to produce such a technically sophisticated drama as a weekly series (Katz, cited in Alexander, 1994, p. 224). Having satisfied themselves that Desilu was capable of producing the series, NBC ordered a second pilot from a new selection of story outlines chosen specifically to sell the series to advertisers. Indeed, NBC did go on to transmit the first pilot in a re-edited two-part story entitled 'The Menagerie' that went on to win a Hugo Award.

Furthermore, the promotional document produced by NBC Sales for *Star Trek* ahead of the 1966–7 season, did not shy away from the series' 'cerebral' treatment of its narrative themes.

> In the manner of every successful piece of speculative fiction from the classics of Jules Verne, H. G. Wells and Aldous Huxley to the works of such current masters of the art as Ray Bradbury, Isaac Asimov and Kingsley Amis, the *Star Trek* storylines will stimulate the imagination without bypassing the intellect. While speculating in a fascinating way about the future, the series also will have much to say that is meaningful to us today. (Reproduced in Solow and Justman, 1996, pp. 202–3)

In this document, the associations of *Star Trek* with the 'intellectual' narratives of literary science fiction are actually emphasised, suggesting that far from opposing the potential for intellectually stimulating stories in *Star Trek*, the network actively promoted this aspect of the series' format.

However, despite the references to authors of literary science fiction in this promotional document, the use of the term 'speculative fiction' in favour of 'science fiction' points to the anxieties the network had about the generic expectations associated with science fiction. Herbert Solow and Robert Justman claim that NBC's audience research suggested that while

NBC's advertisement for the first episode of *Star Trek*, which ran in *The Los Angeles Times* (8 September 1966) and in the *TV Guide* (fall preview edition, September 1966), places the youthful human hero Kirk (William Shatner) in the foreground (reproduced from Solow and Justman, 1996, p. 264)

women in their twenties and thirties were not opposed to action-adventure series, they were definitely not fans of science fiction (Solow and Justman, 1996, p. 64). NBC was particularly keen not to alienate this section of the audience, who were considered an attractive demographic by advertisers because of their perceived control over family spending. The newspaper advertisements for *Star Trek* placed by the network prior to its initial transmission on NBC in September 1966 indicate the possibilities and difficulties offered by the series' associations with science fiction. The full-page advertisements claimed that *Star Trek* was going where 'no program has ever gone before ...'. This tag-line, which makes use of the series' opening narration to emphasise the novelty of its futuristic format, suggested that *Star Trek*'s generic difference from other television drama was understood as an important element in attracting viewers to the series. The bulk of the advertisement consists of a drawing reflecting the key elements of the series' format. A large dark planet dominates the centre with a small sketch of the starship *Enterprise* flying across it, leaving in its wake the words *Star Trek* in large print. The dynamism of the distinctive spaceship is indicated but relegated to a small section of the background. Underneath and dominating the foreground are artist's sketches of the faces of William Shatner 'as Capt. James T. Kirk (Earthman)' and Leonard Nimoy 'as Science Officer Spock (from the planet Vulcan)' in front of a group image of officers on the bridge of the *Enterprise*. The sketch of Kirk, emphasising his youthful attractiveness, dominates the page, while Spock's unusual features are much less prominent in the background. The advertisement signals the series' unusual elements which associate *Star Trek* with science fiction – a spaceship, an alien co-star, interplanetary travel – but relegates them to the background, allowing the character of the youthful human hero to dominate.

The emphasis in this advertisement on the characters is also apparent in Roddenberry's series outline for *Star Trek*, which placed a stress on the series' use of identifiable characters and situations.

> *Star Trek keeps all of science fiction's variety and excitement, but still stays within a mass audience frame of reference* ... By avoiding 'way out' fantasy and cerebral science theorem and instead concentrating on problem and peril met by our very human and very identifiable characters. Fully one-third of the most successful of all science fiction is in this 'practical' category. Tales of exotic 'methane atmosphere worlds with six-headed monsters' are rare among the science-fiction classics. The best and most popular *feature highly dramatic variations of recognizable things and themes.* (Cited in Whitfield and Roddenberry, 1991, p. 23)

The 'cerebral' aspects of science fiction are here associated with scientific theorem, rather than the exploration of intellectual themes or contemporary concerns, and Roddenberry is keen to stress that despite the generic associations of science fiction with technically and scientifically complex narratives, *Star Trek*'s stories will remain within the viewer's frame of reference.

These documents appear to challenge the notion that, in producing *Star Trek*, Roddenberry used the science-fiction genre to 'disguise' the series' address to contemporary social concerns. Rather than indicating that the networks aimed to produce television drama that overtly avoided contemporary issues, these documents suggest that NBC's major concern was to produce a long-running series that would attract regular, large audiences. Their primary anxiety in promoting *Star Trek* was not that it may tackle socially relevant issues, but rather that its futuristic setting may make its narratives too remote and removed from the viewer's frame of reference. Consequently, the promotion for the series stresses the relevance of the stories and the centrality of the characters. Here the series' generic associations with science fiction are both valuable, offering product differentiation and story latitude, and problematic, potentially alienating important audience demographics. The innovative ways in which *Star Trek* attempts to create a new form of science-fiction television are regulated through an emphasis on those elements that will offer a familiar point of reference for the audience.

The emphasis placed on creating these familiar points of reference in the series' promotion is carried over into the construction of the crew of the *Enterprise*. The three leads in the series are constructed as recognisable character types. Captain Kirk (William Shatner) is the determined action-adventure hero, Doctor McCoy (DeForest Kelley) the humorous and cynical doctor and Spock (Leonard Nimoy) the intelligent and efficient second-in-command. This point of identification is enhanced through the narrative device of the Captain's log. In each episode, this voice-over narration by Captain Kirk orientates the viewer.[15] The Captain's narration is always reliable and frequently provides a privileged point of view. For example, in the first season episode, 'The Enemy Within', Captain Kirk is divided into two characters, one good and one evil, by a transporter malfunction. The teaser depicts Kirk walking out of the *Enterprise*'s transporter room as a second Kirk materialises in the transporter chamber. The unusual nature of this second appearance of Kirk is enhanced through the use of strong lighting from below and the dark background that frames Kirk's face, underscored by rhythmic drums building in intensity. After the credits, the first act returns to this manifestation of 'evil' Kirk in a tracking mid-shot. Over this shot, Kirk's voice-over explains the situation from a privileged point of knowledge as he narrates: 'Unknown to any of us during this time, a duplicate of me, some strange alter-ego had been created by the transporter malfunction.' This explains the story to the viewer; clarifying any ambiguity and providing the exposition absent in the teaser's dramatic cliff-hanger.

The narrative device of the Captain's log therefore allows the series to comment upon its own story and to indicate to the audience what is 'strange' and what is 'normal' in this futuristic world. Captain Kirk becomes one of the primary means through which the audience gains access to the rules and conventions of this futuristic world and takes a position upon them. The voice-over also provides a point of intimacy between the character of Kirk and the audience. The viewer is privy to his personal thoughts and comments on the action that is unfolding. This is reiterated through the frequent use of 'asides' in which recurring lead characters direct dialogue away from the other characters and in the direction of (but not directly out to) the camera. These asides are moments in which the regular characters provide their appraisal of the situation at hand, offering exposition and narrative explanation. For example, in 'Errand of Mercy', Kirk and Spock beam down to the planet Organia to secure it as a Federation outpost in the continuing war between the Federation and the Klingons. The sets and costumes used to represent Organia resemble that of medieval Earth. In a verbal exchange between Spock and Kirk, directed out towards the camera and away from the Organians, Spock reveals that his scientific measurements of the planet do not correspond with the Federation's computer records. He states

> Our information on these people and their culture is not correct. This is not a primitive society making progress towards mechanisation. They are totally stagnant. There is no evidence of any progress as far back as my tricorder can register.

This exchange situates the visual references to medieval Earth in the representation of Organia within the narrative context of the episode, while also intimately drawing the viewer into the private space of Kirk and Spock's discussion.

This 'frontality' as a visual device places an emphasis on the *reactions* of characters to the unknown over the representation of the fantastic itself. Therefore, although this intimacy is balanced by action sequences, it is not unusual for the climactic cliff-hangers to end with a close-up of the face of a recurring character, rather than with a dramatic special effect or action sequence. The moments of tension and drama in *Star Trek* are therefore predominantly dependent upon the representation of the consequences of the events depicted for its main characters. For example, in 'Errand of Mercy', acts one to three all end with a close-up of either Kirk, or Kirk and Spock. The emphasis in these dramatic moments is on the escalated threat to these central characters. For example, act two ends with Kirk being threatened with death by the Klingons. The camera tracks in to a close-up of Kirk's concerned face, accompanied by a dramatic music sting. The use of a close-up here draws the viewer into an intimate relationship with these familiar recurring characters, emphasising audience identification by locating the drama in the reaction of the characters to the escalation of the threat, rather than in a fast-paced action or special effects sequence. Thus, the excitement and drama of *Star Trek* is constructed less through the depiction of alien creatures and fantastical planets than in an exploration of the consequences of the meeting of its familiar recurring characters with the threat of the unknown. *Star Trek* therefore domesticates its representation of futuristic space flight by grounding its fantastic narratives in the experiences of its familiar characters, emphasising the construction of an intimate relationship between the protagonists and the audience over the representation of alien creatures or spectacular conflict.

Regulated Innovation and Narrative
Familiarity is enhanced further by the series' use of the conventions of the action-adventure series, which had become the dominant form of episodic television drama by the mid-1960s. The origins of the action-adventure series in the US lie with the episodic series that emerged in the late 1940s. Although the 1940s and 1950s have been characterised as a 'Golden Age' of anthology dramas and single plays (see above) that were superseded by the episodic series, the episodic drama can be traced back to the late 1940s with live series such as the half-hour crime drama, *Man Against Crime* (CBS, 1949–53, Dumont, 1953–4, NBC, 1953–4, 1956). However, once the networks were no longer trying to attract viewers to television as a medium, competition began to emerge between networks, and sustaining audiences became as important as attracting them in the first place. These changes favoured the episodic series which offered audiences familiar characters, settings and stories which were repeated each week. Preferred by sponsors, the filmed episodic series enabled identification with a cast of recurring characters which, as Barnouw points out, had merchandising advantages as stars could be used to promote sponsor's products (1990, p. 166). Filmed series were also generally cheaper to produce than single plays, using a recurring range of sets, actors and props. By the late 1950s live drama (both episodic and anthology) was gradually eclipsed by the production of filmed episodic telefilms which became the main battleground for network ratings.

While in the mid- to late 1950s the Western series dominated primetime telefilm production (with series such as *Cheyenne* [ABC, 1955–63] and *Gunsmoke* [CBS, 1955–75]), other genres of telefilm appeared over the 1960s, such as the crime, spy, science fiction and fantasy series. Despite the generic differences between these series, they all shared certain characteristics. There was an emphasis on dramatic action and on the presentation and resolution of conflict, often through violence and gunplay. The narrative structure maintained familiarity by using a regular cast of characters and storylines based around set themes that were resolved each week in the twenty-five or fifty-minute episodes. Indeed, Osgerby and Gough-Yates (2001) unite the Western, crime, spy and fantasy series of this period under the generic category of the 'action-adventure series', in which a cast of heroic, recurring characters is placed in a different perilous situation each week from which they must use their skill and ingenuity to escape.

It is these action-adventure telefilms which came under particular attack in Newton Minow's 'vast wasteland' speech as 'a procession of ... blood and thunder, mayhem, violence, sadism, murder, western badmen, western good men, private eyes, gangsters, more violence' (Minow, reproduced in Kahn, 1984, p. 285), and which were understood to constitute a move away from the quality of performance, writing and stylistic innovation associated with Golden Age anthology drama towards the 'low culture' of Hollywood B-movie serial production. Yet, to characterise the telefilmed series as simply formulaic genre productions, is to fail to allow the episodic series any kind of aesthetic value.[16]

As Horace Newcomb (1997) argues, a deeper examination of the form of the Western telefilms reveals a strong element of the anthology drama within their narrative structures. While these series were based on a conflict/resolution narrative structure in which a regular cast in a familiar setting encountered and resolved a problem, the conflict within these dramas frequently came from the guest stars rather than the recurring characters. In part this was a necessary consequence of the narrative format of the episodic series, as the resolution of conflict and the return to the status quo tended to inhibit significant character and narrative development. Yet, as a consequence of this, the filmed episodic series actually enabled the treatment of a wide range of relevant social issues. As Newcomb argues of the Western telefilm:

> Like the live anthology dramas they replaced, then, and similar to the anthological filmed drama found in series as distinctive as *Route 66*, *The Twilight Zone*, *The Defenders*, or *The Fugitive*, the television western as narrative was open to a huge range of topics and plot configurations. (1997, p. 296)

The format that Newcomb identifies as linking the Western telefilm with the anthology series – a primary concern with conflict that is located with the recurring cast's engagement with a guest character – is a basic element of all action-adventure series. As such, Newcomb's defence of the Western from cultural criticism can equally be applied to other generic forms of action-adventure drama.

Star Trek's narrative structure certainly follows the broad conventions of the action-adventure series. Each week the crew of the *Enterprise* encounters a new problem that brings them into conflict and each week they must use their ingenuity to overcome the conflict and return to their status quo. As with Newcomb's definition of the Western telefilm, the conflict frequently occurs through the crew's interaction with an external force. This narrative device allowed the series to deal with a wide range of different issues without compromising its basic format. However, the narrative fluidity of *Star Trek* was greatly enhanced by its fantastic premise. As a consequence, *Star Trek*'s world is one in which great transformations are possible, allowing it to explore the consequences of a human's personality being split into 'good' and 'bad' ('The Enemy Within'), of a human being given the powers of a god ('Where No Man Has Gone Before') or of a human's inhibitions being removed ('The Naked Time'). As with *The Prisoner*, the fluidity of the format is also used to enable the series to play with its own narrative format, turning the rational Spock into an emotional being ('This Side of Paradise') or creating an alternative 'evil' version of the starship *Enterprise* ('Mirror, Mirror'). This fantastic premise also enables *Star Trek* to reference a range of different generic expectations. For example, 'The Devil in the Dark' makes use of the generic expectations of the crime mystery as the *Enterprise* is called in to investigate mysterious deaths in a mining colony. 'Assignment: Earth' references the spy genre; 'Spectre of the Gun' is set in the Wild West; and 'A Piece of the Action' is clearly indebted to the gangster genre as the *Enterprise* visits a planet reminiscent of the US in the 1920s. These generic references expand the story potential, while still functioning within the narrative expectations of the series' action-adventure format. They also function to combine the dual demands of story latitude and audience identification, offering a wide range of different stories within one format and enhancing audience identification by drawing on familiar generic expectations.

Despite the seemingly limitless possibilities opened up by this use of the fantastic, the series never wavers from the action-adventure format. At the end of each episode, the narrative disruption is overcome and equilibrium is re-established. Following the expectations of the action-adventure format, the viewer can be assured that every week the crew of the *Enterprise* will be placed in a perilous position from which they will inevitably escape. Each episode ends with the restoration of 'normality', ensuring that the basic elements of *Star Trek*'s format remain consistent from week to week. The stories never refer to other episodes and the characters, procedures and basic elements of the series do not substantially change over the course of its three seasons. As Ilsa J. Bick points out:

> A large portion of ST's [*Star Trek*'s] psychological agenda is invested in the maintenance of sameness, most explicitly in the fact that the Enterprise, as symbolic of this self-enclosed, hermetic stasis, opens and closes every episode of the original series except one. (1996, p. 45)

This apparent paradox, between allowing extensive narrative fluidity on the one hand, and maintaining sameness on the other, is a general feature of the action-adventure format. While, as Newcomb argues of the Western telefilm, theorists frequently criticise the 'easy' resolutions offered in these series, such a critique should not be at the expense of an equal recognition of the ways in which these series expose and tackle social conflicts. Indeed, to create regulated innovation, *Star Trek* aims to offer innovation and difference while retaining a certain level of familiarity. *Star Trek*'s basis in fantasy enables extensive story latitude, allowing the series to disrupt its own narrative conventions and to draw on a wide range of generic expectations in order to explore metaphorically issues of social concern, while its recurring elements – the *Enterprise* and its crew – remained largely unchanged.

As a consequence, as Buxton (1990) argues, the series' ideological project remains contradictory. While it is premised on an optimistic conception of human development into an egalitarian future in the twenty-third century, its individual episodes undermine the progressive future represented. Each week the crew encounters a problem as a consequence of engaging with alien beings. To understand and solve these problems, Kirk and his officers apply a form of logical reasoning which, as Buxton argues, imposes the norms of human evolution 'as a standard for all intelligent development' (1990, pp. 61–2). Yet the series' application of these norms frequently conflicts with its optimistic conception of a peaceful future for mankind. For example, in 'This Side of Paradise', the crew of the *Enterprise* beam down to the planet Omicron Ceti III, where a human colony had settled three years previously. Despite being exposed to deadly 'Berthold' rays, the colonists are in perfect health, living in a paradisaic pre-modern society with no vehicles, weapons, violence, disease or unhappiness. It soon becomes apparent that the colony's idyllic existence is a consequence of their infection by the spores of an alien plant, which soon infect the crew of the *Enterprise* too. As a consequence, the usually rational Spock feels emotion for the first time, falling in love with Leila, one of the colonists, and the rest of the crew mutiny, leaving Kirk alone on the ship. In fighting the infection from the spores, Kirk discovers that violent human emotions are the only cure. He engages Spock in a violent battle, and uses a subsonic ray to incite the rest of the crew and the colonists to feel aggression, ultimately freeing them from the effect of the spores. This episode, while metaphorically critiquing the 'drop-out' counter-cultures of the 1960s, presents a notion of humanity that is ultimately contradictory. The passive, emotional and peaceful life on Omicron Ceti III is problematic because its ethos goes against the project of the *Enterprise* – the ambitious project to seek out new civilisations, to explore the universe. As Kirk argues of the life of the colonists, 'No wants, no needs. We weren't meant for this, none of us. Man stagnates if he has no ambition, no desire to be more than he is.' The conclusion to the episode is ultimately critical of the 'paradise' offered by the spores. Once the hold of the spores over the colonists is broken, their leader agrees to allow them to be taken to a new colony, exclaiming dejectedly of their life on Omicron Ceti III, 'We've done nothing here. No accomplishments, no progress'. Yet, at the same time, the use of violence to break the hold of the spores reveals an inherent conflict in the *Enterprise*'s 'peaceful' mission, suggesting that the ideology of the *Enterprise* rests on a conception of humanity whose 'ambition' is impossible without violent and aggressive emotions. Furthermore, much of the emotional resonance of the episode lies with Spock's experience of emotion for the first time. This plotline has a poignancy that opens up the space for the ideology of the *Enterprise* to be drawn into question. Indeed, while the overarching narrative thrust of the episode upholds Kirk's ideology, this is undercut as the episode ends with Spock exclaiming of his time under the influence of the spores that 'for the first time in my life, I was happy'. Here, the resolution that is required to return the crew to its status quo is far from 'easy' and offers a potential critique of the *Enterprise*'s apparently egalitarian mission.

Regulated Innovation and Representation

The contradictory nature of Star Trek's narratives is further apparent in the strategies it adopts to represent the fantastic visually. Despite the possibilities for story latitude in Star Trek's narrative premise, the series' ability to represent space as 'a place of infinite variety' (Roddenberry's series outline, reproduced in Whitfield and Roddenberry, 1991, p. 23) was severely limited by the financial restrictions under which it was produced. Star Trek was budgeted at $200,000 per episode, with NBC contributing $160,000 per episode, and Desilu making up the deficit.[17] While the average cost for a comparable action-adventure series at this time was $160,000, this higher budget was necessary to fund the series' special effects and in particular, the extensive use of optical effects (between fifteen and twenty per episode). As a consequence of financial limitations, only four types of alien planet are represented in the series: a generic rocky planet set; a lush green 'paradise' planet shot on location; a planet which equates with earth, either through the use of backlots or location shooting; Federation planets which allowed the re-use of permanent Enterprise sets.

However, the series' 'innovation' was premised in part on the expectation that it would take the viewer 'where no man has gone before'. In order to fulfil this expectation within its budget, the series turned to the use of colour. Roddenberry stressed the importance of shooting the series in colour in a memo to Grant Tinker at NBC in July 1964:

> Further research and preparation on Star Trek has so convinced me of the necessity of color photography that I felt I owed you this early note on the subject. It is important to effectively meet the challenge of giving continuing variety to the new planets we visit from week to week – plus that extra 'something' which suggests the mystery and excitement of other worlds. Color solves many problems here. For example, the occasional converting of our blue sky to violet or other hues can be accomplished via filters, mats, and other methods. Along the same line, color can also convert even common vegetation into something new and exciting. Whereas fabricating entirely new vegetation can be quite a budget factor, the spraying of an occasional bush and tree to a new tint can be economical and highly effective. Costumes which might seem rather Earthly in recognizable colors can take on an entirely different identity in the same way. And without expensive changes in form and configuration, a vegetable-dyed green woman can be at once very attractive and still highly alien. (Cited in Alexander, 1994, p. 201)

Star Trek's extensive reliance on colour to represent the fantastic future of space travel made it an attractive product for NBC, a network financially invested in the sale of colour receivers. In the mid-1960s, NBC was engaged in a campaign to become the first 'all-colour' network in the US. NBC was owned by RCA, who in 1954 won the battle for colour television against CBS with the adoption of their three-colour-gun system by the FCC. However, it was not until 1960, when the market for black-and-white receivers was reaching saturation, that RCA made a profit from the sale of colour receivers for the first time (see Barnouw, 1990, p. 100, and Bilby, 1986, p. 210). Throughout the 1960s the market for colour receivers gradually increased. By 1965, twenty companies were manufacturing colour sets and all three networks had begun to transmit in colour. When in 1966, RCA commissioned A. C. Nielsen

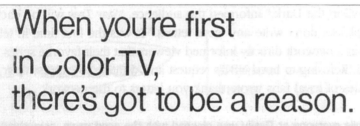

When you're first in Color TV, there's got to be a reason.

See "Star Trek" on RCA Victor Color TV. Shown above, The Hathaway

- Like Automatic Fine Tuning that gives you a perfectly fine-tuned picture every time.
- A new RCA tube with 38% brighter highlights.
- Advanced circuitry that won't go haywire.
- And over 25 years of color experience.
- You get all this and more from RCA VICTOR.

The Most Trusted Name in Electronics

RCA used *Star Trek* in a promotional campaign in *TV Guide* to encourage viewers to purchase colour receivers (reproduced from Solow and Justman, 1996, p. 306) to study the popularity of networked colour television series, the research revealed that *Star Trek* was the highest-rated colour television series on the air at that time. RCA went on to use *Star Trek* in a promotional campaign to encourage viewers to purchase colour receivers. Herbert Solow argues that this research was a factor in the network's decision to renew the series for a second season despite its relatively poor performance in the ratings (Solow and Justman, 1996, p. 307).[18] Furthermore, RCA actively associated its colour sets with the technical advancements of the space race through a promotional campaign that claimed, 'Color TV custom-engineered the Space Age way' (cited in Spigel, 1997, p. 56).

Colour is used extensively in *Star Trek*, in the design of the recurring elements, such as the *Enterprise* and her crew, and in the representation of alien planets and creatures. In the design of the *Enterprise*, colour is used to signal the futurism of the spaceship and her crew, and to enhance audience identification by offering a distinctive and intelligible representation of futuristic space travel. For the interiors of the *Enterprise*, set designer Matt Jeffries used bold primary colours (particularly red and yellow), doors that open automatically, and banks of flashing lights, to create a futuristic-looking environment. The distinctive use of colour in the sets is reinforced through the lighting design, which uses pools of primary colours through-out the *Enterprise*, frequently backlighting the stars with strong colours in close-up. However, these futuristic sets are also made intelligible through references to contemporary socio-cul-tural verisimilitude. The interior design of the *Enterprise* has a contemporary nautical feel with curved walls and visible trunking, complemented through the use of contemporary sailing terms such as port, starboard, captain, crew, ship, and so on. The crews' uniforms bear little resemblance to twentieth-century military dress, but they follow a similar logic in their con-ception. The arms of each tunic are adorned with gold wavy bands which indicate rank – one for a lieutenant, two for an officer, three for a captain – and all uniforms carry a Federation insignia on the chest. The colours of both the male and female crew costumes indicate their relative departments (blue for science; red for engineering and security; yellow for the cap-tain, helmsmen and so on) while also complementing the use of colour in the set and lighting designs. This regimentation in the costumes takes twentieth-century concepts about uniform dress and transposes them into the future, enabling them to be both futuristic and believable.

The construction of the recurring setting of the *Enterprise* as futuristic and intelligible can also be understood in relation to the contemporary discourses surrounding space flight in the representation of the space race in the 1960s. Much of the visual iconography of futuristic space travel in the design of the *Enterprise*, such as the curved console chairs, drew on con-temporary designs associated with space travel. However, as Lynn Spigel points out, in the 1960s, such designs were mass marketed for consumption in the domestic space of the sub-urban home (1997, pp. 55–6). Such visual elements signal the *Enterprise* as both futuristic and familiar, and draw a link between the private domestic space of the home and the pub-lic/private spaces of the *Enterprise* sets. *Star Trek* not only takes you into space and into the future from the comfort of your own home, it does so in a ship and with a crew that, while recognisably futuristic, are also reassuringly familiar. However, this is a suburban domesticity that was predominantly only open for consumption by white, middle-class Americans, sug-gesting that the familiarity offered by the recurring elements of the series' design might be more open to certain audiences than others.

This is also apparent in the casting of the crew of the *Enterprise*. *Star Trek* represented an integrated cast on the *Enterprise*, in which both women and ethnic minorities have positions of responsibility in the Federation's voyages into space. Such multiculturalism was particularly significant at a time when NASA was criticised for its marginalisation of women and ethnic minorities in its space project (Spigel, 1997). However, despite putting an African woman, a Japanese-American man and a Russian man on the bridge of the *Enterprise*, these characters are all relegated to supporting roles (see Bernardi, 1998, pp. 39–42). The familiarity offered by this integrated cast is one in which, for example, women undertake traditionally gendered roles, such as Uhura's role as Communications Officer and Christine Chapel's role as the ship's nurse.

Meanwhile, the 'otherness' of the aliens encountered by the *Enterprise* is indicated by contemporary socio-cultural signifiers of racial difference. As the series could not afford to regularly commission expensive effects to create vastly different creatures, the alien beings that the *Enterprise* meets are primarily humanoid. To rationalise this, the series drew on a notion of 'parallel evolution', which, as Bernardi points out 'allowed the creative decision-makers to construct alien societies with which both the audience and the network could identify' (1998, p. 56). Costume and make-up are frequently used to suggest the alien through reference to contemporary visual codes associated with the 'exotic'. For example, the enemies of the Federation, the Klingons, are differentiated through make-up and skin colour, which as Bernardi argues,

> include cosmetically darkened skin and sinister goatees cut in the fashion of stereotypes of the Chinese. In fact, Klingons in the original *Trek* bear a striking resemblance to the diabolical Fu Manchu character made famous by Warner Oland in the early 1930s and revived in both the serials of the 1940s and in such 1960s films as *The Vengeance of Fu Manchu* (1968).
> (1998, p. 63)

The series therefore used contemporary racial signifiers to make the Klingons not only identifiable as alien, but also as the enemy.

However, these signifiers could also be used to confound audience expectations. The half-human and half-alien character of Spock, for example, was a point of contention between NBC and Desilu because of his satanic-looking pointed ears. NBC Sales feared that the association of pointed ears with the devil would not only make audience identification with Spock impossible, but would actually affect sales of the series to the Bible belt of America.[19] However, their fears were misplaced as Spock came to be one of the most loved members of the crew of the *Enterprise*. Although Spock's ears certainly carry demonic associations, his character is far from devil-like, with his scientific rationality and propensity for logic. The disjuncture between Spock's personality and his appearance is a means for the series to comment upon racial prejudice based on assumptions about physical characteristics. This point is actually explicitly made in the season one episode, 'Balance of Terror'. The crew of the *Enterprise* is called to investigate the brutal destruction of a number of Federation outposts by a Romulan vessel. When the physical appearance of the Romulans is revealed to be almost identical to the Vulcans (humanoid with pointed ears) the *Enterprise*'s helmsman, Styles, displays racial prejudice towards Spock. The basis for his prejudice – the physical similarity between Spock and the warlike Romulans – is condemned by Kirk and the episode goes on to empha- sise the similarity in nature between the Romulan captain and his human counterpart, Kirk. In the character of Spock, the juxtaposition of incongruous elements – demonic facial fea- tures on a placid and intelligent alien being – has a dual function. First, the pointed ears situate Spock in an understandable frame of reference, indicating him as an alien by differ- entiating him from humans. Second, the juxtaposition of such signifiers with the rational and logical character of Spock creates a cognitive estrangement, drawing into question their association with the demonic. This disruption of socio-cultural verisimilitude is then used by the series to comment on racial prejudice.

The complexity of *Star Trek*'s representations of racial difference can be understood in part in relation to the complex position which NBC was attempting to negotiate at this time. On the one hand, the networks faced criticisms for their marginalisation of ethnic minori- ties and in addition, advertisers began to recognise African-Americans as a demographic with disposable income (see Woll and Miller, 1987, pp. 75–6, and MacDonald, 1992, p. 112). On the other hand, the networks needed to attract broad consensus audiences and to maintain positive relationships with their affiliates. Series such as *I Spy*, which depicted an interracial pair of spies as its lead protagonists, had countered criticisms by introducing an African-American actor into a lead role (MacDonald, 1992, pp. 119–22). However, in the 1965–6 season (the year before *Star Trek* was launched), a number of NBC affiliates in the South had refused to carry *I Spy* because of its interracial cast (see Pounds, 1999, p. 41). While this problem was resolved by the 1966–7 season when *Star Trek* premiered on NBC, this was a period when the representation of ethnic minorities was a difficult issue for the networks to negotiate. A statement from Mort Werner to Desilu in 1966 directly associated the network's desire to promote racially integrated casting with its responsibilities as a national broadcaster:

> since we are mindful of our vast audience and the extent to which television influences taste and attitudes, we are not only anxious but determined that members of minority groups be treated in a manner consistent with their role in our society. (Reproduced in Solow and Justman, 1996, p. 76)

Star Trek is an interesting case in point because its basis in the future raises questions as to how a policy framed in terms of representing minorities 'in a manner consistent with their role in our society' (ibid.) should be accurately implemented. On the one hand, the series places women and ethnic minorities in positions of authority on the *Enterprise* at a time when space flight was primarily the purview of the white male. On the other hand, their roles on the *Enterprise* and the use of racial signifiers in the representation of aliens, largely reinforces contemporary racial stereotypes about the superiority of the white male. As Bernardi argues,

> [*Star Trek*] brings extraterrestrial nations and dissimilar aliens together, yet it also marks and segregates difference as Otherness ... The paradox of *Star Trek* is that, despite or because of its liberal humanism, it supports a universe where whites are morally, politically, and innately

superior, and both colored humans and colored aliens are either servants, threats, or objects of exotic desire. (1998, p. 68)

This paradox in many ways reflects the complexity of the discourses surrounding the space race in the 1960s, which was the focus for debates about racial and gender discrimination, while also offering at times a source of inspiration and pride for US ethnic minorities (see Spigel, 2001, pp. 141–82). The space race itself was paradoxically rooted in a sexist and racist ideology of colonisation while being conducted in the name of democracy and multiculturalism. As Lynn Spigel argues:

the space race was predicated on racist and sexist barriers that effectively grounded 'racially' marked Americans and women in general. This is especially paradoxical given the fact that space exploration was conducted in the name of democracy and a 1960s version of multiculturalism. (1997, p. 48)

This paradox arises in *Star Trek* primarily through its displacement into the future. In order to create a fictional world that is futuristic and intelligible, *Star Trek* both relies on dominant social conventions (situating Uhura in the gendered role of Communications Officer) and disrupts them (representing an integrated cast of 'astronauts' at a time when the profession was almost exclusively white and male). Such representational strategies also fulfilled the network's desire to represent racial minorities without alienating certain audience demographics. This paradox has opened up the space for the series to be applauded for tackling contemporary concerns about prejudice and critiqued for largely relying on contemporary constructions of race and gender difference. *Star Trek*'s representation of an integrated cast, while relegating minorities to supporting roles, did enable questions of prejudice to be articulated in mainstream television and its representation of space engaged with questions of racial prejudice, even while these narratives ultimately reasserted a Eurocentric history and future for space flight.

Familiar Space: Audience Identification and Repetition

Although *Star Trek* can be seen to have offered NBC regulated innovation in terms of its genre, narrative and representational strategies, the series was not particularly successful in the ratings when it was initially transmitted. *Star Trek*'s low ratings in its first season failed to fulfil the network's expectations for the primetime slot it was scheduled in at 8.30pm on a Thursday. When the series was renewed for a second season it was moved to Friday at 8.30pm after *Tarzan*, which NBC hoped would lead new audiences to the series.[20] However, *Star Trek* continued to underperform in the ratings, and in its third and final season, it was moved to the 10.00pm slot on Fridays where it would have less impact on the rest of the schedules. However, this was also a time when the series' core audience of teens and college students were not habitually watching television and after a drop in its ratings, the series was cancelled.

However, despite its relatively unsuccessful performance on primetime network television, *Star Trek* went on to run successfully in syndication after its cancellation in 1969. Kaiser Broadcasting (which owned five major UHF stations: Philadelphia, Detroit, Boston, Cleveland and San Francisco) made a deal to buy *Star Trek* to run in syndication in 1967, although the contract was not drawn up until the series' cancellation in 1969 (see Solow and Justman, 1996, p. 418). The early sale of the series enabled Kaiser Broadcasting to negotiate a lower price and guaranteed Paramount (who had recently merged with Desilu after Gulf and Western's purchase of their adjacent studios) a financial return from the series. The seventy-nine episodes that made up the three seasons of the original *Star Trek* series would normally have been considered an insufficient number to make up a syndication package as it fell below the usual limit of 100 episodes. However, Kaiser Broadcasting felt that *Star Trek* would perform particularly well in syndication. Kaiser's UHF stations were unable to compete directly with the VHF stations in their markets in terms of audience range or size. The approach they took to scheduling was therefore based on providing a different type of programming from their competitors. Rather than scheduling *Star Trek* against other action-adventure series, they placed it against their competitors' news programmes at 6.00pm, to provide an alternative form of programming. The episodes ran in the same order as on NBC, but daily instead of weekly. After the final episode aired, the whole series was repeated again and again. These runs were successful on all five of Kaiser Broadcasting's stations and the series went on to find similar success in the international export market. Although *Star Trek*'s fan followings originated when the series was initially transmitted on NBC, it was through its success in syndication (and abroad) that the series became such a cult phenomenon (Tulloch and Jenkins, 1995, p. 11). This was enhanced by the regulatory changes to syndication brought in with the Financial Interest and Syndication Rule in 1970, which prevented the networks from engaging in domestic syndication or owning the programmes they aired. The consequent growth of the syndication market over the 1970s contributed to the elevation of *Star Trek* to cult status by providing a wide market through which it could be re-run over the decade.

The reasons for the success of *Star Trek* in syndication compared to its relative lack of success on NBC herald the reasons for the success of telefantasy in the US in the 1990s. While network television in the 1960s aimed to appeal to the largest possible audience, the UHF stations adopted strategies closer to the niche marketing of 1990s US network television, targeting specific audiences and adopting a scheduling policy of differentiation (see Chapter 4). Syndication (in terms of scheduling and viewing patterns) is based on repetition and familiarity. *Star Trek* performed well in syndication because it offered a distinctive form of programming that stood up to repeated viewing and rewarded the loyal viewer. The reasons for this stem from the way in which the series' futuristic world was created. In order to signal the futurism of its fictional world, *Star Trek* is premised upon a highly distinctive and unique visual style characterised by the strong use of colour which is instantly recognisable. In addition, this distinctive visual style is complemented by a soundscape that is unique to the series. Each set of the *Enterprise* is accompanied by electronic sounds that provide an aural background to the series overall. In addition, technical instruments (such as the transporter, the phasers, the tricorder) are given their own unique sounds which signal use and function. A viewer familiar with the series can immediately recognise an episode of *Star Trek* from overhearing its distinctive aural design or glancing at its iconic visual design. Furthermore, loyal (and repeat) viewers come to understand the layout of the *Enterprise*, the mechanisms of the

Doctor's medical kit, the procedures for engaging another ship in battle, and so on. These are all elements that are specific to the fictional diegesis of *Star Trek* and cannot be encountered in any other context. *Star Trek*'s representation of the fantastic therefore enables it to create a world which, while accessible to the occasional viewer, rewards the loyal devotee. A series with a distinctive visual and narrative style, which stands up to repeated viewing and attracts a loyal audience, while not necessarily the qualities desired for network television in the 1960s, is particularly valuable to the strategies of product differentiation and niche marketing which characterised syndicated television in the US at this time.

Conclusion

Star Trek was produced at a period in the history of US television which has been characterised as financially profitable and aesthetically impoverished, leading to a mythologisation of Gene Roddenberry as its maverick creator who used the 'cloak' of science fiction to disguise the treatment of contemporary socio-cultural issues. As Tulloch and Jenkins have argued, *Star Trek* fandom has increasingly distanced itself from Roddenberry (1995, p. 19), and academic and non-academic histories of the series have attempted to provide a more nuanced account of its production. However, there remains a dominant and pervasive understanding of *Star Trek* as an unusually intelligent and creative series in a decade dominated by homogenous and formulaic television series. For example, Bernardi reiterates Stephen Whitfield and Gene Roddenberry's understanding of the use of science fiction to disguise the treatment of contemporary issues when he states 'The science fiction nature of the series gave Roddenberry and the rest of the creative decision-makers the space to address contemporary issues while avoiding some network censorship' (Bernardi, 1998, p. 37). I do not want to argue here that the network did not attempt to censor the production of *Star Trek* or influence the content and form of the programme. The network adopted the industry-wide National Association of Broadcaster's Television Code, which regulated the use of expletives, cautioned against 'the use of horror for its own sake' (cited in Alexander, 1994, p. 207), and forbade the representation of open-mouthed kissing and other explicitly sexual behaviour. Furthermore, the network was concerned with making a profit, and was cautious to produce programmes which would appeal to its desired viewers and sell to its advertisers. However, to understand fully the use of fantasy in *Star Trek*, it is important to consider what the series offered to the network within this commercial context.

This chapter has firstly demonstrated that the generic associations of *Star Trek* with science fiction were both valuable to Roddenberry, in order to differentiate the series from other networked programmes, and problematic for the network, which was anxious about the perceived appeal of science-fiction narratives. The network's desire not to alienate the female audience (a key segment of the desired primetime audience) led to an emphasis in the promotion of the series on the human characters over the elements more easily associated with science fiction, such as spaceships, aliens and interplanetary travel. However, the fantastic premise of the series did fulfil two of the key requirements in network television production at the time – product differentiation and story latitude. The basic format of *Star Trek*, in which a futuristic spaceship travels the galaxy, offers a wide range of stories and the possibility for extensive narrative transformations, differentiating it from existing television science fiction and enhancing longevity. However, these narrative disruptions are contained within the action-adventure format, ensuring that 'normality' is restored at the end of each episode. The story latitude of *Star Trek*'s fantastic premise is also contained by the need to retain production practicality and audience identification. Within the dramatic action, emphasis is placed on the characters rather than on the display of special effects, which both reduces production costs and invites audience identification. Furthermore, the design of the series uses signifiers of socio-cultural verisimilitude to make its futuristic world intelligible to the viewer, although this is also a world that is premised in part on its difference to contemporary socio-cultural reality. The series' simultaneous dependence upon and disruption of socio-cultural verisimilitude in its representation of the fantastic (apparent for example in its representation of race and gender) has opened up the space for the series both to be redeemed as a progressive drama, and critiqued for its reliance upon racial and gendered stereotypes.

This analysis of the function of fantasy within *Star Trek* complicates some of the myths that surround histories of the series' production. It suggests that far from being merely a 'cloak' within which to disguise the treatment of contemporary issues, fantasy actually works at the service of the action-adventure format within the demands of 1960s network television production. However, while *Star Trek* gained a loyal audience and critical success when initially transmitted, this was not enough to keep it on the air at a time when the network's revenues were directly linked to the Nielsen ratings. By contrast, the familiarity of the series' distinctive visual and aural landscape proved particularly valuable for the scheduling practices of syndication (where the series went on to function particularly successfully) by rewarding the loyal viewer.

As with the *Quatermass* serials and *The Prisoner*, the representation of the fantastic in *Star Trek* enabled experimentation with the dominant form of television drama: the action-adventure series. In *Star Trek*, this experimentation does not challenge or undermine the form of the action-adventure series. Rather, fantasy is used to fulfil the demands of network television production and its potential narrative and visual disruptions are contained within the action-adventure format. However, this is not to suggest that *Star Trek* is not at all innovative. The premise of a futuristic spaceship travelling the galaxy peopled by cast of familiar and recurring characters was an innovative concept. However, this was a 'regulated innovation', conceived to fulfil the demands of network television, providing product differentiation by proving that such a fantastic premise could be integrated into the action-adventure format to appeal to a primetime adult audience.

Notes

1. All references to *Star Trek* in this chapter refer to the seventy-nine episodes of the original television series, rather than to the *Star Trek* franchise as a whole.
2. Although definitions of science fiction are contested, the genre has its origins in the novels of Jules Verne and in the magazines of the 1920s and 1930s that contained stories whose fantasies were extrapolated from science. Hugo Gernsback, the editor of a number of such magazines, even set up a panel of experts to maintain the scientific accuracy of the stories published in *Science Wonder Stories* (Parrinder, 1979, p. 68).
3. Although the original *Star Trek* series ended on NBC in 1969, it went on to run

regularly in syndication in the US over the 1970s and 1980s, was sold across the world and has generated ten spin-off films, four spin-off television series (*Star Trek: The Next Generation* [Syndicated, 1987–94], *Star Trek: Deep Space Nine* [Syndicated, 1993–9], *Star Trek: Voyager* [UPN, 1995–2001], and *Enterprise* [UPN, 2001–]) and numerous toys, computer games, books, models, websites, and so on. For a comprehensive guide to the written material about the *Star Trek* franchise published before 1991, refer to Gibberman (1991).

4. See Barnouw (1990), Boddy (1993) and Hilmes (1990).

5. The move away from sponsorship was partly a response to the quiz-show scandals in the late 1950s, in which networks and sponsors were found guilty of rigging televised quizzes (see Boddy, 1990).

6. After the FCC removed its freeze on licence allocations, the number of stations increased from below 200 in 1952 to 400 in 1955. It went on to increase to 600 by 1965, expanding the markets to which programmes could be sold in syndication (see Head *et al.*, 1994, p. 61).

7. See Hilmes (1990, p. 166), and Anderson (1994, p. 255).

8. See Boddy (1993, pp. 216–19) and Barnouw (1990, pp. 243–8).

9. 'Address by Newton N. Minow to the National Association of Broadcasters, Washington D.C. May 9 1961', reprinted in Kahn (1984), from which all quotations here are taken.

10. 'Statement from the Editorial Board', *Television Quarterly*, 1962, p. 4.

11. Whitfield and Roddenberry's account of the production of *Star Trek* is widely adopted in histories of the series. See, for example, Gregory (2000).

12. Alvey broadly retains the traditional definition of independent studios in the television industry as firms that only produced television programmes or that did not own a studio and hired their facilities from the major Hollywood studios. While he accepts that this definition becomes complicated over the history of television production, he maintains that the significant role played by the independents in television production reflected the increasing decentralisation of production in Hollywood in line with the decline of the studio system (1997, p. 143).

13. By the time *Star Trek* was actually transmitted in September 1966, the number of science-fiction and fantasy series on network television had vastly increased. Irwin Allen had produced two more family-orientated continuing series, *Lost in Space* (CBS, 1965–8), *The Time Tunnel* (ABC, 1966–7) and a range of domestic fantasy sitcoms had been developed, such as *The Munsters* (CBS, 1964–6), *The Addams Family* (ABC, 1964–6), *Bewitched* (ABC, 1964–72) and *I Dream of Jeannie* (NBC, 1965–70), which were also aimed primarily at a family audience (see Spigel, 2001).

14. CBS rejected *Star Trek*, in part because it was in production with its own science-fiction series, *Lost in Space*, but did purchase *Mission: Impossible*, a gadget-filled spy series, from Desilu.

15. Occasionally, an 'acting' captain provides this narration, if Kirk is indisposed.

16. It also offers too simplistic an understanding of the development of US television drama in this period, one that ignores the presence of the episodic series from the

1940s and the continuance of the anthology series into the 1960s with series such as *The Alfred Hitchcock Hour* (CBS, 1962–4, NBC, 1964–5), *Kraft Suspense Theater* and *Bob Hope Presents the Chrysler Theater* (NBC, 1963–7).

17. For its third season *Star Trek*'s budget was cut to $185,000 per episode (see Solow and Justman, 1996, p. 374).

18. Solow is arguing against the dominant historical account of *Star Trek*'s renewal, which focuses on the letter-writing campaigns from fans of the series (see Tulloch and Jenkins, 1995, pp. 8–10, and Roddenberry and Whitfield, 1991, pp. 345–7). It is likely that both the Nielsen report and the fan letters were contributing factors to the series' renewal.

19. In the document produced for *Star Trek* by NBC Sales ahead of its 1966–7 season, Spock's 'demonic' ears and pointed eyebrows are actually air-brushed out to make him appear more human (reproduced in Solow and Justman, 1996, pp. 202–3).

20. This was the slot in which *The Man from U.N.C.L.E.*, another action-adventure series with elements of the fantastic, had successfully run in the previous season.

4

QUALITY/CULT TELEVISION

The X-Files and Buffy the Vampire Slayer in US Television of the 1990s

Introduction

Over the 1970s and 1980s, the US broadcasting industry underwent a period of accelerated technological, economic and ideological change that altered the shape of network television. Satellite and cable technologies developed to enable stations to offer viable alternatives to the networks' television services. These developments, combined with the deregulation of the telecommunications industry, increased competition for the three networks (ABC, NBC and CBS) and allowed new media conglomerates (such as Rupert Murdoch's Fox Corporation) to enter network television broadcasting for the first time since the mid-1950s. By the 1990s, the three-network oligopoly that had dominated the US television industry over the 1960s and 1970s had collapsed as the total television audience commanded by the networks fell from over 90 per cent to around 60 per cent (see Caldwell, 1995, p. 11). These developments had a particular impact on the production of telefantasy. Although telefantasy remained a part of network programming over the 1970s and 1980s, in the early 1990s, it emerged as a dominant form of primetime series drama on the US networks. This chapter explores the relationship between the industrial changes in US network television broadcasting and the development of telefantasy in this period by analysing two series produced for network television in the 1990s: *The X-Files* (Fox, 1993–2002) and *Buffy the Vampire Slayer* (WB, 1997–2001, UPN, 2001–3).

As with the other series discussed in this book, both *The X-Files* and *Buffy the Vampire Slayer* have been the subject of a great deal of academic attention, primarily concerned with the significance of both series as popular cultural phenomena.[1] These analyses have tended to focus on the series' relevance to contemporary culture, through textual analysis and fan studies.[2] In contrast, this chapter explores these series as products of a crucial moment in the history of US network television as the industry gradually adjusted to the increased market fragmentation brought about by the expansion of new satellite, cable and pay-TV services and the deregulation of the communications sector. Both series were produced by new networks moving into hour-long drama production for the first time. Why did these networks choose to produce fantasy series within this context, and what problems does the dominance of telefantasy in the 1990s have for academic studies of such series?

The Origins of Quality Television

The increase in telefantasy programmes on the network schedules in the 1990s can be attributed to two related developments in US network television over the 1970s and 1980s: 'quality' television and niche marketing. As explored in Chapter 3, in the 1960s, the costs of advertising slots on US network television were calculated in relation to an estimation of the *total* number of viewers tuned to a particular programme at any one time. However, as NBC's anxieties over *Star Trek*'s generic status as science fiction suggest, as well as trying to maximise their audiences, the networks were also concerned with the *kind* of viewer they attracted. In the case of *Star Trek*, they were particularly keen not to alienate the important female viewer who was understood by advertisers to control family spending. Over the 1970s, this consideration of the demographic *composition* of the television audience became an increasingly important factor in network programming.

There are a number of reasons for this. Audience research in the late 1960s indicated that adults (particularly women) aged between eighteen and forty-nine living in urban areas were the prime consumers of the kinds of goods advertised on television. Programmes that targeted this audience were therefore more attractive to advertisers. The urban audience was also crucial for the networks as these were the geographical areas in which the satellite-delivered pay-television services that developed in the 1970s had the greatest market penetration and therefore offered the greatest threat to network television services (see Hudson, 1988, p. 222). With this increased competition for audiences, it was important for the networks to be able to deliver to advertisers the kinds of audiences that would buy their products. As a consequence, from the 1970s, the economic profitability of the networks no longer resided purely in the total number of viewers, but also depended on the type of viewer.[3] While attracting large consensus audiences remained important for the profitability of the national networks, the desire to attract specific audience groups altered the kinds of programming that the networks favoured, leading in the early 1970s to the production of what Feuer *et al.* (1984) termed 'quality' television.

The emergence of quality television in the early 1970s has been explicitly linked to the rise of sitcoms (and later dramas) produced by two production companies, MTM and Tandem for the network, CBS.[4] These programmes attempted to appeal to a specific audience demographic: urban, 18–49, liberal, professional and culturally educated. In commissioning and promoting these programmes, CBS drew on traditional criteria of aesthetic value, such as authorship, artistic freedom and creativity, formal and narrative experimentation, complex characters and sophisticated writing, to attract what was perceived as a discerning 'quality' audience that was ambivalent towards the aesthetic and cultural value of television as a medium. Such quality television was therefore concerned with promoting itself as different from 'regular' television, even though as Feuer points out, the quality series created by MTM for CBS signalled 'quality' and 'regularity' simultaneously, inscribing a number of different positions within a single text.

> The appeal of an MTM programme must be double-edged. It must appeal both to the
> 'quality' audience, a liberal, sophisticated group of upwardly mobile professionals; and it
> must capture a large segment of the mass audience as well. Thus MTM programmes must be

readable at a number of levels, as is true of most US television fare. MTM shows may be interpreted as warm, human comedies or dramas; or they may be interpreted as self-aware 'quality' texts. In this sense also, the MTM style is both typical and atypical. Its politics are seldom overt, yet the very concept of 'quality' is itself ideological. In interpreting an MTM programme as a quality programme, the quality audience is permitted to enjoy a form of television which is seen as more literate, more stylistically complex, and more psychologically 'deep' than ordinary TV fare. The quality audience gets to separate itself from the mass audience and can watch TV without guilt, and without realising that the double-edged discourse they are getting is also ordinary TV. (Feuer, 1984, p. 56)

The 'quality' television produced by MTM therefore accommodated multiple readings to combine an appeal to the 'quality' demographic with a broader consensus appeal. These programmes signalled themselves as literate, complex and 'deep', while simultaneously offering the familiar pleasures of 'everyday' television, inscribing different reading positions within one text. As a consequence, the representation of a working single woman in her thirties in *The Mary Tyler Moore Show* can be interpreted as both 'reactionary' (replicating the ideological structures of the patriarchal family in Mary's worklife) and/or 'progressive' (exploring and valuing the experiences of single working women) (see Feuer, 1984, pp. 56–9).

The valuing of programmes that are open to multiple readings in US television is both specific to this particular historical period and a general characteristic of US television production (as demonstrated in relation to *Star Trek* in Chapter 3). As Todd Gitlin argues, 'television entertainment takes its design from social and psychological fissures' (1994, p. 217). For the US networks, whose profitability is based on audience numbers, programmes with messages which are open to divergent interpretations are favoured, as these are most likely to attract the largest audience. As a consequence, in television success often comes from finding the main fault lines of value conflict in society, and bridging them' (Gitlin, 1994, p. 218). However, Gitlin argues that, while television may attempt to resolve these social and cultural conflicts, it is not always successful, particularly when the industry attempts to appeal to the desires of conflicting social groups (1994, p. 248). In attempting to attract the 'quality' audience while not alienating other network viewers, 'quality' television is precisely concerned with appealing to divergent desires. As a consequence, programmes such as *All in the Family* and *The Mary Tyler Moore Show* do not simply explore or expose contemporary social conflicts, but offer their viewers the possibility of divergent, even conflicting, interpretations within one text.

Quality Television in the 1980s and 1990s

John Thornton Caldwell argues that the 1970s MTM and Tandem series constructed their quality status in relation to content rather than to style (1995, p. 57). The production practices and budgets of serial television had led to the favouring of stylistic techniques based on efficiency, rather than on visual style. As Gitlin argues, 'instead of style there were techniques' (1994, p. 290). However, Caldwell argues that in the 1980s there was a significant shift in the definition of 'quality' television, a shift that encompassed an increasing emphasis on visual style as an indicator of quality. Caldwell sees this as partly a consequence of the rise of quality television itself, arguing that 'once the aura of artistry became a conscious part of the industry hype, *a critical expectation for stylistic accomplishment* followed' (1995, p. 61). Series such as *Hill Street Blues*, often cited as the initiator of the development of visually stylish quality television in the 1980s, led the way with a new form of quality television whose visual distinctiveness and stylistic flourishes were as much an indicator of its 'quality' status as the complexity and depth of its characters and scripts.[5] Caldwell terms this shift 'televisuality' and posits it as a pervasive trend in US television which has permeated across network and cable programming, dramatic and non-fiction forms.[6] What characterises the televisual turn in US television broadcasting is that the *performance* of style becomes an increasingly prevalent feature of US television, with a growing number of programmes drawing attention to and showcasing their visual styles. This self-consciousness of style is an activity rather than a look. It describes therefore not just what television programmes look like, but also the way in which they display and draw attention to their own style. Style is no longer subsidiary to dialogue and narrative, but becomes the text of the show.

While (as has been demonstrated in the previous chapters), this display of visual style is apparent in television produced in the 1950s and 1960s, what changes in the 1980s is that shows such as *Hill Street Blues* demonstrated the potential *economic* return of visually distinctive 'quality' television, garnering critical and financial success for NBC despite initial low ratings.[7] As Caldwell states, 'a shift in cultural capital has clearly occurred by the early and mid-1980s, one that made stylistics a more valuable kind of programming currency' (1995, p. 67). The increasing emphasis on style was, therefore, not just a formal development, but an industrial strategy in a saturated media market, that responded to the economic crisis in US network television production in the 1980s.

Although the networks faced increased competition in the 1970s, it remained a relatively secure time for NBC, CBS and ABC.[8] However, in the early 1980s, President Reagan's Republican government pushed for the deregulation of the telecommunications industry, and the appointment of Mark Fowler as chairman of the FCC signalled the end of anti-monopoly regulations resulting in conglomerate takeovers of CBS, NBC and ABC.[9] The expansion of syndication and cable also increased competition for the networks. Although the FCC attempted to regulate cable in 1972, from 1975 the development of satellite services which could be delivered through cable enabled cable services to expand. In 1984, new FCC regulations significantly deregulated cable television enabling the service to expand, increasing competition even more (see Head *et al.*, 1994).[10]

As a consequence of these changes, the networks' ability to attract large consensus audiences was undermined and they began to target their programmes at differently defined (although not necessarily mutually exclusive) 'niche' markets. Celia Lury argues that, with the shift to niche marketing, 'taste cultures' became as, if not more, important than socio-economic criteria in delineating and targeting market segments:

> The term [taste cultures] was introduced in market planning as a way of exploring the role of non-demographic factors in the organisation of the audience-as-market, and as part of the recognition of the often fleeting and overlapping nature of audiences within a market. It is used to group individuals according to acts of media choice seen to display similarity of

content or style – in short, according to market notions of taste – rather than to demographic variations, and has begun to be used as a basis on which to plan new products. (1993, p. 46)

With the growing fragmentation of the US television market over the 1980s and 1990s, the television audience was increasingly conceived and addressed as a coalition of taste markets (rather than demographics). Within this increasingly fragmented marketplace, the display of a distinctive visual style was a means by which the networks differentiated their programmes from the competition and attracted specific audiences defined in terms of their tastes.

The X-Files as Quality/Cult TV

Robert J. Thompson sees *The X-Files* as an extension of earlier 'quality' television (1997, pp. 184–5). However, I want to argue that the series represented a new form of 'quality/cult' television that marked a shift in network programming in the 1990s and facilitated the rise in telefantasy on network television. Unlike the earlier quality television discussed by Thompson, Feuer and Gitlin, *The X-Files* was not produced by one of the three established networks, but was part of the nascent Fox network's move into hour-long primetime drama. Fox had emerged in the wake of a series of corporate mergers following the deregulation of the broadcasting industry in the mid-1980s and first became profitable in 1989. By the early 1990s, Fox was keen to build on its reputation for successful comedies (*The Simpsons*, 1989–, *Married . . . with Children*, 1987–97) and teenage dramas (*Beverly Hills 90210*, 1990–2000) by moving into hour-long drama production that would extend its demographic range into the 18–49 age group (Caldwell, 1995, p. 11). *The X-Files*, scheduled alongside the Western drama *The Adventures of Brisco County, Jr.* (1993–4), made up Fox's first full evening of hour-long drama series, competitively scheduled at 9.00pm on Friday against ABC's successful comedy line-up. As a consequence of Fox's position as a new network, the production strategies it adopted differed from those of the three established networks. While NBC, CBS and ABC were trying to retain their audiences under the threat of the new cable and satellite services, Fox was attempting to break into the network market. Fox was therefore concerned with attracting viewers from the existing networks *and* from the rival cable and satellite stations. This balancing act is central to understanding the particular way in which *The X-Files* was situated as 'quality/cult' television.

The X-Files depicts the investigations of two young FBI agents, Fox Mulder (David Duchovny) and Dana Scully (Gillian Anderson) into 'X-files', inexplicable cases of supernatural phenomena rejected by the Bureau mainstream.[11] The series combines stories of detection and investigation with the iconography and narratives of the science-fiction and horror genres, as Mulder and Scully explore reports of alien abductions, poltergeists, artificial intelligence, human mutations and demonic creatures, as well as becoming embroiled in a government plot to conceal the existence of paranormal phenomena from the general public. The series therefore signals its distinctiveness in part through its generic hybridity, a strategy that Thompson argues is particularly indicative of quality television (1997, p. 15). Furthermore, the series' sophisticated scripts, complex multilayered narratives, and visually expressive cinematography, combined with its exploration of contemporary anxieties concerning late capitalism (such as *The X-Files'* treatment of environmental issues, the role of medicine, the threat of scientific experimentation and most overtly, the duplicity of the US government) is characteristic of quality television.

However, in addition to this appeal to the 'quality' audience, the series was also produced to appeal to another market segment, the fan-consumer.[12] As Reeves *et al.* (1996) point out, when *The X-Files* was initially produced, there were two different kinds of cult television in the US. The first, like *Star Trek*, were primetime network shows that failed to gain high ratings when initially released on the networks but subsequently attracted large fan followings. These network shows were not produced specifically for the fan audience but went on to gain fan followings, often (as was the case with *Star Trek*) through repeat runs in syndication. The second kind of cult television, such as *Mystery Science Theater 3000* and *Beavis and Butt-head* were series that were narrowly targeted at niche audiences on smaller cable channels with the precise aim of attracting small but loyal fan audiences (Reeves *et al.*, 1996, p. 31). For these smaller, non-network channels who could not expect to gain the large audience figures of the networks, the loyalty of the fan audience was particularly valuable. Reeves, *et al.* argue that the production of *The X-Files* marked a new form of cult television that can be attributed to the Fox network's nascent status in the early 1990s (1996, p. 31). *The X-Files* differed from earlier cult television in two ways. First, unlike earlier series that had been produced for the niche fan audience, this was a series produced by a new network attempting to compete with NBC, ABC and CBS. Second, rather than being a network series produced for a consensus audience that was 'found' by fan audiences and subsequently gained the status of a cult, *The X-Files* was actively produced by Fox as a cult series designed to attract the fan-consumer taste market.

The fan audience was valuable to a network such as Fox, attempting to break into an increasingly competitive environment, because of its loyalty. As a consequence, as Matt Hills argues, in the 1990s, 'fandom has begun to furnish a model of dedicated and loyal consumption which does, in point of fact, *appeal* to television producers and schedulers within a fragmented multichannel environment' (1999, p. 5). In addition, fans are not only loyal consumers of television programmes, but also of the ancillary products generated by such programmes. The exploitation of the ancillary market was particularly valuable for Fox, a media conglomerate with holdings in a range of different companies. As Reeves *et al.* argue, Fox was able to exploit *The X-Files'* appeal to the fan market in order to promote their other media holdings and to offset the financial risks of investing in the series.

> In Britain, first-run episodes of the series appear only on Sky One, part of Rupert Murdoch's satellite network. Fox also attempted to use *The X-Files* to promote Delphi, its online service; Delphi became the official home of *The X-Files*, and writers and producers were encouraged to frequent the discussion areas related to the show. By using the show's cult status to multiply its revenue streams, Fox has taken away some of the pressure on *The X-Files* to be a ratings hit. (Reeves *et al.*, 1996, p. 31)

The X-Files therefore combined the production strategies of the existing networks with those of the rival cable channels in an attempt to infiltrate the network primetime market and to minimise risk by attracting a specific, commercially valuable niche fan audience. In doing so it combined quality television's dual address to the 'everyday' and 'discerning' viewer, with an additional address to the fan-consumer.

The negotiation of this layered address to different taste markets is apparent in the series' use of fantasy. Immediately before the production of *The X-Files*, there was relatively little fantasy television drama on US network television. However, the success of the *Star Trek* spin-off, *Star Trek: The Next Generation* in syndication had demonstrated the appeal of fantasy series beyond the small fan audiences gained by other non-network cult shows such as *Mystery Science Theater 3000*. *The X-Files'* use of the fantastic can therefore be understood as a strategy designed to exploit the generic appeal of science fiction and horror to fan audiences and as a strategy of product differentiation designed to offer a form of television drama not previously found in the US network schedules. *The X-Files'* creator, Chris Carter, claimed that the idea for *The X-Files* stemmed from a desire to redress the lack of horror in the primetime network television schedules. Carter stated that when working on the initial premise for *The X-Files* he sensed a void: 'You look at the TV schedule, . . . and there's nothing scary on tele-vision' (cited in Lowry, 1995, p. 10). As Glen Morgan, former co-executive producer on the series, explained, 'Horror had been relegated to the slasher movies, and I think the networks felt that you couldn't do horror without lots of blood' (cited in Coe, 1995, p. 57). Here, the series' use of the horror genre is evoked in a rhetoric of distinctiveness. The implication is that *The X-Files* appealed to Fox because it offered something different from the other networks (horror), in a new way (without 'lots of blood'), allowing Fox to fill a void left open by its competitors. However, the precise nature of this difference is constructed in relation to the generic conventions of existing forms and the network's conception of acceptability. The attempt at horror functions as a viable aesthetic strategy as long as the series avoids the generic associations with 'lots of blood', which would be unattractive to a network broadcaster keen to maximise its audience and extend its demographic reach.

The negotiation of difference and acceptability is further apparent in the construction of the series' visual style. *The X-Files* has a distinctive 'signature' style, a production strategy that Caldwell (1995) argues is increasingly important as a form of product differentiation within the saturated media environment of US television. Signature styles immediately signal the distinctiveness of a television programme and for series with high production values, are also important indicators of quality. Distinctive signature styles are also useful in the production of ancillary merchandising as they are immediately associated with the series and can be replicated across a range of products. Carter claims of *The X-Files*, 'When you read the scripts they're very visual in terms of what the writer is asking the director to see at any particular moment. It's a very visual show' (cited in Martinez, 1995, p. 21). While all television is visual, Carter points here to the mode of storytelling employed by *The X-Files* in which the image is particularly significant, in part because of the series' thematic treatment of the fantastic. Fantasy narratives open up a particular space for the display of visual style through the representation of the unreal. While not all telefantasy is *primarily* concerned with this kind of visuality, the representation of the fantastic in *The X-Files* offered the possibility for the visual flourishes and stylistic distinctiveness which were particularly valuable for Fox as markers of difference and indicators of quality. However the creation of *The X-Files'* signature style needs to be understood in relation to Fox's strategy of balancing product differentiation and an appeal to the quality and cult audiences, with existing notions of acceptability in US network television.

The X-Files' Signature Style

Both John Bartley (Director of Photography for the first three seasons) and Chris Carter have described the logic behind The X-Files' visual style in terms of *lack*. Bartley claimed, 'You don't want to show the audience too much. You just want to feel that there's something there' (cited in Probst, 1995, p. 32), while Carter stated, 'You're always more scared of what you don't see than what you do see' (cited in Martinez, 1995, p. 22). In an article in American Cinematographer (Probst, 1995), Bartley discussed the techniques he used on the series to evoke a visual style that Carter described as 'dark, moody, mysterious and sometimes claus-trophobic' (cited in Probst, 1995, p. 28). Bartley explained how he consistently underexposed actors' faces to create a shrouded image and used blue lights in the background to give the effect of a dark hue while still showing some detail and allowing background and foreground to be distinguished. While this is most pronounced in frightening and mysterious scenes, the series as a whole tends to avoid high-key lighting. The exception to this is the use of strong bright lights. A visual motif is established over the series, which associates brightness with alien abduction, medical invasiveness and memory. These three elements are repeatedly con-nected in the series, in which alien abduction is characterised by memory loss and medical intrusion. However, these white lights, in their blinding intensity, are not a revealing source of brightness but are as obscuring as the shadowy darkness.

The series' characteristic use of darkness and bright lights to obscure rather than reveal, places a visual emphasis on concealment. When the series does represent the fantastic it tends to be glimpsed in the shadows rather than clearly displayed. Both Bartley and Bill Roe, the Director of Photography who replaced him for the series' subsequent seasons, have empha-sised their reliance on 'practicals' – lights that have a real and discernible source – in shooting the series.[13] This gives the visual style of the series a plausible basis and also makes the light sources very directional, enabling the general look to be dark, while allowing beams of light to illuminate necessary details. This effect is heightened through the use of smoke, which gives the image an underlying ambient glow while picking up beams of light as they cut through the murky darkness. This particular style of lighting is most pronounced in what can be described as a signature X-Files shot, in which Mulder and Scully enter darkened spaces shining bright flashlights.

Bartley described how they shot such a scene for the season two episode, 'Dod Kalm':

> In 'Dod Kalm', which ends up in a frigate that is supposed to have been dormant for thirty years, the only lighting sources in the halls and cabins are the Xenon flashlights. . . . I use the pebble-bounce [off screen reflectors] so the actors can shine the flashlights into the reflector, which bounces the light back into their faces. (Cited in Probst, 1995, p. 30)

The extent of the darkness in these scenes is pronounced. At times the screen is almost entirely black. Yet the use of strong directional light, combined with close-ups, allows the

In the shadowy scene in which Mulder and Scully enter the dormant ship in *The X-Files*' 'Dod Kalm', the actors' Xenon flashlights are the only source of lighting

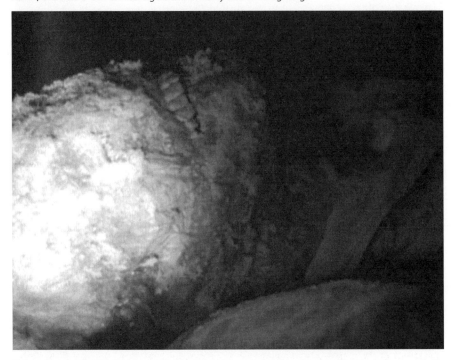

The gruesome details of this scene in 'Dod Kalm' are glimpsed in close-up, illuminated momentarily by the moving beams of light

pertinent (and rather gruesome) details to be glimpsed within the bright beams of the flash-light. The series' signature style can be characterised therefore, not only by the extremes of darkness and brightness on the screen, but also by the use of strong contrast. This enables the series to employ a visual rhetoric whose emphasis on concealment (what is hidden or obscured by the dark shadows and bright flashes) simultaneously opens up spaces for the fantastic to be occasionally and fleetingly exposed. This visual 'lack' functions as an ideological strategy, whereby the series can *suggest* all manner of horrors, rather than represent them. This allows the series to explore such topics as necrophilia, childhood abduction and torture without compromising the network's notions of acceptability.

These characteristic elements of *The X-Files'* signature style are established from the open-ing of the pilot episode. The episode begins with a short sequence in which a girl is killed in a forest. It opens with a series of tracking shots following a girl in a nightgown as she runs distractedly through a forest at night. The dark image, rapid editing, and shaky camerawork provide mere glimpses of the girl as she stumbles through the trees. She falls into a clearing and a bright light fades up behind the trees to expose a dark figure in silhouette walking towards her. As the stranger reaches her, leaves begin to engulf them in an unnatural cir-cling motion accompanied by an eerie whirring soundscape. The image gradually fades to white, and as the whirring sounds fade out, there is a dissolve to a close-up of the girl's dead body being discovered in daylight the following morning. All the characteristics of *The X-Files'* signature style are in this sequence. The extreme darkness shrouds the image, while the fade to white acts as an ellipsis in which the potentially fantastic event is implied yet obscured. The narrative of this sequence is also told in visual terms rather than through dialogue. Style is not subsidiary to dialogue here, but is used to present the basic themes of the series: the possibility of alien abduction and paranormal events, and the impossibility of fully represent-ing or witnessing such events.

Indeed, this signature style reinforces the basic narrative logic behind *The X-Files*, in which a central ambiguity remains about the existence of paranormal phenomena because Mulder and Scully can never prove what they have experienced. The emphasis on *suggestion* in the series' representation of the fantastic further reinforces the narrative and thematic lack of the series by problematising perception and representation. The series frequently re-enacts scenes, inviting the audience to question how to interpret what has been represented. For example, the opening sequence from the pilot episode is re-enacted later in the episode as Mulder and Scully visit the same spot in the forest late at night. The second sequence repeats the visual iconography of the first, however this time the bright white light and the shadowy figure are revealed to be the local sheriff in his car. Here the series' characteristic darkness and emphasis on visual storytelling is used to undermine the reliability of the image. This is then reiterated at a thematic level at the end of the episode when Scully admits that she is unable to objectively substantiate what she has witnessed. This relationship between per-ception, belief and proof is at the heart of the series and is consistently undermined. In a later episode, 'EBE', it is suggested that Mulder and Scully's physical encounter with a UFO and the photographic evidence that they produce as proof, is a hoax orchestrated by the US gov-ernment. Even when the fantastic is visually witnessed and even when physical proof of the paranormal is gained, uncertainty remains.[14] The series is therefore fundamentally concerned with the performance of visual style, inscribing the relationship between sight and belief as a central dramatic drive of its format. Mulder and Scully's consistent inability to gain proof of what they have witnessed, accompanied by the frequent unreliability of the image as a means of establishing the truth, is reinforced by the visual logic in which the fantastic is often shrouded in darkness or only fleetingly depicted.

This signature style works in tandem with the series' narrative structure to create a basic formula that can be sustained over time. Drawing on the emphasis placed on continuing story-lines in quality television over the 1980s, *The X-Files* combined one-off 'genre' episodes cen-tred on a single investigation, with an ongoing and increasingly complex 'mythology' narrative about a government conspiracy to conceal the paranormal from the US public. As *The X-Files* moved into its second season the unexpected pregnancy of Gillian Anderson (Dana Scully) resulted in the creation of a story arc that continued over a number of episodes in which Scully is abducted by an unknown force. The consequent interweaving of character history and conspiracy narratives became a prevalent feature of the series. *The X-Files* thus serialised the narrative structure of the series by combining one-off stories traditionally characteristic of episodic series such as *Star Trek*, with ongoing narratives more usually associated with the narrative structure of the serial. This dual narrative structure enabled the series to be access-ible to the casual viewer, while simultaneously rewarding the loyal viewer with character and story development, indicating the increasing importance attached to the loyal viewer in 1990s US television production.

However, despite the use of a series structure that provided space for character and story development, *The X-Files* depended on the maintenance of sameness. The series' basic premise is constructed around Mulder and Scully's search for *elusive* proof about the exist-ence of paranormal phenomena. In order to give this quest value and meaning, the series must continually suggest that 'the truth is out there' (to borrow from the series' tag-line), while never allowing it to be fully established. The signature style, based around suggestion in which the fantastic is glimpsed rather than displayed, is central because the narrative logic of the series is constructed around continuation, which is possible only if ambiguity remains about the reality of the fantastic.[15]

The X-Files and the Aesthetics of Television

When *The X-Files* transferred to the cinema for a spin-off movie, this visual style of contrast and suggestion was significantly altered. *The X-Files* movie (Rob Bowman, 1998) differed most dramatically from the series in its two big-budget special effects set pieces. The first is the finale of the opening sequence, in which Mulder fails to defuse a bomb and just man-ages to escape before a large city skyscraper is blown up. The narrative logic of opening with an exciting action sequence mirrors that of the television series' use of the teaser. Yet the film's extensive use of special effects flaunts its difference from the series: it is bigger, more expensive, more expansive. Similarly, the film ends with a dramatic, effects-laden climax in which Mulder rescues Scully from an alien spaceship buried beneath the snow moments before it takes off. An overt attempt is being made here to exploit the particular advantages of film-making (larger budgets, extended production and post-production schedules) to dis-play what the cinema can offer to the television series (see Duncan, 1998). The film does retain elements of the series' signature style, largely replicating its use of darkness and contrast. However, these particular set pieces are brightly lit, to display the special effects to the viewer. Here, *The X-Files* is not simply transferred to film; it is recreated as a blockbuster.

To suggest this is not to denigrate the technical sophistication of the television series. The extremes of bright light and darkness in the series skirt the boundaries of NTSC's transmission capabilities and are only possible because the Director of Photography exploits the developments in film stock, pushing the emulsion to its limits (see Probst, 1995). The series also takes advantage of the decreasing costs of special effects technology and advances in computer graphics to create its own exciting set pieces, such as the circling leaves at the climax of the pilot's opening sequence. The difference between the visual style of the film and the television series is one of scale and context. The use of effects-laden set pieces in the film relates in part to the economic context within which it was produced, but also to the conventions of science-fiction, horror and action cinema, where the large-scale display of effects is the norm. Within the television series, the *emphasis* is on suggestion. Week after week the series must imply the presence of the supernatural, while maintaining a central ambiguity about its reality, in order to validate Mulder and Scully's continued search for an elusive truth and thus maintain the *continuity* of a long-running series. This aesthetic strategy is also in line with the demands of the network, enabling the series to function within the economic and temporal demands of weekly television production and avoiding the potentially controversial representation of excessively horrific or violent images.

I am not suggesting here that a comparison of the movie with the television series verifies the binary oppositions through which television's small screen and intimate address have been characterised against cinema's big-budget spectacles. The centrality of visual style to *The X-Files* challenges an understanding of television aesthetics which argues that television subsumes visual style to narrative and character. Thus *The X-Files* television series counters assertions such as that made by Conrad Schoeffter that 'the content of a television movie you can get with your eyes closed. Television is an oral medium' (1998, p. 114). Not only does *The X-Files* largely rely on the image to tell its stories but it is thematically concerned with the role of the image in structures of knowledge and belief. However, to argue that the image is central to the series is not to argue that it simply adopts a 'cinematic' style. As a comparison of the film and television versions suggests, *The X-Files'* visual style differs significantly from the cinematic blockbuster and needs to be understood in relation to the specific demands of US television production in the 1990s.

However, *The X-Files'* 'televisuality' does challenge a number of the dominant assumptions about the aesthetics of television, including flow and glance theory. The notions that television can be understood as a 'flow' of programmes arranged into an ongoing schedule, rather than as individual texts (Williams' theory of flow (1994)), and that television is primarily glanced at by a distracted domestic spectator (Ellis's theory of glance (1982)), have been dominant paradigms for understanding the specificity of television for the last two decades. However, as Caldwell has argued in relation to televisuality more broadly, flow and glance theory are no longer fully adequate paradigms in an environment in which 'the committed television viewer is overtly addressed' (Caldwell, 1995, p. 26) and in which much television 'self-consciously rejects the monotonous implications of the flow' (Caldwell, 1995, p. 19).[16]

The X-Files' dense visual landscape demands attentive viewing, rewards the loyal viewer and is constructed to signal the series' difference from other television programmes. In the increasingly competitive environment of US network television broadcasting, these qualities are particularly attractive to television producers and are increasingly characteristic of US network television. Hence, the changing landscape of US television production is challenging the adequacy of these dominant paradigms for understanding television as a medium.

Buffy the Vampire Slayer as Teen Fantasy

From the early 1990s, when Fox consolidated its position as the fourth network, the environment of US network television broadcasting further fragmented. By the mid-1990s, two more networks had joined the existing four (NBC, CBS, ABC, Fox), WB and UPN.[17] With the increased competition, the strategy of niche marketing became increasingly prevalent and new audience segments and taste markets emerged as prime targets for the new networks. At the same time, the consolidation of the media industries continued with a number of corporate mergers increasing media conglomeration. One consequence of this was that teenagers became a particularly valued audience. Like the fan audience, teenagers were valued for their conspicuous consumption, making them attractive to media conglomerates with holdings in a wide range of media industries, including television, gaming, music, publishing and the Internet. Teenagers were also an attractive demographic to advertisers and networks were able to charge high rates for advertising slots within series which appealed to teen viewers. Edward Helmore notes that although WB's teen series, *Dawson's Creek* ranked only seventy-sixth among all viewers in the US in 1998, the network was charging advertisers $250,000 for a thirty-second slot during the series, equivalent to the amount charged for the same slot during the CBS nightly news, a programme that attracted twice as many viewers (Helmore, 1998, p. 27). Over the 1990s, the quality teen drama series became increasingly visible in the network primetime schedules (see Moss, 2001).[18] Many of these series adopt characteristics of the quality television series, with ensemble casts, sophisticated writing and psychologically complex characters. These attributes are combined with a focus on adolescent issues which appeals to the teen audience but is not restricted to this demographic. Indeed, in contemporary Western society, 'youth' is not merely a demographic category, but also a sensibility that can extend (and be sold to) audiences outside the teen generation (Davis and Dickinson, 2004, p. 11). In an era in which 'staying young' forms a central part of the drive of consumer culture, youth programming (particularly if it has the articulate, liberal, sophisticated edge of 'quality' television) has a valuable appeal to advertisers and broadcasters.

   Buffy the Vampire Slayer can be situated within this history of the development of teen television on US network television. After the initial transmission of the two-part pilot episode of the series (between 8.00 and 10.00pm), the first season of *Buffy the Vampire Slayer* was scheduled to run between 9.00 and 10.00pm after WB's other hour-long drama *7th Heaven*, WB's highest-rated series in the 1996–7 season. The scheduling of these two series as WB's first *full* evening of primetime *hour-long* drama series was designed to contribute to the creation of a particular signature for the WB network. WB's 1996–7 season was dominated by half-hour sitcoms designed to appeal to a teen and/or family audience. Of the eight half-hour series which returned for the 1997–8 season, three were set in a high school (*Nick Freno:*

Licensed Teacher, The Steve Harvey Show, Smart Guy) while the other five were based around a family unit (*The Jamie Foxx Show, The Parent 'Hood, Sister, Sister, Unhappily Ever After, The Wayans Bros.*). The commissioning of *Buffy the Vampire Slayer* with *7th Heaven* to lead WB's move into hour-long drama contributed to the development of a defining signature for WB as 'the "family" network' (De Moras, 1997, p. 11). *7th Heaven*, a series about a minister, his wife and their seven children appeals to family values in its depiction of a stable, loving, Christian family. *Buffy the Vampire Slayer*, with its young cast, high-school setting and thematic treatment of adolescent anxieties, appeals to teens and young adults.

However, WB's linking of *Buffy the Vampire Slayer* with *7th Heaven* smoothed over some of the potential conflicts in combining family and teen appeal. While *7th Heaven* extolled traditional family values, *Buffy the Vampire Slayer*'s treatment of adolescent themes through horror narratives did not always sit easily with WB's 'family' signature. Joss Whedon claimed that during the production of the first season of the series, WB expressed concern about the use of potentially controversial words, such as 'slut' and 'virgin'.[19] *Buffy the Vampire Slayer*'s treatment of adolescent anxieties included potentially contentious issues such as teenage sex, homosexuality and domestic violence. However, following its first season, the series' treatment of controversial issues grew, with the development of a lesbian relationship between Willow and Tara, the increasingly sexual nature of Buffy's relationship with her boyfriend Riley in season four (and subsequently with Spike in season six) and Willow's 'addiction' to witchcraft in season six. Despite these potentially contentious storylines, the series ran successfully on the WB network for five seasons and moved to UPN for its sixth season in September 2001 after UPN offered to pay $2.3 million per episode for the series. Concurrent with the success of *Buffy the Vampire Slayer*, WB shifted its signature to the 'teen' (rather than the family) network.[20]

The need to create a distinctive identity in order to distinguish itself from its competition was an important commercial strategy for WB, a new network attempting to break into the competitive environment of network television broadcasting, while also competing with an expanding number of cable and satellite stations. Despite WB's initial anxieties about the series, *Buffy the Vampire Slayer* contributed to the network's developing 'teen' signature, depicting its eponymous heroine struggling with the everyday anxieties of adolescent life with a mixture of articulate dialogue and playful irony typical of the 1990s teen series, such as *Dawson's Creek* (WB, 1998–2003) and *Clueless* (UPN, 1996–9). Valerie Wee has argued that one of the characteristics of 1990s teen television is the use of 'rich, organic visuals characteristic of the filmic, rather than the televisual image', with programmes often making intertextual references to specific films or music videos within their visual and narrative styles (2004, pp. 92–3). The emphasis on the display of visual style apparent in quality television is thus evident in 1990s teen television, but in specific ways. First, teen television often displays its visual style in order to promote the consumption of specific products (music, clothes, media texts and so on) associated with the lifestyles offered in the shows. Second, teen television is frequently intertextual in its visual and narrative references to other media texts. As Wee argues, these intertextual references function to introduce young audiences to older media texts, facilitating their continued circulation to a new generation of consumers, and the profitability the media conglomerates who hold the rights to transmit and distribute them

(2004, p. 95). However, these two characteristics, while features of teen television, are also characteristics of cult television. While teen television might promote music, films and fashions through its display of visual style, cult television creates series with distinctive signature styles which can be transferred and exploited across a range of ancillary merchandising, such as toys, computer games, calendars, and so on. In *Buffy the Vampire Slayer*, which combines stories of growing up in contemporary America with tales of demons, witches and monsters, the display of visual style functions both within the context of teen television, to promote consumption associated with specific lifestyles, and within the context of fantasy/cult television, to enable the exploitation of ancillary merchandise.

The Combined Appeal of *Buffy the Vampire Slayer*

From the opening title music, in which a Gothic organ is rapidly replaced by grungy rock and roll, *Buffy the Vampire Slayer* announces its playfulness with generic expectations, combining monsters with prom dresses, action sequences with an emphasis on the style and costuming of the characters. By using the representation of the fantastic metaphorically to deal with adolescent themes, *Buffy the Vampire Slayer* creates a fictional world in which the line between the 'real' world of the high-school adolescent and the 'fantasy' world of demons and monsters is unstable and consistently violated. Joss Whedon, the series' creator claims that 'nothing is as it seems' is the mission statement of the series.[21] Vampires conceal their demonic nature beneath a human face, allowing Buffy to fall unwittingly in love with 'vampire-with-a-soul' Angel in the first season. Frequently, incidental characters are revealed to be hiding their 'true' nature. Buffy's mother falls for a 'perfect' man who turns out to be a robot in 'Ted', while in season five, Buffy's sister is introduced and then later revealed as a mystical key to an alternative world. While Buffy conceals her secret identity as the slayer, Sunnydale, the town in which she lives, conceals its alternative identity as the location of the 'Hellmouth', a portal to the world of demons and vampires.

Buffy the Vampire Slayer is therefore premised on the creation of two different worlds that are intricately and inseparably connected. This is reflected in the series' signature style, in which certain shared characteristics are used across the teen and demonic worlds. As Jean Oppenheimer states of the creation of the series' visual style by Michael Gershman (Director of Photography),

> the show needed a visual style that would reflect its mix of genres and emotions. For the daytime 'reality' world, in which kids attend high school and engage in typical teenage activities, Gershman fashioned a bright, colourful landscape. For nighttime sequences he shifted to a dark, edgy, textured look, replete with deep blacks and bold slashes of frequently coloured light. (1999, p. 91)

However, while the series differentiates visually between the high-key 'real' world of the high school and the dark and shadowy 'fantasy' world of the demons, there are also certain distinctive visual elements that run across its two 'worlds', contributing to the narrative and thematic blurring between the everyday and the fantastic. As with *The X-Files*, visually *Buffy the Vampire Slayer* is unusually dark for a US mid-1990s primetime television series. The night and interior sequences, particularly those featuring demons, are shadowy and obscure. However, the series uses a much richer palette of colours than *The X-Files*, making extensive use of ambers, browns, greens, reds, purples and blues in its lighting, costume and set design. This use of colour stems partly from the need to compensate for the lack of depth provided by 16mm film, used to shoot the first two seasons of the series. As Michael Gershman states,

> it's hard to get depth with 16mm ... It tends to flatten everything out, so one of the early lighting concepts I came up with was to create depth in the frame. If I put a cool light in the middle and a different color light on the actors, the frame doesn't look quite as flat. (Cited in Oppenheimer, 1999, p. 91)

The series' characteristic use of backlight (what Oppenheimer refers to as one of the series' 'trademarks' (ibid.)) and sharp beams of light across the characters' faces contributes to the creation of this illusion of depth in the frame. However, directional light also creates strong shadows, allowing both night and day scenes to be pervaded by a sense of foreboding. The use of directional light combined with the use of strong colours in the design for both night and day scenes helps to create a visual synergy between the dark nighttime and brightly lit daytime sequences in the series, allowing it to adopt two different looks within one broader signature style.

The combination of fantasy and teen drama in *Buffy the Vampire Slayer* therefore has a number of different functions. The playful mix of generic references and expectations appeals to the media-literate audience. Economically, the series' generic mix enables it to appeal to, and be marketed to, a range of audiences (the teen audience, the 'cult' fan, male and female viewers, and so on). However, the combination of teen and fantasy in *Buffy the Vampire Slayer* is valuable to WB not simply because it integrates an appeal to a range of market segments; it also functions as the way in which the series distinguishes itself from other television series. In interviews to promote the series, generic references are not used to categorise or situate the series within a recognisable framework, but to draw attention to its difference. For example, Edward Gross described the series as 'unique' because it 'effortlessly manages to combine humour, action and horror, while somehow managing to address the overall high-school experience' (Gross, 1999, p. 21). Therefore, while *Buffy the Vampire Slayer*'s combination of teen and fantasy contributes to WB's signature as the 'teen' network, and appeals to a coalition of valuable taste markets, it also functions to differentiate the series within a television market saturated with telefantasy. I want to go on to examine the ways in which the use of generic hybridity as a marker of distinctiveness functions in the contemporary US network television market by exploring its relationship to the increasingly dominant practice of branding.

Distinctiveness, Branding and *Buffy the Vampire Slayer*

Celia Lury argues that as a consequence of the circulation of cultural works as commodities in the culture industries of the late twentieth century, questions of authorship, innovation, novelty and creativity have become increasingly assessed in terms of 'distinctiveness as experienced by the intended audience, rather than the creative will or expression of the cultural producer' (1993, p. 56). Linked with this is the undermining of authorship as a basis for the adjudication of intellectual property rights. Intellectual property law states that, for a cultural product to be designated a 'work of art', it must display two kinds of originality: creativity, 'some indication of the producer's contribution'; and distinctiveness, 'some variation in the nature of the work itself' (Lury, 1993, p. 26). Lury notes that, in the latter part of the twentieth century, there is an increasing shift from copyright law to trademark law in the assessment of intellectual property rights, which has led to the terms of this creativity and distinctiveness being recast. She notes a tendency, particularly in the US,

> to use trademark law in preference to copyright as the preferred means of securing the profitability of popular titles and characters. A trademark provides a legal shield around the name, logo, slogan, shape, or character image and, in conjunction with product licensing, makes it possible for the original proprietor to transfer this sign to second and third parties for a limited period of time in exchange for royalties. (Lury, 1993, p. 85)

Whereas copyright law protected the author as a signifier of originality, trademark law licenses the image and/or text enabling it to be exploited as a brand across a range of products. Lury argues that, as a consequence of this shift, 'what might be called *branding*, the forging of links of image and perception between a range of products, has become an increasingly significant production strategy within and across the culture industry' (1993, p. 87).

In television, Lury argues that the shift to branding is characterised by an intensification of strategies of serialisation and the creation of flat characters. Lury differentiates here between rounded characters who 'develop and change along the chronology of classical narrative time' (1993, p. 86) and flat characters, such as Superman, who endlessly repeat their actions. Flat characters are particularly valuable because they can be licensed under trademark law, enabling the exploitation of the character across a range of goods to be protected and therefore open to financial exchange. In this way, the character is recreated as a trademarked brand and consequently replaces the author as the basis for the adjudication of intellectual property rights. Thus, 'the cultural producer's protected position as originator has been undermined by the commercial exploitation of the possibilities of replication offered by the technologies of cultures in so far as they employ strategies of regulating innovation as novelty' (Lury, 1993, p. 51). The regulation of innovation is particularly facilitated by the use of the series form, 'which attempts to achieve a dialectic between predictability and novelty' (1993, p. 43). Lury argues that the series form offers repeatable pleasures evoked by the familiarity of repetition and the subtlety of slight variations, recasting distinctiveness as the simulation of innovation rather than innovation itself. She links the narrative structure of the series to the construction of 'flat' characters, claiming that in the series form of television, 'the flat character has found the ideal form for ensuring his or her immortality' (1993, p. 43). Thus, Lury argues, in the move towards branding in which the trademark replaces copyright law, innovation is recast as simulation. Where the author retains his/her author-function, it is only insofar as it can be understood to contribute to the effects of a cultural product, through audience ratings and sales. In trademark law creative labour is able to retain privileged conditions in so far as it is able to lay effective claim to having made a contribution to the commercial 'effects' of a cultural good, including, most notably, that of producing audience ratings. (Lury, 1993, p. 54)

The move towards trademark law is particularly apparent in the production of US television series. The logos for *The X-Files* and *Buffy the Vampire Slayer* are both protected by trademark law and are used across a wide variety of products. The consequences of the move towards branding are also apparent in the function of authorship in *Buffy the Vampire Slayer*. The series is a spin-off from the 1992 film of the same name written by Joss Whedon and directed by Fran Rubel Kuzui. The film was a co-production between 20th Century-Fox and the independent production companies, Kuzui Enterprises and Sandollar Productions. Despite the initial box-office failure of the film, after being released on video it went on to acquire a small cult fan following. Gail Berman, then running the television wing of Sandollar, partnered with Fran Kuzui to turn the film into a television series. They hired Joss Whedon to act as 'creator' of the series, effectively overseeing the development and production of the programme. The presence of Whedon is significant in relation to Lury's assessment of the author-function in contemporary cultural production. In Berman's account of the series' development, she claimed that she never expected Whedon to be interested in a television spin-off of one of his early and unsuccessful film scripts. Berman stated of *Buffy the Vampire Slayer*,

We were contractually obliged to offer this to Joss [Whedon]. Everybody said he was a big movies guy now, and he'll never want to do this, including his agent, who said that to me on the phone. Then his agent called me back and said that, in fact, this was the only thing that Joss *was* interested in doing. (Berman cited in Golden and Holder, 1998, p. 249)

Elsewhere, Berman claimed that it was Whedon's presence on the series as creator that influenced their decision to sell the series to network television, rather than for syndication (see Kutzera, 1997, p. 54).

Berman's account raises two central points about the author-function in the production of *Buffy the Vampire Slayer*. First, it highlights the value attached to the authorial voice of Whedon in relation to the series' marketability to network television. This is reiterated in published accounts of the series' production where the crew repeatedly identify *Buffy the Vampire Slayer* as Whedon's creation.[22] This marketing strategy utilises the aesthetic value attached to creative authorship as a commercial strategy. Second, it recasts distinctiveness as a commercial attribute by drawing on the associations between individual authorship and originality. This has a further function in relation to the series' appeal to a cult audience as cult texts are frequently identified with a single creative author by their fans.[23] Whedon's name has been used to promote ancillary merchandise aimed at the media cult market, such as the comic book, *Tales of the Slayers*, in which a number of renowned comic book artists illustrate stories about earlier slayers. While Joss Whedon writes only two of the stories (the others being authored by writers associated with the show), the book is promoted by a tagline above its title proclaiming 'from the creator of *Buffy the Vampire Slayer*'.

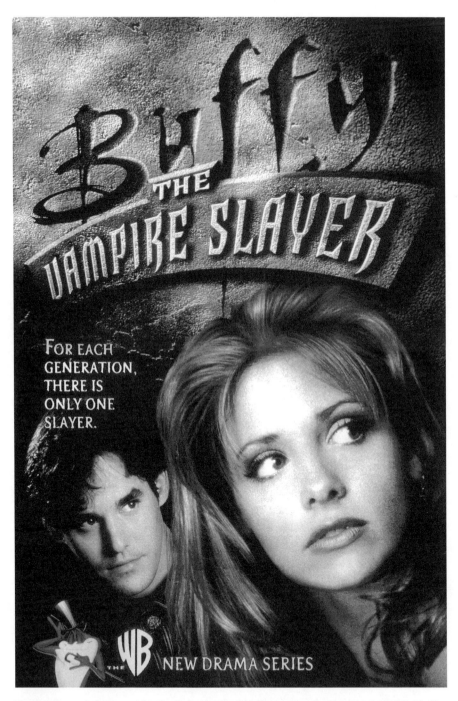

The full-page advertisement for the first episode of *Buffy the Vampire Slayer* in the *TV Guide* (8 March 1997) places an emphasis on the character of Buffy Summers, the series' young female lead

However, although Whedon is clearly attributed authorship status of the television series in associated publications targeted at a fan audience, the WB marketing produced to initially advertise the series makes no reference to Whedon, or any other author. In the issue of *TV Guide* for the series' first week of transmission, the series is advertised with a full-page poster. Across the top is the series' trademarked logo, which is replicated on the merchandising produced from the series. Underneath and dominating is a large image of Buffy Summers (Sarah Michelle Gellar) facing the camera and looking off to the right, with a smaller image of her friend Xander (Nicholas Brendon) behind and to her left. The image is accompanied by the text 'for each generation, there is only one slayer', offering a simplified premise for the series. Here, the emphasis is clearly placed on the young female lead, the character of Buffy, rather than on the authorship of the series. The advertisement essentially captures the basic format of the series, which focuses on the reactions of its protagonists to the bizarre events that they encounter, using these events to explore their adolescent anxieties.

Here, and across a great deal of the merchandising for the series, the character of Buffy acts as a brand; a recognisable and transferable image used to sell calendars, chocolate bars, mugs, magazines, games, posters, and so on. However, the image of Buffy does not function on its own, but is constructed in relation to the visual style of the series, allowing the actor Sarah Michelle Gellar to be differentiated from the character Buffy in ancillary merchandise. This is achieved in part by the use of the trademarked *Buffy the Vampire Slayer* logo that accompanies the official merchandise. However, it is also facilitated by the creation of a strong signature style for the series. Star shots of Sarah Michelle Gellar can generally be distinguished from images of the character Buffy by a combination of pose and style. Images of Buffy adopt the characteristic elements of the series' signature style, using directional light and strong colours, combined with the costuming and pose of the character. In contrast, star shots of Sarah Michelle Gellar tend to be lit in a more high-key style and substitute the strong gaze of Buffy with more traditionally feminised facial expressions and physical poses.

The series' signature style, which uses directional light and strong colours to combine the teen and horror 'worlds' of the series, also enables the ancillary merchandise to be exploited across a range of differently targeted markets. For example, the eponymously titled magazine published by Titan to accompany *Buffy* in the UK tends to emphasise the horror elements. The second issue includes a cartoon strip based on the series, interviews with two regular vampires from the second season of the series (Spike and Drusilla) in character, and an article on the creation of the series' special effects. Its two-page colour poster depicts Buffy threatening Drusilla with a stake in the foreground, as Spike leans aggressively forward in the background. The image predominates with ambers and browns in the series' characteristically shadowy style. This 'action' image in an industrial setting is in contrast to the covers of the fictional novels accompanying the series, which have a much clearer address to a female teen audience than the predominantly male market of fantasy comic magazines. The colour plates on the covers of these books tend to be posed shots of the characters in soft focus, looking directly towards the camera. The emphasis tends to be on the on the style of the characters' dress and image, rather than on the recreation of an action pose. Despite this, they still display the same use of directional light and strong ambers and blues in the colour palate.

This promotional image of Sarah Michelle Gellar as Buffy Summers uses directional light, the colour palate of the series, a strong direct gaze and an assertive, yet feminised, pose

This star shot of Sarah Michelle Gellar is more traditionally feminised in its pose and expression, and uses high-key lighting

Such ancillary merchandise exploits the different modes of address combined within the series in order to maximise its potential revenue. The generic mix of *Buffy the Vampire Slayer* not only maximises its appeal across a range of differently defined markets, but also extends the markets to which ancillary merchandise from the series can be marketed. This is particularly facilitated by the creation of a series format and signature style whose distinctiveness is constructed through generic hybridity, enabling the series to maintain its originality while still appealing to extant taste markets. The series' signature and format are both distinctive enough and flexible enough to be exploited in quite diverse ways. The generic hybridity of the 'brand', *Buffy the Vampire Slayer*, is then sufficiently malleable to be marketed to a range of different taste markets and demographics, enabling the potential revenue from the series to be maximised.

Seriality and Characterisation in *Buffy the Vampire Slayer*

Lury argues that branding favours the 'repetitive flow of the series' and 'the flat character … defined precisely by his (sic) abstention from experiences which might produce change or personal growth' (1993, p. 86). *Buffy the Vampire Slayer* certainly established a format that offers certain repeated narrative and stylistic pleasures. Each episode depicts Buffy and her friends fighting demonic foes, addresses themes about growing up in contemporary America, has a characteristic visual style, and contains certain elements, such as fight sequences, ironic humour and moments of horror. This format grounds the viewer's expectations and provides the network with a recognisable product that offers predictable pleasures repeated each week. However, unlike the narrative structure of earlier action-adventure series such as *Star Trek*, *Buffy the Vampire Slayer* also develops a continuing narrative. Actions carry over from episode to episode so that the events of one episode have consequences for the series overall. While *The X-Files* balanced this paradox through the construction of genre and mythology episodes, this distinction is much less clear cut in *Buffy the Vampire Slayer*.

There are episodes in *Buffy the Vampire Slayer* which can be distinguished as primarily 'stand-alone' stories, structured around the battle against a specific demonic foe. However, it becomes increasingly difficult to distinguish between the one-off and continuing narrative strands within each episode of *Buffy the Vampire Slayer* as the single episode plot devices become inextricably bound up with the continuing narratives. An example of this is the season six episode 'Tabula Rasa', in which one of Willow's spells goes wrong and causes each character to lose their memory. The primary action of the episode is concerned with the main characters attempting to escape from vampires while trying to reconstruct their memories. However, the emotional resonance of the episode lies with the way that the consequences of the memory loss relate to ongoing narrative strands. While in the continuing series' narrative, Willow and Tara's relationship is faltering, under the memory loss spell they fall in love all over again. While Buffy has lost her will to live after being brought back to Earth from heaven, under the spell she rediscovers her calling and the thrill of vampire slaying. The one-off plot convention of memory loss here works with the series' ongoing narratives, functioning metaphorically to explore the emotional resonance of loss experienced by a number of the series' primary characters. While this episode has a stand-alone narrative that is resolved by the end when the spell is broken, the meanings constructed by the episode appeal to the viewer's knowledge of the ongoing and changing relationships between the characters.

Therefore, although *Buffy the Vampire Slayer* works within certain formulaic conventions established during its first season, this does not restrict it to the creation of repetitive narratives and flat characters. Rather, the primary emphasis in *Buffy the Vampire Slayer* is on the development and growth of its characters over time. As Buffy struggles with her role as the slayer, she rejects her duties, struggles for her independence, returns with renewed commitment to her role in season five, only to have to re-evaluate her life after the death of her mother and her own death and resurrection in season six. Meanwhile, Willow gradually overcomes her insecurity and low self-esteem to discover an increased sense of self-worth through her growing Wicca skills and sexual awareness, and has to struggle to deal with the consequences of her increasing dependence upon magic as a source of self-esteem in seasons six and seven. In addition to these character changes, the situation of the series shifts as the characters move from high school, to college, to work. Giles has to cope with unemployment and an increasing feeling of redundancy, eventually leaving the series as a regular character in season six; the high-school students have to adjust to moving away from home and becoming increasingly independent. The series is not afraid to change its regular cast. At the end of season three, Angel and Cordelia leave the series to star in the spin-off, *Angel*. In season four, Willow's boyfriend Oz leaves and Tara, her girlfriend, is introduced as a new regular character, only to be killed in season six. The vampire Spike, who was introduced in season two becomes a regular character as he loses his ability to harm people and develops a growing love for Buffy. Most drastically, in season five, both Buffy and her mother die. Through these changes the series is able to treat (metaphorically and directly) the experiences of growing up in contemporary America.

The use of the serial/series narrative structure in *Buffy the Vampire Slayer* contains the dialectical demands of contemporary US television production to attract and maintain loyal audiences while not alienating the occasional viewer. The series constructs a narrative structure that allows it to combine repetition and change. As argued in relation to *The X-Files*, the move towards increasing serialisation in US television drama series reflects the increasing value attached to loyal audiences who are rewarded by series with dense storytelling which refers back to previous episodes. This shift can also be understood in relation to the development of the VCR and DVD player, which enables viewers to record series off-air or to buy sell-through copies of their favourite programmes. The VCR/DVD is an important element in the commercial valorisation of the fan-consumer as it creates a new market (the sale of videotapes and DVDs) through which series with fan followings can be exploited. As television becomes less ephemeral, series with ongoing and complex narrative structures become more commercially viable.

These developments challenge Lury's argument that the shift to trademark law and the development of branding leads to an emphasis on repetitive narratives and flat characters. In contrast, *Buffy the Vampire Slayer* is constructed around a format which allows the character of Buffy to be both 'flat', in that her character's function is defined by her role as the slayer, and 'rounded', in that the series is centrally concerned with exploring Buffy's changing emotional response to her given role. It is therefore necessary to rethink Lury's argument that the move away from copyright to trademark law has resulted in innovation being recast as a simulation. To do so, it is necessary to return to some of the debates addressed earlier about the developments in quality television.

Debating Quality Television: Commercial Aesthetics

Lury's exploration of branding (1993), and Feuer (1984), Gitlin (1994) and Thompson's (1997) histories of 'quality television', are all concerned with the relationship between the aesthetic and the economic. Lury argues that with the move towards branding, the mark of distinctiveness, which had traditionally functioned as an indicator of originality in the designation of a work of art, no longer functions as a signifier of innovation, but merely as the simulation of innovation. Essentially, she is exploring the ways in which the shifts in cultural production in the late twentieth century have challenged the signifying function of traditional aesthetic criteria. Thompson tackles a similar problem in his analysis of quality television. He argues that by the 1990s,

> 'quality television' has become a genre in itself, complete with its own set of formulaic
> characteristics. As is the case with any genre – the cop show, the western, the doctor show –
> we come to know what to expect. All of the innovative elements that have come to define
> 'quality television', even its unpredictability, have become more and more predictable. By
> 1992, you could recognise a 'quality show' long before you could tell if it was any good.
> Quality television came to refer to shows with a particular set of characteristics that we
> normally associate with 'good', 'artsy', and 'classy'. (1997, p. 16)

In Thompson's analysis, the traditional criteria of aesthetic value evoked by quality television, such as creative authorship, formal innovation, complex writing and so on, can no longer be relied upon as markers of 'good' television, but have come to serve (in part) the signifying function of generic elements that offer the viewer a particular and predictable product.

The difficulty in these accounts of dealing with the notion of the aesthetic in relation to commercial television recalls the difficulties encountered in the production of *The Prisoner* in reconciling the generic and the avant-garde in its textual and production strategies (see Chapter 2). The difference in the cases of *The X-Files* and *Buffy the Vampire Slayer* is that the aesthetic and the commercial aims of such productions are co-dependent. The aesthetic signifiers of 'quality' used by both series, such as distinctiveness, single authorship, complex narratives and so on, function at the service of the commercial demands of the networks, while the commercial networks demand programmes which can be read as aesthetically valuable. While in the case of *The Prisoner*, there was a conflict at the level of production between the commercial and the aesthetic aims of the series, in the quality US television series, this conflict is removed but resurfaces at the moment of academic analysis.

In many ways, Thompson's understanding of 'quality' television as a genre is astute, in that it recognises the function of traditional criteria of aesthetic value as markers of expectation, much as generic elements are used to shape viewer expectations. Yet in doing so, Thompson implies that by adopting the aesthetic characteristics associated with 'good' television as a production strategy, quality television undermines our ability to assess the value of television drama. This is particularly apparent with *The X-Files* as much of the academic debate surrounding the series is concerned with its interpretation as either a (valuably) subversive/ progressive, or a (problematically) reactionary text. For example, Douglas Kellner argues that the series attempts to subvert dominant ideologies to comment 'on some of the most frightening aspects of contemporary society, including government out of control, science and technology out of control' (1999, p. 174). Adrienne L. McLean, borrowing from the theories of Marshall McLuhan, takes this a step further by arguing that the series has progressive potentiality. In her argument, the divergent responses to *The X-Files* suggest that the series offers spaces for counter-hegemonic resistance to consensual ideology. At its most progressive, she argues, 'it helps us achieve what McLuhan calls a consciousness of the "revolutionary transformations caused by new media," thus giving us the means by which to "anticipate and control them" rather than being their slaves' (1998, p. 9).

However, the series' representation of the fantastic and its deliberate refusal of narrative resolution has led other theorists to argue that, far from being a progressive text, the series 'demonstrates the infantilism of the American psyche, where a loss of faith in a political vision has given way to the ingenuous belief in everything else' (O'Reilly, 1996, p. 6). In this counter argument, the series' critique of traditional institutions of knowledge and power (such as science, technology and government), which Kellner sees as progressive, is interpreted as a reactionary attack on rationality, which is solidified by the series' foregrounding of the paranormal and mythological over the sceptical and logical.[24] As John Lyttle writes,

> Mulder and Scully don't want you to wake up, and be responsible for, say, CIA involvement in the illegal overthrow of Chile's President Allende, or even the budget deficit. They want you to wake up, and be responsible for, the Loch Ness monster, for liver-eating mutants who live for hundreds of years, for Bigfoot. Which is no responsibility at all. . . . *The X-Files* promotes the very powerlessness it pretends to challenge. (1996, p. 17)

Lyttle argues, therefore, that the series functions as an apolitical attack on capitalism, which rejects rationalism in favour of ill-formed insecurity and paranoia based on nebulous and unproveable phenomena.

While these readings might on the surface seem opposed, for Booker they reflect the ways in which the series 'presents a postmodern view of the world while simultaneously straining against and protesting certain characteristics of the postmodern age' (2002, p. 126). However, while Booker offers a complex reading of the series, he ultimately refutes the arguments for *The X-Files*' 'subversiveness', arguing that 'those who see the series as subversive . . . are probably underestimating the ease with which the style and content of *The X-Files* can be absorbed by the commercial television context in which it exists' (2002, p. 148). For Booker, *The X-Files* can never be truly subversive because of 'the thorough embeddedness of commercial television within the system of late consumer capitalism' (2002, p. 156). Yet Booker's rigid ideological model, which ultimately implies the dismissal of all commercial television because of its mode of production, does not adequately address either the context of production or the context of reception for television drama.

As I have argued, the ambiguity of *The X-Files* can be understood in relation to the industrial context within which the series was made, in particular its attempts to combine an appeal to the 'quality', fan and network audience markets. As Gitlin (1994) argues, by attempting to generate programmes with mass audience appeal, the networks are inevitably drawn towards social and cultural conflicts. While some television offers resolutions for these conflicts, the histories of 'quality' television and telefantasy indicate that television drama is quite capable of generating programmes that build in multiple (and potentially opposed) readings. Indeed, this strategy has become particularly valued by networks which are attempting to appeal to a number of different taste markets and demographics. To suggest that the capitalist mode of production of US network television ultimately contains such contradictions is an oversimplification of the context of production. Furthermore, it fails to address the reception of television programmes. Indeed, Fox's specific attempt to appeal to the fan audience creates an emphasis in the production of *The X-Files* on complex, multilayered and open storylines which are deliberately constructed to leave the space open for audience engagement and debate, which is clearly evidenced by the wide range of fan sites, chat rooms and academic debate generated by the series.[25]

However, this is not to suggest that we should privilege the progressive reading of the series over the reactionary reading. Rather it is to suggest that *The X-Files* invites both of these readings. For example, Booker argues that *The X-Files'* insistence that 'the truth is out there', combined with its inability to ever offer this truth to its audience, replicates the deferral of desire that characterises the ideology of late capitalism (2002, p. 148). Yet, while the series certainly defers any definitive 'truth' about the paranormal, in doing so it also offers this very deferral as a central problematic. As a consequence, the deferral of desire becomes not just a characteristic of the series, but a central theme, explored through Mulder and Scully's struggles to keep the 'X-Files' open and through the increasing personal sacrifices they have to make in order to continue searching for the truth. In the later seasons, Mulder and Scully defer their desire to be together shortly after their relationship is first consummated, as Mulder goes into hiding and Scully is left to bring up their child alone. This deferral of desire becomes increasingly difficult for Scully, who ultimately gives her child up for adoption. If, as Booker argues, the postponement of the fulfilment of desire is a characteristic of late capitalism, then *The X-Files* does not simply replicate this logic, it also represents the deferral of desire as a problem. By both replicating the deferral of desire in its overarching narrative and thematic structure, and problematising it through the experiences of the central characters, the series is able to be read as both critical of and conforming to the logic of late capitalism. Rather than trying to close down analysis of such series into these either/or dichotomies, it is important to examine how these dichotomies function as a specific characteristic of US television production. As I have argued, this openness to divergent interpretations is not an historical anomaly but a consequence of the series' historical position as 'quality' television and telefantasy, and a prevalent feature of the contemporary US television series.

Conclusion

The shifts in US network television over the 1980s and 1990s present a challenge for the dominant aesthetic paradigms for understanding television as a medium. Not only do these series challenge the adequacy of the notions of glance and flow for describing the television experience, they also threaten the previous dichotomies upon which aesthetic criteria such as quality, distinctiveness, innovation and so on, were based. In negotiating the demands for series that combine longevity and an appeal to the aesthetic criteria of quality with the propensity to be exploited through branding, both *The X-Files* and *Buffy the Vampire Slayer* combine flat characters and repetitive narratives (Mulder and Scully are defined by their continued search for the truth about paranormal phenomena, Buffy is defined by her role as the slayer), within a narrative structure that allows for character growth and narrative development. This suggests that the dichotomies (repetitive narratives and flat characters versus complex narratives and changing characters) through which Lury argues that innovation is recast as simulation, cannot adequately address the complex negotiation between familiarity and distinctiveness apparent in these texts. This chapter therefore suggests that it is necessary to move beyond such dichotomies in order to understand how aesthetic criteria such as distinctiveness and innovation function in relation to the commercial demands for long-running series that can be easily branded and marketed to a range of different niche audience segments.

Telefantasy has flourished in 1990s US television because the representation of the fantastic facilitates a number of these commercial demands. The propensity for visual display in the representation of the fantastic facilitates the creation of distinctive series signatures that can be exploited through branding across a range of ancillary products. The tendency towards generic hybridity in fantasy texts enables the marketing of these series to a range of different niche demographics and taste markets. Fantasy narratives also retain associations with cult texts, suggesting the representation of the fantastic as a useful strategy in appealing to the valued fan-consumer taste market. The next chapter explores the place of telefantasy in Britain in the same historical period. If the growth of telefantasy responds to the move towards niche marketing in the face of increased competition in US network television, what function does it have in the public service environment of British terrestrial broadcasting?

Notes

1. McLean refers to *The X-Files* as a 'popular culture phenomenon' (1998, p. 4), while the sleeve to Kaveney's (2002) edited collection on *Buffy the Vampire Slayer* describes the series as 'one of the most original and popular television programmes of the last decade'.

2. On *The X-Files* see, for example, the essays in Lavery, Hague and Cartwright's edited collection (1996). On *Buffy the Vampire Slayer* see, for example, the essays in Kaveney's edited collection (2002).

3. The reasons for this shift are complex, arising from competition from satellite- and cable-delivered pay-TV, changes in syndication, shifts in personnel at the networks, and socio-cultural changes (such as the women's liberation movement, youth culture and civil rights). For more details see Feuer *et al.*'s edited collection on MTM (1984), Gitlin's study of the Hollywood television industry (1994) and Thompson's study of the 'quality television' debate (1997).

4. MTM produced *The Mary Tyler Moore Show* (CBS, 1970–7), a number of spin-off

series such as *Lou Grant* (CBS, 1977–82) and *Rhoda* (CBS, 1974–8), and *Hill Street Blues* (NBC, 1981–7). Tandem had a reputation for more socially 'relevant' sitcoms, such as *All in the Family* (CBS, 1971–9) (based on the BBC's *Till Death Us Do Part*), *Maude* (CBS, 1972–8) and *Sanford and Son* (NBC, 1972–7) (based on the BBC's *Steptoe and Son*).

5. For discussion of *Hill Street Blues* as quality television see Thompson (1997), Gitlin (1994) and Feuer *et al.* (1984).

6. Caldwell stresses that although in televisuality 'a new aesthetic sensibility has emerged' (1995, p. 21), it is one of many competing and contradictory paradigms in 1990s US broadcasting.

7. *Hill Street Blues* averaged in the low-20 share of the audience for most of its first season (Gitlin, 1994, p. 302). However, the series went on to receive twenty-one nominations and eight awards in the 1981 Emmy ceremony. After this, the audience ratings increased and by autumn 1982, it was the top-rated show in primetime for male viewers aged 18–34 (Gitlin, 1994, pp. 322–3).

8. The regulation brought in by the FCC in 1970 to curb the power of the networks actually helped secure their financial position over the decade. Although the Financial Interest and Syndication Rule (which prevented the networks from engaging in domestic syndication or owning the programmes that they aired) enabled the syndication market to flourish, it also forced the networks to sell their syndication divisions and focus on networked programming. Its companion regulation, the Prime Time Access Rule, was designed to reduce the network's hold on primetime by restricting the network hours between 7.00 and 11.00pm to three. However, the effective reduction in the network primetime hours worked in the networks' favour by reducing the number of advertising slots available within primetime network programmes, enabling the networks to increase their charges for advertising (see Brown, 1998, pp. 157–8).

9. ABC was taken over by Capital Cities in 1985, CBS by real estate company Lawrence Tisch, and NBC by General Electric (see Barnouw, 1990, p. 510).

10. Re-regulation of cable was introduced in 1992 to curb its effect on the networks, for example by enabling the networks to charge or force cable providers to carry their signals. However, this re-regulation did not reduce the fragmentation of US television broadcasting or the increased competition faced by the networks.

11. At the start of the eighth season David Duchovny left the series as a regular cast member and was replaced by Robert Patrick as John Doggett. Later in that season, Monica Reyes (Annabeth Gish) also joined as a regular cast member, and in season nine, Reyes and Doggett are assigned to *The X-Files* in the place of Mulder and Scully, although Scully continued as a regular character throughout the series.

12. This is not to imply that the fan and quality audiences are mutually exclusive, but that the network differentiated between them.

13. For Bartley see Probst (1995), for Roe see Holben (2000).

14. The exception to this may be the 'mutant' human episodes such as 'Squeeze' in which Mulder and Scully are instrumental in capturing a man who is able to squeeze through

impossibly small spaces, but must consume human livers in order to do so. However, even when such human mutants are captured, there is no clear explanation (other than evolutionary mutation) for these 'monsters' and the series emphasises the penal system's inability to understand and therefore deal with such cases.

15. The final two-part episode of *The X-Files* does offer some narrative resolution. As Mulder is placed on trial for murder, a number of characters from across the history of the series offer testimony that brings together and explains previously unresolved narrative strands. However, this evidence is dismissed by the court because of the lack of corroborating evidence, ultimately maintaining the series' premise in which the existence of the fantastic can be witnessed but never proved.

16. Indeed, as I will argue in the conclusion, the display of visual style apparent in all of the programmes examined here suggests that flow and glance theory may not be adequate paradigms for understanding television before, as well as after, the 1980s.

17. As with Fox, these new networks are part of larger conglomerates, UPN being owned by Paramount and WB by AOL Time Warner.

18. As Rachel Moseley (2001, p. 41) notes, this has coincided with a growth in the production of teen movies such as *Clueless* (1995), *She's All That* (1999), and *Cruel Intentions* (1999).

19. Joss Whedon's audio commentary for the pilot episode 'Welcome to the Hellmouth', DVD release of season one box set (Fox, 2000).

20. Other teen series transmitted by WB since it began transmitting *Buffy the Vampire Slayer* include *Dawson's Creek* (WB, 1998–2003), *Felicity* (WB, 1998–2002), and *Roswell* (WB, 1999–2002).

21. Joss Whedon's audio commentary for the pilot episode 'Welcome to the Hellmouth', DVD release of season one box set (Fox, 2000).

22. See for example, the interviews in Golden and Holder (1998).

23. Examples of individuals attributed with authorship of cult texts are Gene Roddenberry (*Star Trek*), Patrick McGoohan (*The Prisoner*) and Chris Carter (*The X-Files*). Hills argues that a 'designated "author" is ... likely to be offered up by shows which aspire to any sort of cult status' (Hills, 2002, p. 133).

24. In his 1996 Dimbleby Lecture on BBC1, Richard Dawkins took a similar line in criticising the series' attack on reason. As Thomas Sutcliffe wrote of the lecture, 'week after week, he [Dawkins] pointed out, sceptical enquiry is vanquished in favour of moronic credulity' (1996, p. 36).

25. *The X-Files*' ambiguous representation of the fantastic and complex conspiracy narratives, leave 'a space for interpretation, speculation and fan affect which cannot be closed down by final "proof" or "fact"' (Hills, 2002, p. 143). This 'space for interpretation' is apparent in both the extended debate and speculation generated by fans of the series, and the continuing academic debates about how the series should be understood.

5

PROBLEMATIC HISTORIES

US and UK Telefantasy in British Television of the 1990s/2000s

Introduction

As examined in Chapter 4, the industrial, economic and aesthetic changes in the US television industry since the 1980s led to the alignment of certain aesthetic and economic attributes in the programming of primetime network television. Value was attached to network series that functioned within a generically defined notion of 'quality television', that appealed to a specific range of niche taste markets, and that displayed a distinctive visual style that could be branded and exploited across a number of products. Telefantasy emerged as a successful form of programming in this environment with series such as *The X-Files* and *Buffy the Vampire Slayer* fulfilling these requirements, with their striking visual style, complex narratives and appeal across a range of valuable taste markets. This chapter will explore how the industrial, economic and aesthetic changes associated with the rise of satellite, cable and digital television resonated in the different context of the British television industry. In Britain, these technological changes, alongside shifts in cultural and aesthetic values, have been understood to threaten received notions of British public service broadcasting through the increase in commercial pressure. This chapter assesses these claims. It begins by examining the scheduling of US telefantasy series, *The X-Files*, *Buffy the Vampire Slayer* and *Angel* on British terrestrial television. Then it goes on to examine the production of British telefantasy, focusing in particular on a case study of the production of *Randall and Hopkirk (Deceased)*, a remake of the 1960s British telefantasy series, produced in 2000–1. If telefantasy has thrived in the US following the expansion of satellite and cable services, what effect do these shifts have on the scheduling and production of telefantasy in British terrestrial television?

Scheduling US Telefantasy on British Terrestrial Television

For its first run on US network television, *Buffy the Vampire Slayer* was scheduled in a prime-time weekday evening slot between 9.00 and 10.00pm for its first season, and between 8.00 and 9.00pm for all subsequent seasons. In the UK, *Buffy the Vampire Slayer* got its first transmission on the subscription satellite, cable and digital channel Sky 1 about four months after it was originally screened in the US. On Sky 1, *Buffy the Vampire Slayer* was scheduled much as it is in the US, on a weeknight in the primetime slot between 8.00 and 9.00pm. Generally, each season of *Buffy the Vampire Slayer* was first transmitted on UK terrestrial television a year after it was transmitted on US network television.[1] However, rather than being scheduled in a mid-evening primetime slot, the series was placed between 6.45 and 7.30pm on the second BBC channel BBC2, which has a remit to provide minority and specialist interest programming. The specific slot within which *Buffy the Vampire Slayer* was situated further emphasised its status as minority or specialist interest programming as it provided an alternative to the early evening news bulletins transmitted by the two main terrestrial channels, BBC1 and ITV, between 6.00 and 7.00pm.

Annette Hill and Ian Calcutt have argued that the scheduling of *Buffy the Vampire Slayer* on BBC2 situates the series in a slot for family and children's programmes. They argue that the 'teatime slot may be suitable for the younger fans [of *Buffy the Vampire Slayer*], but not for viewers aged 16–24 who are the core audience for this series' (Hill and Calcutt, 2001). However, an analysis of the history of this slot reveals that it has a distinctive identity as a site for programmes aimed precisely at an audience of teens and young adults. On two nights a week in the late 1980s and early 1990s, BBC2 scheduled dedicated youth programming in this slot, under the collective title of *Def II*. In addition to programmes created specifically for an audience of teenagers and young adults, such as the *Rough Guide* travel series and the music show, *Rapido*, *Def II* also consisted of repeats of telefantasy series from the 1960s and 1970s.[2] After *Def II* was cancelled by the BBC in the early 1990s, repeats of telefantasy series, such as *The Addams Family, Star Trek, Stingray* (1964–5), *The Man from U.N.C.L.E.* and *Dr Who* continued to form a large part of this slot. This was also the place in which the first *Star Trek* spin-off series, *Star Trek: The Next Generation*, premiered in the UK.[3] Over the 1990s, the 6.00–7.30pm slot on BBC2 continued to be the primary site in which imported, contemporary US telefantasy was scheduled in the UK, with primetime US network series such as *Star Trek: Voyager* and *Sliders* scheduled here.

What is apparent in this scheduling history is that 1990s primetime US telefantasy series, such as *Buffy the Vampire Slayer*, were being associated with alternative, special interest youth programming in the UK. This had a direct impact on the form in which audiences were able to view these programmes on UK terrestrial television. In order to conform to the expectations of its pre-watershed early evening slot, *Buffy the Vampire Slayer* was cut by the BBC for language, and violent and sexual content.[4] The pattern for scheduling *Buffy the Vampire Slayer* on BBC2 was repeated with the scheduling of *Buffy's* spin-off series, *Angel* (WB, 1999–2004), on Channel 4, a terrestrial channel funded by advertising but with a public service remit to provide diverse, experimental and minority interest programmes. The first season of *Angel* was scheduled between 6.00 and 7.00pm on Channel 4, in contrast to its 9.00–10.00pm slot on the WB network in the US.[5] As with the 6.00–7.30pm slot on BBC2, this slot on Channel 4 was also associated with alternative programming with a strong youth appeal. Channel 4 scheduled a number of US sitcoms here such as repeats of *Friends*, in addition to their youth-orientated soap opera, *Hollyoaks*, and imported teen dramas such as *The O.C.* They have also placed a number of telefantasy series here, such as the US series, *Babylon 5* and *Smallville: Superman the Early Years*, and the 1960s series *The Avengers* and *The Time Tunnel*. Produced as a more adult-orientated spin-off of *Buffy the Vampire Slayer*, *Angel*'s violent action sequences and occasionally coarse language were cut for its early evening transmission on Channel 4. Jay Kandola, Channel 4's head of series' acquisition, defended this decision by arguing that, 'Channel 4 has made minimal cuts [to *Angel*] to make sure that it can be viewed by all of its fans and not just some' (from an interview in *Right to Reply*, UK, Channel 4, tx. 6 October 2000).

The scheduling and cutting of *Buffy the Vampire Slayer* and *Angel* needs to be understood in relation to received notions of public service broadcasting in Britain. Jay Kandola's defence of Channel 4's scheduling of *Angel* appeals to a particular understanding of television's social responsibilities in which television scheduling safeguards the rights of all viewers to watch programmes that are both appealing and appropriate. Simon Frith has argued that in the current climate of British broadcasting, audience research indicates that for viewers in Britain, '*access* [to television programmes] is as significant as *content*' (Frith, 2000, p. 47). It is precisely through this argument that the terrestrial broadcasters are here defending cutting the *content* of *Angel* in order to enable *access* by all its potential viewers.

Part of the problem raised by series such as *Buffy the Vampire Slayer* and *Angel* stems from their generic hybridity, combining horror and action with a strong address to adolescent themes. In the competitive, fragmented environment of US network television, the appeal of *Buffy the Vampire Slayer* to valuable niche taste markets makes it an economically viable primetime series. However, on UK terrestrial television, this multiple address has to be negotiated in order to fulfil the perceived requirements of public service broadcasting. The association of US telefantasy with youth programming in the UK schedules further exacerbates this. While the combination of appeal to the teen and fan taste markets contributes to the value of *Buffy the Vampire Slayer* in the US network schedules, the categorising of *Buffy the Vampire Slayer* and *Angel* as youth programming has proved problematic for its scheduling on UK terrestrial television. For while on the new US networks, programmes with a strong youth appeal are considered a valuable element of primetime television drama, in the UK they tend to be understood as fulfilling 'alternative' tastes to the mainstream.[6]

Quality, Value and British Public Service Television

What is particularly striking about the scheduling of *Buffy the Vampire Slayer* and *Angel* in Britain and the US is the differing terms under which such decisions are justified by programmers. As argued in Chapter 4, the production and scheduling of *Buffy the Vampire Slayer* in the US can be understood in relation to industrial attempts to unite aesthetic and economic value through a redefinition of quality television as a generic style combined with an appeal to a number of valuable niche markets. By contrast, Jay Kandola's defence of the scheduling of *Angel* on Channel 4 is not couched in terms of the economic or aesthetic value of the series. Rather it appeals to public service notions of the role of the broadcaster to protect and meet the needs of the majority of viewers. Implicit in such decisions is an evaluation of the programme and its perceived audience(s).

In an article in the British journal *Screen*, Simon Frith (2000) reported on the findings of the Economic and Social Research Council's Media Economics and Media Culture Research Programme, which was set up in 1995 to explore the impact of economic and regulatory frameworks on the value judgments made in the process of producing and delivering programmes in Britain. He identified three interrelated notions of value in British television: quality television, valuable television and good television. This division provides a useful starting-point for considering the ways in which the shifts in the context of television production over the 1980s and 1990s have affected the types of programmes being aired on terrestrial television in Britain and the forms of value associated with them. In Frith's model, 'quality television' refers both to a type of programme and a mode of production. As with Thompson's (1997) definition of quality in US television, quality television is here understood as the exception rather than the norm. However, Frith's notion of quality is constructed within the context of British public service broadcasting. Thus, quality television in Britain stands in contrast to popular television and is produced for aesthetic rather than commercial gain. Frith argues that, 'The idea of quality television comes ... from the concatenation of two strands of British regulatory history: high cultural disdain for the mass media; and the defence of public service broadcasting against various forms of commercialization' (2000, p. 40). While arguing that the definition of quality television stems largely from broadcasters, Frith claims that 'valuable television' is defined by viewers in terms of what they like and what they are prepared to pay for. By contrast, 'good television' refers more directly to received notions of aesthetic value, such as imagination, authenticity, social relevance and so on (Frith, 2000, p. 45).

These three concepts interrelate in the negotiations that take place across the industry, text and audience about the value of television as a medium and as individual programmes. Within Britain, they are constructed specifically through the notion of public service broadcasting. Thus quality television has traditionally been associated with non-commercial television produced within institutions protected from the denigrating effects of market forces by state regulation.[7] In this public service model, quality television is defined through aesthetic criteria associated with high culture that is differentiated from mass mediated and commercial cultural production. Within this definition of quality television, commercially produced television series such as *Buffy the Vampire Slayer* and *Angel* are automatically situated as the kind of programming *against* which judgments of quality are made.

However, these criteria of quality television not only problematise the place of commercially produced US television in the UK, they also problematise any intrinsic aesthetic value of television programmes themselves, suggesting that television can only be of 'quality' if it refuses or subverts the mass mediated nature of the medium. The implication that television programmes in themselves are not of the same aesthetic value as other cultural products is reflected in Channel 4's differing policies on cutting films and television programmes. Channel 4 has a policy of not cutting films purely to fulfil scheduling requirements. By contrast, by claiming that in the scheduling and cutting of *Angel*, 'I have to please everybody, and I think I have pleased the majority of people' (from *Right to Reply* interview, 6 October 2000), Jay Kandola implies that it is part of the channel's requirements as a public service broadcaster to censor a television series like *Angel*. What Jay Kandola is implying is that Channel 4 has a greater responsibility to schedule a series such as *Angel* in a slot which is accessible to the majority of the public to whom the series will appeal, than to ensure that the series remains uncut. The channel's remit to serve the public is defined here in terms of enabling viewers to *access* the programme at the expense of any intrinsic aesthetic value that the series may have.

As examined in Chapter 2, the relationship between the commercial imperative and aesthetic value has long since been a contentious and problematic issue in British public service broadcasting. However, this is an issue that is further exacerbated by the growth of satellite, cable and digital television, which has made commercial US television an increasingly central part of the landscape of British television culture. Technologically, new forms of programme delivery, such as satellite, cable and digital television, have led to a proliferation of television programmes across a greatly expanded range of channels. This not only threatens the status of terrestrial television as the sole provider of programmes across a limited number of channels, it also introduces new approaches to television production, such as niche marketing and branding (discussed in Chapter 4), which extend across programmes to new, branded 'genre' channels such as the Sci-Fi Channel. Economically, this proliferation of channels challenges the terrestrial services, while simultaneously providing them with extended markets through which to exploit their own products.[8] For example, in 1991, the BBC launched a commercial satellite channel, *BBC World Service TV*, to exploit the international demand for BBC programmes, suggesting that in the expanded market of international television, the BBC itself can be understood as a brand associated with quality. A year later it partnered with the US cable operator, Cox and the commercial company, Thames Television, to set up *UK Gold*, a UK-directed satellite channel screening repeats from the archives.

Furthermore, the 1990 Broadcasting Act stipulated that terrestrial broadcasters commission not less than 25 per cent of their programmes from independent production companies, a move that corresponds with the gradual reduction of the BBC's role as an in-house production company. In combination with the increasing importance of global markets, this shift affects criteria of quality as an appeal to British tastes and standards may no longer be the primary financial incentive in television production. It also challenges the power of commissioning editors in the UK to dictate the types of programmes made, as the terrestrial television market becomes just one of a number of potential points of sale. As a consequence, notions of quality in British public service broadcasting which had previously been defined in opposition to commercial mass media are becoming increasingly difficult to sustain.

However, despite the growth in satellite, cable and digital television, terrestrial television still remains the primary form of television in Britain. In 2000, the audience share for public service broadcasters in homes with satellite, cable or digital television was as high as 61.6 per cent of the total audience, rising to 70 per cent in primetime.[9] Although the Christmas statistics for 2003–4 indicated that for the first time the non-terrestrial channels reached the same audience share as ITV1 (23.6 per cent), both ITV1 and BBC1 were still regularly gaining the same or a larger share of the audience than all of the digital, satellite and cable channels put together (see <www.barb.co.uk>). Terrestrial broadcasters maintain control over the scheduling of series which, as in the example of *Buffy the Vampire Slayer*, conform to nationally specific criteria of appeal and value. However, the precise nature of these criteria is constructed in the interface between producer and viewer, and the erosion of the terrestrial broadcasters as the primary providers of television broadcasting is challenging previously accepted criteria of aesthetic value. Frith notes a paradox in the public service approach to television production in which there is both a suspicion of popular aesthetics (the tastes of the viewers) and a need/desire to appeal to audience interests, whether in the production of minority programming for a specific audience or in the creation of mainstream programming with a wide appeal (Frith, 2000, p. 46). This is apparent in the transmission of an episode of *Right to Reply* on Channel 4 in which an irate viewer challenged Channel 4 programmers about the scheduling of *Angel*, and from which the quotations from Jay Kandola have been taken.[10] In this programme, the viewer's identification of *Angel* as a 'valuable' programme comes into conflict with the programmers' criteria of 'quality' television.

Frith also suggests that these evaluative criteria may be further complicated by the social shifts in the make-up of the audience and production personnel.

> The question now, then, is whether different patterns of recruitment (Media Studies rather than Oxbridge graduates), different cultural reference points (US cinema rather than the British stage) are ... leading to a different, more populist, set of evaluative criteria even of drama. (Frith, 2000, p. 45)

What this suggests is that this period of change in the landscape of British television broadcasting is one in which previously accepted criteria of aesthetic value which were central to definitions of public service broadcasting are under threat. This threat comes from changes within the British industry and British society, and from the increasingly significant impact of global markets.

British Telefantasy: Responding to *The X-Files*

As in the US, the success of *The X-Files* in Britain demonstrated the potential for telefantasy series with high production values to appeal to a broad audience. *The X-Files* was initially transmitted on British terrestrial television on BBC2 between 9.30 and 10.15pm. However, over its first season it gained exceptionally high ratings for this minority interest channel and was moved to a primetime BBC1 slot during its second season.[11] This scheduling move represented a shift in strategy for the BBC and recognition of the mainstream appeal of this 'cult' US hit with a majority British audience. Janet McCabe (2001) argues that the scheduling of *The X-Files* by the BBC exemplified the shift in British public service broadcasting from the notion of the 'vulnerable' viewer defined in the Pilkington Report in the 1960s to the 'informed consumer' defined in the Peacock Report in 1986. The Peacock Report signalled a shift in the definition of British public service broadcasting by suggesting that 'viewers and listeners are the best ultimate judges of their own interests' (Peacock Report cited in McCabe, 2001, p. 149). With an increasing recognition of the plurality of British society over the 1970s and 1980s (exemplified by Channel 4's remit for diversity) and the expansion of viewer choice with the multiplication of television services, the imagined 'public' of public service broadcasting has come into question.[12] McCabe argues that the scheduling of *The X-Files* reflects the BBC's difficulties in negotiating its position within this environment. She suggests that, while the move of the series from BBC2 to BBC1 responded to the judgments of its viewers, the subsequent erratic scheduling of the series on BBC1 was justified by an understanding of the series' audience as loyal and devoted viewers who would follow the series regardless of its scheduling (2001, p. 150). McCabe argues that these scheduling decisions reflect not the actual audience gained by the series (which increased by two million when the series moved from BBC2 to BBC1), but the BBC's 'imagined' audience for the series. Hence it reflected how 'the BBC, on the verge of change, finds a consensual notion of the public more difficult to sustain' (McCabe, 2001, p. 152).

The above debates suggest that the changes in British television over the 1980s and 1990s have brought earlier definitions of public service broadcasting into question by challenging the possibility of conceptualising or appealing to the British 'public' as a consensus audience. However, while in the US the *consensus* audience has been replaced by a notion of the television audiences as a *coalition* of viewers, the problematic space that US telefantasy series occupy in the UK terrestrial schedules suggests that within the tradition of public service broadcasting in Britain, this shift is much more difficult to negotiate. The tensions between commercial imperatives and a tradition of public service; popularity and quality; mass media and high culture; the national and the global; problematise the criteria by which telefantasy is valued both industrially and culturally in the UK. This is apparent not only in the scheduling of imported telefantasy, but also in the production of contemporary British telefantasy.

A number of indigenous British telefantasy series followed the success of *The X-Files* in the UK and adopted a range of different strategies. *Neverwhere* (BBC2, 1996) followed in the tradition of British telefantasy drama characterised by the long-running series *Dr Who*, with its emphasis on using studio sets and costumes to depict an 'ordinary' man's adventures in a fantastical world beneath the streets of London. The six-part series, *The Last Train* (ITV, 1999) reinvigorated another tradition of British telefantasy. In following the survivors of a global holocaust with a gritty, realist style, *The Last Train* is clearly indebted to series such as *Survivors* (BBC1, 1975–7) from the disaster strand of British telefantasy from the 1970s. Other series attempted to transfer the themes and style of *The X-Files* to a British setting. The six-part serial *Ultraviolet* (Channel 4, 1998) updated the vampire myth to the 1990s, following the work of a covert government agency set up to deal with the vampire threat. The series' dark visual style and combination of conspiracy narratives with tense action and suspense is clearly indebted to *The X-Files* and comparisons were made between the two series by David Pirie (1996). In contrast, *The Visitor* and *Invasion Earth* were more concerned with exploiting the developments in special effects technology in their invasion narratives. Both series premiered in spring 1998, *The Visitor* on ITV1 and *Invasion Earth* on BBC1. Jed Mercurio situated his creation of *Invasion Earth* directly in relation to *The X-Files*, stating in an interview about the series that, 'Because of the ratings success of *The X-Files*, TV executives have been looking for a British version' (cited in Millar, 1998, p. 2). The series, a co-production between BBC Scotland and the Sci-Fi Channel, was reportedly the most expensive drama ever made for British terrestrial television with each episode costing approximately £750,000 (Millar, 1998, p. 2). The high budgets were used to exploit the developments in CGI technology to create a vast alien entity, an expense that Mercurio justified in terms of a desire to disassociate the series from the comparatively low production values of earlier British telefantasy (cited in Millar, 1998, p. 2).

Thus it is apparent that in the response to the success of *The X-Files* in Britain there were two broad trends. First, to build on the renewed interest in telefantasy by reinvigorating British traditions in telefantasy. Second, to integrate the thematic and stylistic possibilities opened up by *The X-Files* within indigenously produced British programming. The most apparent difference between these British series and their US counterparts is their narrative structure. All these British programmes adopt a much shorter narrative structure than their US counterparts. Each series is relatively self-contained and, although a series such as *Ultraviolet* was based on a format that could run over a number of seasons, it still functioned on a much

smaller scale, limited to six episodes. None of these contemporary British telefantasy programmes have been long running. This difference in narrative structure can be understood
in part in relation to the differences between the national industries. In the US, the television
industry is relatively standardised around a particular scheduling routine that favours the production of series with twenty to twenty-six episodes. The location of the industry in Hollywood
means that production tends to be dominated by a number of key conglomerates and production companies have access to a wide range of specialist services. In addition, as discussed
in Chapter 4, the commercial imperative in US broadcasting places an emphasis on the production of programmes that can be exploited across a range of media and sold to syndication.
All these elements combine to favour the long-running series.

By comparison, the British terrestrial schedules are constructed along more diverse lines.
The public service remit in British broadcasting is based on the notion that the British public
is best served by a mixed schedule of programmes. While there is room within this schedule
for long-running series and soap operas such as *The Bill* and *EastEnders*, there is a greater
emphasis on a diversity of programme types than on the US networks. However, as we saw
in Chapter 2, British television drama has historically adopted the structure of the US television series. The different narrative structure of 1990s British telefantasy therefore cannot
simply be attributed to the greater diversity of narrative forms on British terrestrial television.
Another factor here is the impact of US programmes on UK production values in the 1990s.
As Jed Mercurio's comments suggest, there was a perceived need in the production of
Invasion Earth to compete with the production values of US telefantasy. However, with the
relatively lower production budgets in British television production, such a financial investment is less risky in a series that only runs for four or six episodes. One consequence of the
shorter length of British telefantasy series is the effect that it has on their broader cultural
impact. Programmes that run for four or six episodes are less likely to have the cultural impact
of the US series that run for a number of seasons and are consequently less likely to develop
cult fan followings. I want to explore these differences between contemporary US and UK
telefantasy by examining an example from early 2000, *Randall and Hopkirk (Deceased)*. As a
remake of a late 1960s British telefantasy series, the differences between the earlier and later
productions suggest a number of ways of thinking about the changes in British television as
it has moved from what Ellis (2000) has termed the era of scarcity to the era of availability.

British Telefantasy on British Terrestrial Television: *Randall and Hopkirk (Deceased)*

The original series of *Randall and Hopkirk (Deceased)* ran for one season of twenty-six fifty-
minute episodes in 1969. It was produced by Lew Grade's ITC, who were responsible for a
number of telefantasy series in the 1960s and 1970s, including *The Prisoner* (see Chapter 2).
The two protagonists, Jeff Randall and his partner Marty Hopkirk, run a detective agency and
the series followed a basic detective narrative as they investigated cases, assisted by Hopkirk's
wife, Jeannie. The 'twist' in the series came in the first episode when Hopkirk was killed and
returned as a ghost, visible only to his partner Randall, to solve his own murder. The original
series was essentially constructed around the detective genre with the fantastic elements
confined to the appearance and disappearance of Marty, simply produced through stopping

the camera and removing the actor from the frame, and Marty's paranormal powers were predominantly limited to observation. The series was reasonably light in tone, particularly with the casting of Kenneth Cope as Marty, an actor best known for his appearances on the satire series, *That Was the Week That Was*. As with much of ITC's production in the 1960s, *Randall and Hopkirk (Deceased)* was produced for both a British and a US market. Re-named *My Partner the Ghost* for US audiences, the series was not a ratings success, but did run in syndication through the 1970s.

Randall and Hopkirk (Deceased) was revived in the late 1990s by WTTV for the BBC and the remake was first transmitted in March 2000 on BBC1. WTTV (Working Title TV) was formerly owned by PolyGram, and was sold in 1997 to the US conglomerate, Universal. Working Title is best known for the productions of its sister arm, Working Title Films, responsible for a number of internationally successful British films in the 1990s, including *Four Weddings and a Funeral* (1994), *Elizabeth* (1998) and *Notting Hill* (1999). The television arm of the company by contrast had a significantly low output, producing around twenty major television dramas and films between its formation in 1984 and the production of *Randall and Hopkirk (Deceased)* in 2000. WTTV's managing director, Simon Wright, claimed that the company's ownership by a large US conglomerate like Universal was financially and aesthetically valuable in the television market in the late 1990s. He argued that the international market had become increasingly central to television production, with series which perform badly in Britain still being financially viable as a product for sale abroad and often proving successful in the international market (see Elliott, 2000, p. 21). Much of WTTV's television output has been in the form of international co-productions, a strategy facilitated by Universal's powerful international distribution arm. Furthermore, Wright claimed that while most independent production companies in Britain struggled to increase their production output at a low cost in order to maximise profits, the economic pressures on WTTV were offset by the financial presence of Universal.

> Most [independents] are trying to make as much as possible because the amount of work you do equates with the amount of profit you make. We have a long-term interest in sharing ownership of programmes and exploiting their library value. (Cited in Elliott, 2000, p. 21)

As a consequence WTTV could develop projects independently from the broadcasters without the pressure to raise a percentage of the production costs from them. Wright argued that this gave them the creative freedom to select scripts, directors and principal cast before approaching potential broadcasters (ibid.). This creative independence was combined with the financial backing of Universal to enable them to produce high-quality, big-budget series.

WTTV's production of *Randall and Hopkirk (Deceased)* arose out of PolyGram's desire to exploit its ownership of the ITC catalogue (which has since been purchased by the British company, Carlton). Wright's reasons for the choice of this series point to the factors that he argued were particularly economically viable in the 1990s television market. He saw the original series as 'high-concept cult TV' (Elliott, 2000, p. 21), whose previous simplistic effects could be improved with modern special effects and an increased budget. It provided a high-concept template upon which the larger budgets from Universal could impose higher production values.

In this account, Wright attached value to particular attributes which contribute to the economic value of the series for development. As with the US network television market, high-concept series (whose premise can be easily reduced to a simple phrase – a detective series in which one of the partners is a ghost) are prioritised as more saleable across a range of markets. These economic criteria of value are combined with aesthetic criteria as Wright drew attention to the creative independence of his production company from the rigors of the market, and the high production values of their version of the series. As with the accounts of the production of *Buffy the Vampire Slayer*, for Wright the economic and aesthetic are interdependent, suggesting that higher production values and creative authorship lead to a more financially viable product (ibid.).[13]

There are a number of similarities between *Randall and Hopkirk (Deceased)* and a US telefantasy series such as *Buffy the Vampire Slayer*. Both series combine elements of telefantasy with a significant address to a youth audience. They both play with different levels of audience expectation (*Buffy's* use of genre and *Randall and Hopkirk's* status as a remake) structured around various levels of generic and narrative 'known-ness'. Furthermore, both are scheduled as mainstream primetime drama when initially transmitted in their countries of production. However, there are a number of significant differences in the particular strategies employed in the production of each series that need to be understood in relation to nationally specific notions of aesthetic and economic value.

Randall and Hopkirk (Deceased) as Mainstream Family Television

Randall and Hopkirk (Deceased) was commissioned by the BBC and transmitted on BBC1 between 8.55 and 9.45pm every Saturday night for six weeks between 18 March and 22 April 2000.[14] This is a post-watershed slot, allowing the treatment of material considered unsuitable for younger viewers. However, the Saturday-evening schedules are also traditionally constructed for family viewing, consisting of game shows, variety, soap operas and mainstream drama series (such as *Jonathan Creek* about a magician who solves mysterious crimes) which are seen to have a broad demographic appeal and can be viewed by the whole family.[15] The commissioning of *Randall and Hopkirk (Deceased)* for this slot points to the particular evaluative judgments that lie behind the BBC's construction of both appropriate and appealing family viewing.

As a remake of a 1960s television series, *Randall and Hopkirk (Deceased)* functions in relation to the appeal of the original. Meg Carter (2000a) argues that the appeal of 'retro TV' in the 1990s stemmed from the increasing economic pressures on broadcasters and programme-makers. She quoted Jim Reid, head of development at Channel X, who claimed that 'Dusting off old programme formats is a way of minimising the risks. Certain series, such as *Randall and Hopkirk (Deceased)*, are widely known even by those who can't remember them. You don't have to explain the concept' (cited in Carter, 2000a, p. 20). The 1990s remakes of telefantasy series from the 1960s and 1970s into Hollywood blockbusters, such as *Lost in Space* (1998) and *The Avengers* (1998), would seem to back up Reid's argument. Certainly, the remake of *Randall and Hopkirk* is part of an economic strategy by WTTV to exploit the economic potential of Universal's ownership of the ITC catalogue. However, it can also be understood in relation to the perceived audience appeal of such series.

Charlie Higson, who adapted *Randall and Hopkirk (Deceased)* for WTTV, described his initial interest in the series in nostalgic terms. He claimed, 'I'd always wanted to have a go at making the kind of show I enjoyed as a kid. Big, imaginative shows, like *The Avengers* and *The Prisoner*, with a strong fantasy element' (Higson, 2000, p. 19). Higson's own nostalgia for these programmes suggests that part of the appeal of the series for BBC1's Saturday-night schedules stemmed from a recognition of the changing make-up of the family audience, many of whom, like Higson, would have watched such series as a child. It is a recognition that the audience for 'cult' telefantasy is not necessarily made up of an 18–24 demographic and that such a remake could have a strong resonance across a number of generations – those who watched the original series in the 1960s, those who watched the repeats of the series in the early 1990s on BBC2 in the 6.00–7.30pm slot, and those who have never seen the original but are fans of telefantasy programming.

As an adaptation of a 1960s telefantasy series, therefore, *Randall and Hopkirk (Deceased)* did have a potential cross-generational appeal. However, Charlie Higson went on to cast the primary appeal of the series in terms of the presence of Vic Reeves and Bob Mortimer in the starring roles and the series' generic associations with US telefantasy. Of his approach to adapting the series, he stated:

> I certainly didn't want to tinker with the basic premise and dynamic, but after the first couple of episodes I wanted to get away from the old series and do something completely new. The BBC was keen that we made it very much a detective show. I was told, 'People understand detectives, you know, police and mysteries. They like what's familiar.' But I pointed out that there are at least four detective programmes on every day and that's just on terrestrial TV. What the world didn't need was yet another dull detective show. We had Vic [Reeves] and Bob [Mortimer]; we had a central character that was a ghost – and just look at the success of shows like *Buffy the Vampire Slayer* and *The X-Files*. So my aim was to push the fantasy side of it. (2000, p. 20)

Higson's justification of his approach to the series is significant on a number of levels. There is recognition of the value of the 'basic premise and dynamic' of the original series alongside a simultaneous desire to 'do something completely new'. This tension is then articulated in relation to a struggle between the BBC's desire for the 'familiar' and his emphasis on creating something unusual and different, which is structured in generic terms around the combination of the detective and fantasy genres within the series' format. Finally, Higson situates the difference of the fantastic within known terms – the comic personae of Reeves and Mortimer and the success of US telefantasy. For Higson, the appeal of the series can be seen to lie in the way in which it integrates these two elements into the basic format of an extant programme.

Performing Comedy, Performing Fantasy

I want to explore these two elements that Higson sees as central to the remake's appeal. British comedians, Vic Reeves and Bob Mortimer are a well-known double act from the alternative British comedy scene. They first rose to prominence in the late 1980s with their surreal stage show, *Vic Reeves' Big Night Out*, which was turned into a television series for Channel 4 in 1990. After moving to BBC2 with the sketch show *The Smell of Reeves and Mortimer* (1993–5), the pair went on to combine their act with other mainstream genres, producing four series of *Shooting Stars* (1995–2002), an absurd game-show parody in which two teams of celebrity guests competed against each other. While their previous series had been produced for BBC2 and Channel 4, in 1998 Reeves and Mortimer moved into main-stream television with the family quiz show, *Families at War* (1999). Scheduled to open BBC1's Saturday-evening family viewing, the series pitted two families against each other in a series of bizarre tests of skill and talent set by Reeves and Mortimer. The series combined familiar aspects of the Reeves and Mortimer double act (the bickering between the comedians, the repetitive catch phrases, the bizarre set pieces) with the expectations of the family quiz show (the inclusion of real families, the light tone, the omission of offensive language, and so on).

Although coming out of the British alternative comedy scene, Reeves and Mortimer can also be situated within the context of British light entertainment. They have been frequently compared to the comic double act Morecambe and Wise, who were a staple of British prime-time television over the 1960s, 1970s and 1980s. Morecambe and Wise's double act combined sketches with musical numbers in which the pair parodied well-known routines and songs for comic effect. Ernie Wise played the straight, gullible foil to Eric Morecambe's infantile and mischievous clown. Becoming somewhat of a British institution, the duo's comedy series were frequently scheduled in the primetime Saturday-night variety slot on BBC1. Reeves and Mortimer's double act in *Vic Reeves' Big Night Out* is in many ways an updated (if somewhat anarchic and surreal) version of Morecambe and Wise, with its combination of sketches, musical numbers and dance routines performed in front of a live studio audience.

I want to argue therefore, that the appeal of Reeves and Mortimer extends across a range of potential audiences. As a comic double act coming out of the alternative British stand-up scene, they have an appeal to teenagers and young adults. However, elements of their act can be understood in relation to a tradition of British variety with a strong family appeal. Fur-thermore, the combination of this act with mainstream genres extends this appeal to both a younger and older demographic.

Like Reeves and Mortimer, Charlie Higson is a comedian from the alternative British scene. Higson worked with Reeves and Mortimer on the stage version of *Big Night Out* and since then as a script editor and producer. He also has a reputation in Britain as a comedian in his own right, most prominently with the successful television sketch show *The Fast Show*. *Randall and Hopkirk (Deceased)* was therefore a move, for Reeves and Mortimer, and Hig-son, into drama from sketch comedy. While Higson has insisted that the series is not a spoof, but 'straight drama' (Killick, 1999, p. 9), he has also emphasised a desire to build on its comic potential, a move which is intrinsically linked to the presence of Reeves and Mortimer in the starring roles.

Randall and Hopkirk (Deceased) can therefore be seen as an extension of Reeves and Mor-timer's gradual move into more mainstream television, from the surreal comedy of the sketch show, *The Smell of Reeves and Mortimer* to the more accessible combination of surreal humour with established generic forms in *Shooting Stars* and *Families at War*. The combi-nation of Reeves and Mortimer's double act with the basic format of *Randall and Hopkirk*

(Deceased) conflates stand-up comedy with the narrative drama of telefantasy. What is presented is the transposition of the comic personae of the double act onto the fictional characters of the series. Reeves and Mortimer's double act is constructed around a deeply affectionate yet antagonistic relationship between the pair. This is recreated in the relationship between Marty and Jeff, which is represented as a deep bond despite Jeff's irritation at Marty's frequently infantile behaviour. It is important to distinguish here between the performers, Jim Muir (Vic Reeves' real name) and Bob Mortimer, and the comic personae, 'Vic Reeves' and 'Bob Mortimer', constructed through their double act. Reeves' comic persona is the likeable clown with an absurd sense of humour. Mortimer tends to act as his foil, the voice of reason or incredulity at Reeves' jokes and performances. These constructed comic personae remain reasonably consistent across the body of Reeves and Mortimer's work (although the pair frequently adopt other comic roles in their sketch shows). For example, when the pair hosted the game show, *Shooting Stars*, their performances and the relationship enacted between them was in line with that established in their earlier series. They were not merely chairing a celebrity quiz. Rather, they were comedians presenting a performance of their comic personae acting as hosts.

The strength of Reeves and Mortimer's comic personae is apparent in their performances in *Randall and Hopkirk (Deceased)*. Not only can the characters of Randall and Hopkirk be equated with the comic personae of Mortimer and Reeves (respectively), there is also a strong element of 'performance' in their portrayals of the characters. The childlike, clownish qualities in the character of Marty Hopkirk are emphasised in Reeves' performance in order to highlight the similarities between his comic persona and the character he portrays. This is played against an interpretation of Jeff Randall as Marty's straight, uptight foil, corresponding to Mortimer's comic persona and the constructed relationship of their double act. For example, in episode four, Marty's ability to create a ghostly wind is given a comic twist as he demonstrates to Jeff his ability to move objects through farting. This visual gag plays out the relationship between Reeves and Mortimer's comic personae as Jeff attempts to continue the 'straight' narrative development of the story while Marty disrupts the scene through his ghostly presence. This correlation between the performer, Reeves and the character, Marty is further emphasised in the following episode when Marty performs a song-and-dance routine in Limbo. As Marty sings the song, 'Kick in the Head', the visual effects literally depict him kicking his own head as part of his dance routine. This number does not advance the narrative but rather acts to combine the showcasing of Reeves' trademark comic musical numbers with the display of special effects. As a consequence, in *Randall and Hopkirk (Deceased)*, Jim Muir and Bob Mortimer do not offer psychologically realistic portrayals of the characters of Marty Hopkirk and Jeff Randall. Rather the series represents the comic personae of 'Vic Reeves' and 'Bob Mortimer' performing the characters of Marty Hopkirk and Jeff Randall. Indeed, Mortimer has actually claimed, 'I just do Jeff Randall as Bob Mortimer' (cited in Lane, 2001, p. 57).

The performative nature of Reeves and Mortimer's portrayals of Randall and Hopkirk to appeal to the expectations of their comic personae is extended to other characters within the series, most prominently Marty's mentor, Wyvern, portrayed by Tom Baker, renowned for his role as the fourth incarnation of the Doctor in *Dr Who*.[16] In episode two, Wyvern introduces

Marty to the practicalities of his ghostly existence. He explains that his house is just a construct to make Marty feel more at home and that his physical appearance is also merely fabricated to please Marty. As Marty leans in to ask Wyvern what he really looks like, there is a cut to a close two-shot of them and Wyvern stares into his eyes and replies mystically, 'You don't want to know Marty, believe me, you don't want to know.' Marty and Wyvern then both turn their heads slowly to look directly at the camera (the audience), pausing the conversation, before there is a cut back to a mid-shot and Wyvern rises out of his seat to continue his oration. This look out at the camera is clearly and deliberately marked by the camera work, editing and performances as a significant pause in the narrative thrust of the episode. It can be read simply as an acknowledgment of the unknown, a gaze out as Marty contemplates what possible manifestation Wyvern may possess. However, there is also a deliberate overtness about the look, which addresses the viewer directly. This break with conventional modes of representation at the moment when Wyvern is describing his 'true' appearance self-consciously addresses the cult fan viewer and draws attention to the fabrication of the performances. It adds ironic significance to the question of what Wyvern 'really' looks like, highlighting the presence of Tom Baker in the role of Wyvern. Such moments of knowing irony, also apparent in the cameos by British comedians and actors throughout the series, appeal directly to the knowledgeability of the cult television fan, but also contribute to the emphasis on the performative in the series overall.

While the remake of *Randall and Hopkirk (Deceased)* utilises the expectations associated with the comic personae of Reeves and Mortimer, it also playfully acknowledges the viewer's knowledge of the narrative format of the original series. This is most overt in the first episode in which Marty is killed investigating a case and returns from the dead to enlist Jeff's help in solving his own murder. The first half of the episode plays with the viewer's expectation of Marty's imminent death. The moment of Marty's death is delayed through a number of comic narrative displacements. When a car races towards Marty at high speed, a close-up of Marty adopting a direct copy of the pose struck by Kenneth Cope (as Marty) in the original series just moments before he was killed by a speeding car, invites the viewer to assume that this will be the moment of Marty's death, and then subverts this expectation as the car fails to hit Marty. Marty manages to avoid a series of possible accidental deaths over the episode before ironically exclaiming, 'It's not my lucky day' just moments before he is driven off a cliff to his death. The series' manipulation of expectation for comic effect reveals a delight in narrative and visual play that informs the whole of the series' visual and narrative style.

Despite being based on a detective narrative, *Randall and Hopkirk (Deceased)* privileges visual style over narrative, in much the same way that it privileges the comic personae of Reeves and Mortimer over the characters of Randall and Hopkirk. For example, in episode four, 'Paranoia', Jeff Randall is hired to protect an ex-Government employee, Douglas Milton, who is due to give a potentially damaging exposé at a conference on 'Freedom, Security and Terrorism'. Milton's fear of assassination is confirmed after the opening teaser, as a number of different characters are depicted plotting his death. Once he arrives at the conference, the disastrous failure of each attempt on his life is played for comic effect, while Randall and Hopkirk are oblivious to the danger Milton is in. In the denouement, a new assassin is revealed as Marty witnesses the head of security threatening Milton and Jeannie, and uses his ghostly powers to save them. Finally, the episode ends on a comic gag as Milton's exposé simply re-tells well-known scandals and conspiracy theories. Over the episode, a case is established and resolved. However, Randall and Hopkirk do not use any detective skills and the murderer is exposed through chance rather than through expertise. There are no clues presented over the course of the episode whereby the viewer could piece together the final solution. Each of the potential assassins is clearly displayed as such, while no evidence is provided through which the audience could anticipate the head of security's eventual betrayal. Instead, the episode is constructed for comic effect. The assassins are inept characters played for laughs, and their attempts on Milton's life are farcically plotted as they end up killing each other rather than their intended victim in a series of visual set pieces.

The emphasis on the performative in the series' narrative and visual style extends into the use of special effects. In its first season of six episodes, the series contained over 500 special effects, which accounted for a large part of the series' £5.5 million budget. These are used to manifest Marty in ghostly form and also, in a departure from the original series, to create an environment for him in the afterlife called 'Limbo'. Paul Franklin from Double Negative, the company responsible for creating the effects, described the techniques used as 'cutting edge. This stuff has only been available for a few months' (cited in Richardson, 2000, p. 51). The particular way in which these effects are used in *Randall and Hopkirk (Deceased)* is significant here. The scene in which Marty meets Wyvern, his ghostly mentor, and in which the

In episode five of the first season of *Randall and Hopkirk (Deceased)*, Marty approaches the entrance to Limbo in long-shot against a CGI background of pulsing blue lines

Inside, Limbo is surrounded by shifting rectangular and circular plates of CGI images depicting different brightly coloured places

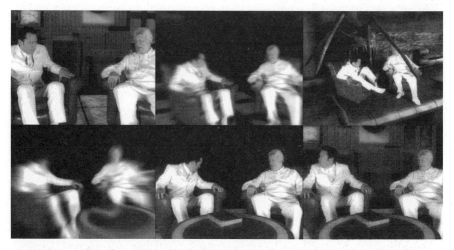

In episode two of the first season of *Randall and Hopkirk (Deceased)*, Wyvern transforms the interior of his room into a scene from one of Marty's computer games in a sequence that puts on display the series' use of CGI

afterworld is represented for the first time, is constructed to showcase the sophistication of the CGI effects. A CGI effect is used to materialise Wyvern out of a stream of smoke against a blank black frame. Wyvern swirls his arms above his head in a majestic gesture and the camera tracks left as a number of moving plates swirl across the screen, oscillating in size and position and eventually coming together to create a large room composed of a number of moving images. This scene self-consciously draws attention to the use of special effects as the room is literally constructed before the audience. After a short scene in which Jeff receives his first client, the action returns to Wyvern and Marty. Wyvern explains that the room is merely a fabrication and demonstrates this by creating two alternate environments for Marty. As he does so, the camera tracks back from a mid-shot of the two seated characters, and the CGI-constructed image of the room is transformed into an airport runway with the shadow of a plane taking off over their heads. The camera tracks once again towards the characters and the background of the room returns. This is repeated a second time, with the space transforming into a scene from one of Marty's computer games, before finally returning to the room interior once more. These two sequences function to showcase the series' special effects through equating the ghostly powers of Wyvern (and later Marty) with the technological trickery of modern technology in a display of special effects that is typical of the series overall.

Higson justifies the use of such sophisticated techniques in terms of the audience's expectations of visual fantasy on television.

> People these days watch a lot of American TV which is very sophisticated, they watch so many films and the level of effects they do in there is extraordinary. So there is a very big special effects budget on this [*Randall and Hopkirk (Deceased)*] because anything with a fantasy, special effects, supernatural element to it, if you don't do it properly you just get laughed off the screen. (Cited in Killick, 1999, p. 9)

Higson's comparison with US television here reflects in part the generally lower budgets available to British television in the 1990s. However, while there are a number of contemporary US series that make extensive use of CGI technology, such as *Lex* and *Stargate SG-1*, this is certainly not a prerequisite of successful telefantasy in the 1990s. For example, *Buffy the Vampire Slayer*'s use of expensive computer-generated special effects is relatively limited. The death of vampires, in which they explode into dust, is created using CGI, as are some of the monsters, particularly in the season finales, such as the transformation of the mayor into a snake-like demon at the end of season three. However, John Vulich (from Optical Nerve, who create the special effects for *Buffy the Vampire Slayer*) claimed that the series' producers do not like 'the look of CGI as much, and prefer the organic, shot-on-the-set look. ... So we're always being pushed to do things practically on sets and come up with creative ways to do them' (cited in Ferrante, 1998, p. 48). The extensive use of CGI effects in *Randall and Hopkirk (Deceased)* must therefore be understood not as a prerequisite of the creation of telefantasy in the contemporary age, but as a specific decision by the producers that can be understood in relation to the national context of the series' production.

The showcasing of special effects in *Randall and Hopkirk (Deceased)* functions to place the series within a particular relationship to the traditional conventions and values of British telefantasy. Both Charlie Higson and Simon Wright argue that part of the rationale for choosing to develop *Randall and Hopkirk (Deceased)* was the relative simplicity of the special effects techniques used in the original production. As such, the series' display of special effects can be understood as an attempt by the producers to differentiate the remake from a tradition of British telefantasy which is associated with low production values and poor special effects, where the fantasy is created through costumes and set, and the focus is on the characters over the action. In showcasing its use of special effects therefore, *Randall and Hopkirk (Deceased)* is not simply adopting the conventions of contemporary US telefantasy but is working *against* a notion of British telefantasy as aesthetically inferior and less appealing to British (and international) audiences than its contemporary US counterparts.

Negotiating Primetime

The BBC's audience research for the first season of *Randall and Hopkirk (Deceased)* revealed that it attracted a younger demographic than was usual for this scheduling slot. Simon Wright claimed that the published reviews also suggested a generational divide, stating that, 'Those critics who liked it generally came from the more stylish, trendy press with a younger audience' (Wright cited in Carter, 2000b, p. 19). He went on to situate this appeal to a comparatively young audience as a failure of the series to fulfil the public service remit of the primetime Saturday-evening slot within which it was scheduled. He claimed, 'Saturday nights on BBC1 are and should be about catering for everyone. Which is something we will be addressing in series two, which will have a broader appeal' (ibid.). Despite the emphasis that WTTV placed on the international market to contemporary television production and despite Higson's understanding of the appeal of the series in relation to the popularity of US tele-fantasy in the UK, it is in relation to public service broadcasting that Wright finally evaluated the success of the series. In this evaluation, it appears that, despite the shifts in British broad-casting since the 1980s, the notion of the 'consensus' audience was still central (if problematic) to BBC1's primetime schedules.

When *Randall And Hopkirk (Deceased)* returned for a second season in autumn 2001, it had incorporated a number of changes in order to appeal to a broader audience. While the series still placed an emphasis on the performative in the depiction of the central characters, the plotting of the narrative and the use of special effects, all three of these elements were subtly toned down. Most apparent was the change to the narrative form of the series. A greater emphasis was placed on the investigative narrative, with plots whose structure was closer to the conventions of the detective genre, allowing the audience to piece together clues over each episode. There was also far less emphasis placed on the display of special effects. All of these changes contributed to diminish the emphasis on the performative that characterised the first season and to increase the emphasis on the narrative. The changes between the first and second season reinforce traditional definitions of television's aesthet-ics. While privileging the performance of the stars and the special effects over narrative complexity in the first season can be understood as a form of post-modern play with con-ventional signifiers, the greater emphasis on narrative structure in attempting to broaden the appeal of the series in the second season reflects a more traditional understanding of British television as a writer's medium more suited to narrative complexity than visual display.

Conclusion

The rise of satellite, cable and digital television, the growth in the number of independent productions and international co-productions and the increasing importance of global markets, have the potential to displace the traditional public service role of the British terrestrial television broadcasters. Despite this, these case studies suggest that, in the early 2000s, there remained a strong and distinctive culture of public service broadcasting on British terrestrial television. However, these case studies also suggest that the changes in British television over the 1980s and 1990s raised new debates that challenged the terms by which public service broadcasting was understood. These debates are concerned in particular with the way in which broadcasters, to borrow Georgina Born's phrase, 'engage imaginatively with "the audience"' (Born, 2000, p. 415). The mixed appeal of a series like *Buffy the Vampire Slayer* cannot be easily reconciled with the scheduling practices of British terrestrial television in the late 1990s. The perceived appeal of the series to teens and young adults and its generic associations with cult fantasy television suggest the 6.45–7.30pm slot on BBC2 was an ideal site for the series. Yet the content of the series conflicted with the perceived address of this slot and the public service broadcaster's responsibility to ensure the appropriateness of its broadcasting. Charlie Higson's attempt to create a primetime British series in response to the success of US telefantasy series such as *Buffy the Vampire Slayer* and *The X-Files* in the UK, was similarly problematic. In attempting to combine an appeal to the audience for US telefantasy, fans of Reeves and Mortimer and of the original series, *Randall and Hopkirk (Deceased)* not only failed to fulfil the public service requirements of its primetime Saturday-evening slot, it also complicated the dominant aesthetic model for British television. The series adopted a self-conscious style epitomised by the display of special effects and the performance of the stars. This was more akin to the 'televisuality' through which Caldwell (1995) defined 1990s US television than the dominant aesthetic model of television in Britain as an intimate, 'writer's' medium.

However, I do not want to argue that this implies an 'Americanisation' of British television in the wake of a threat to British public service broadcasting. If one compares *Buffy the Vampire Slayer* and *The X-Files* (the US series with which Charlie Higson generically equates *Randall and Hopkirk (Deceased))* with *Randall and Hopkirk (Deceased)* itself, the British series actually places a far greater emphasis on the showcasing of visual effects than its US counterparts. Therefore, the 'televisuality' of *Randall and Hopkirk (Deceased)* cannot simply be understood in terms of an attempt to replicate the style of contemporary US telefantasy. Rather, the emphasis that Charlie Higson places on the role of special effects in appealing to the expectations of viewers attuned to the high production values of US telefantasy, can be understood as much in relation to Higson's own construction of British television as less visually 'sophisticated'.

The tensions in the reception of *Randall and Hopkirk (Deceased)* suggest that the established criteria of judgment for quality, valuable and good television in the late 1990s and early 2000s are open to debate. Simon Frith argues that 'until quite recently (the launching of Channel 4 in 1982 marked the beginning of the change) there was a straightforward continuity between ideas of television quality held by the artistic establishment inside and outside television' (2000, p. 45). These aesthetic criteria, which Frith (borrowing from Jay Blumler) lists as 'freshness, imagination, authenticity, education, truth, social relevance, expressive richness,

integrity' (ibid.), are broadly modernist in tone and can be understood in relation to the dominant aesthetic in British television. As has been discussed in Chapters 1 and 2, British television
drama has been predominantly understood within a realist framework. This tradition is apparent in two recent studies of British television. John Caughie's (2000) exploration of 'serious
television' clearly situates quality television in relation to both modernism and realism. Meanwhile, John Ellis's (2000) model of television as a form of 'working through' is most clearly
applicable to news, documentary and forms of drama, such as British soap opera, which belong
to a broadly defined tradition of British social realism. Furthermore, the growth of academic
interest in telefantasy over the 1980s and 1990s has to be understood primarily as a US
phenomenon. Although there are studies of British telefantasy by British academics, such as
James Chapman's (2002) exploration of British action-adventure, these are greatly outnum-
bered by the extensive academic work on US telefantasy by predominantly US academics.

Simon Frith asks whether different patterns of recruitment into the television industry and
different cultural reference points will lead to a shift towards a more populist set of evaluative criteria in the production of television programmes. It would certainly appear that in the
production of *Randall and Hopkirk (Deceased)* both Simon Wright and Charlie Higson
employed evaluative criteria that attempted to address the impact of US television and move
against some of the traditions of British television drama. However, these judgments are made
specifically in relation to perceived audience appeal and, as is apparent in the changes made
to the second season of the series, must be understood as negotiated between viewer and
producer rather than as stemming simply from programme-makers. Implicit in this, is an
appeal to a particular notion of popularity. Far from being an insignificant factor in the evaluation of public service broadcasting, the failure of *Randall and Hopkirk (Deceased)* to gain
popular appeal across a wide demographic is equated with a failure for it to fulfil its function
within a public service remit to appeal to a broad consensus audience. The nationally specific
criteria of value, quality and popularity that circulate in the production and reception of television texts may have become increasingly populist in tone. However, there still exists a
tension within the public service model between high and low culture. While in the US in the
1990s, telefantasy has become equated with the economic and aesthetic value of mainstream
drama, its status in Britain is more problematic. In the US, the popularity of mainstream television drama is defined through reference to specific economically valued audiences. By
contrast, in the UK it is measured in relation to appeal across a broad consensus audience.
In the British context of contemporary public service broadcasting, *Randall and Hopkirk
(Deceased)*'s visual display and stylistic playfulness was ultimately toned down and its narrative complexity was increased in an attempt to fulfil a public service remit to appeal to
'everyone'. Such changes not only draw on a dominant understanding of television as a
writer's medium more suited to the development of complex storytelling than visual display
and stylistic excess, but also reinforce a false dichotomy in which narrative complexity is placed
in opposition to visual style. As a consequence of a continuing understanding of the need for
public service broadcasting to appeal to a broad consensus audience, the criteria for evalu-
ating the success of mainstream terrestrial television drama in the UK tend to be in line with
the traditional criteria of television's aesthetic value as a medium in which visual style is seen
as inferior to (and separate from) narrative and thematic complexity.

Notes

1. See Appendix E for details of the first transmission dates of *Buffy the Vampire Slayer* on WB/UPN, Sky 1 and BBC2.
2. For a more comprehensive discussion of these youth programmes and *Network 7* (the precursor to *Def II*), see Lury (2001).
3. *Star Trek: The Next Generation* premiered in the UK on 26 September 1990 with a feature-length pilot transmitted on BBC2 between 6.00 and 7.25pm. It went on to be regularly scheduled every Wednesday evening on BBC2 between 6.00 and 6.50pm before *Def II*.
4. Fans of the series complained about its treatment in the British schedules. When the series returned to BBC2 in October 1999 to complete its second season, a late-night uncut repeat was scheduled.
5. While *Buffy the Vampire Slayer* remained on BBC2 for its entire run on UK terrestrial television, in its later seasons *Angel* moved to a late-night slot on the commercial terrestrial station, Channel 5.
6. Not all programmes created largely for the youth market are scheduled on BBC2. For example, the pop music series *Top of the Pops* commands a primetime slot on BBC1.
7. It is worth noting here, that commercial television has also been 'protected' from the potentially denigrating effects of market forces by state regulation in the UK. For example, the 1990 Broadcasting Act stipulated that the Independent Television Commission apply a 'quality threshold' when awarding the ITV franchises in 1992. Franchises could not simply be allocated to the highest bidder, and companies had to demonstrate a commitment to quality programming. This regulation implies that commercialisation stands in opposition to quality.
8. International markets have been a significant factor in the production of television programmes since the 1960s (see Chapter 2). However, the expansion of satellite and cable and VCR technology multiplies the number of potential markets through which programmes can be economically exploited.
9. Statistics presented in the report by the Department of Trade and Industry and the Department for Culture, Media and Sport, entitled *A New Future for Communications* (2000), reproduced in Franklin (2001, p. 36).
10. *Right to Reply* is a consumer-interest programme offering viewers the opportunity to air their complaints about television programmes.
11. *The X-Files* continued to run on BBC1 until the end of its sixth season. At the start of its seventh season it moved back to a post-watershed slot on BBC2. See Appendix D for the first transmission dates of *The X-Files* on Fox, Sky 1, BBC1 and BBC2.
12. On Channel 4, see Higson (1989) and Harvey (2000).
13. Unfortunately for WTTV, their remake of *Randall and Hopkirk (Deceased)* was not the great ratings or financial success in the UK that they may have hoped for. The first episode of the series gained good ratings of 10.63 million viewers but this declined to 5.85 million viewers by the final episode of the first season. The second season began with ratings of 5.57 million, which declined to 3.24 million by the final episode (figures from <www.randallandhopkirk.com>, accessed 6 July 2004). At the time of writing the

series had not been sold to the US and the merchandise produced for the series (two novels, a music album and single, and a 'making of' book) had not made a significant impact on the market.

14. A second season of seven episodes was transmitted between 29 September 2001 and 24 November 2001.

15. Indeed Ofcom (the UK's broadcasting regulator) states that while the watershed refers to programmes transmitted after 9.00pm, when scheduling programmes, broadcasters must also take into account the potential overlap in the audience before and after 9.00pm (see <www.ofcom.org.uk>).

16. The series is populated by a number of established British comic and straight actors often in cameos that playfully acknowledge the expectations associated with such stars.

CONCLUSION: GENRE, AESTHETICS, HISTORY

Genre and Television

At the beginning of this book I raised the difficulties that telefantasy presents to the study of genre in television. Each of the series examined displays a pronounced generic hybridity that poses problems for their generic categorisation. Furthermore, while they are all generically linked through the centrality of the representation of the fantastic to their basic series' formats, the fantastic remains a confusingly imprecise term that crosses and complicates the boundaries between generic categories. This book has argued that an approach to genre that attempts to situate these texts within theoretically delineated generic boundaries closes down the possibility for exploring the often complex and contradictory ways in which a number of different genres function within these series. Rather, it has proposed an approach that explores how the production discourses surrounding these series engage with a range of generic expectations and how these are articulated within the texts themselves. Such an approach understands genres as sets of culturally and historically constructed conventions, rather than as theoretically predetermined categories and enables an exploration of the ways in which genre is used within specific historical contexts.

What is apparent from this approach, is that the expectations associated with specific genres such as science fiction and horror function in relation to those associated with broader notions of television as a medium, television drama, serial drama and so on. Thus, for example, the generic expectations of the horror and detective genres function in *The X-Files* in relation to the specific demands on US network television in the 1990s to create a visually and thematically distinctive series that combines ongoing narratives with one-off storylines. Furthermore, within each of these case studies, this range of expectations has been proved to be historically specific. For example, the representation of the fantastic in *The Quatermass Experiment* is negotiated in relation to the generic expectations of US cinematic science fiction (the most visible example of the genre at this time) and in relation to the dominant notion in the 1950s of television as an intimate medium. By contrast, the use of fantasy in *Randall and Hopkirk (Deceased)* is negotiated in relation to the generic expectations which associate fantasy with 'cult television' in the 1990s, which are problematically negotiated in relation to the changing notions of television as a public service medium in the UK. However, if the expectations associated with specific genres (at a micro level) and television as a medium (at a macro level) are so historically specific, what is the value of bringing this range of texts together under the umbrella of 'telefantasy'?

While each chapter has explored a different set of historically and nationally specific debates, bringing these series together as telefantasy demonstrates that certain discourses concerning the representation of the fantastic as a production and a textual strategy recur across these different contexts.[1] By comparing a range of historical and international case studies, the different ways in which these recurring discourses are articulated within specific contexts can be explored. This can bring to the fore the impact of certain historical shifts on the production and textual practices in television without losing the specificity of these historical instances to the generalising tendencies of grand theory.

Telefantasy: Television Aesthetics, Visual Style and Narrative Structure

I have argued that the representation of the fantastic is a particularly valuable site for the analysis of visual style in television drama, an area that has been largely overlooked in television studies in favour of the analysis of theme. In the production debates surrounding these series, the role of the image has been understood as central to the representation of the fantastic. The representation of the fantastic implies the representation of that which confounds socio-cultural verisimilitude, and part of the rhetoric of the fantastic is a rhetoric of vision, structured around seeing or revealing the unknown and the relationship between sight and knowledge. This is a rhetoric that has been apparent in each of these series, from the *Quatermass* serials, that gradually build up to the final revelation (and subsequent destruction) of the alien, to *The X-Files*, which destabilises the relationship between sight and knowledge. The emphasis placed on the visual representation of the fantastic in these series invites (but does not necessarily demand) the *display* of visual style, in which the role of the image becomes a central narrative and thematic element within the text. The display of visual style has proved to be a primary production and textual strategy in the representation of the fantastic, showcasing the potential for spectacle in early British television in the *Quatermass* serials and providing strong signature styles in *The X-Files* and *Buffy the Vampire Slayer* which facilitate branding in the increasingly competitive market of US network television production in the 1990s.

Each case study has also demonstrated that the display of visual style facilitated by the representation of the fantastic needs to be understood in relation to the narrative structure of the programme. The dark visual style of *The X-Files* contributes to its narrative by suggesting (but not confirming) the presence of the fantastic, while the gradual revelation of the fantastic in the cliff-hangers of the *Quatermass* serials builds suspense by escalating the threat of the alien while increasing our knowledge of the danger. The representation of the fantastic also opens up spaces for extensive narrative fluidity, which has been particularly exploited by long-running series such as *Star Trek* and *Buffy the Vampire Slayer* as it enables extensive story latitude while remaining within the series' established narrative format.

The discourses circulating around the role of the image in the representation of the fantastic are further bound up with discourses concerning experimentation. In each case study, the disruption of socio-cultural and generic verisimilitude implied in the representation of the fantastic is understood to offer the opportunity to experiment with the formal possibilities of television as a medium. Within these discourses therefore, the representation of the fantastic is understood to offer the opportunity to adopt new narrative practices, to use new technologies, and/or to explore new generic combinations, in order to represent something that appears completely 'other', alien and unreal. In the discourses surrounding the production of these series, the fantastic is therefore understood as offering a means to innovate formally and thematically. However, the fantastic is also understood to occupy a seemingly contradictory set of expectations in which it is understood as formulaic, thematically and aesthetically unchallenging, responding purely to consumer demand and so on.

The contradiction between the generic expectations associated with the fantastic as both 'low' art (formulaic, commercial, conventional) and 'high' art (subversive, innovative, experimental) can be understood in relation to the formal practices of representing the fantastic. While the representation of the fantastic implies the representation of that which confounds socio-cultural verisimilitude, this book has argued that this process depends on the *maintenance* of socio-cultural and generic verisimilitude. The representation of the fantastic therefore demands the negotiation of a dialectical position, simultaneously depending upon and disrupting the generic and socio-cultural expectations at work in the text. As a consequence, these programmes rely on familiar narrative and visual conventions, while equally challenging dominant representational and expressive strategies in television production.

This dialectic in the representation of the fantastic has enabled these programmes to be read as *both* ideologically progressive *and* conservative. The problems that programmes such as *Star Trek* and *The X-Files* raise within academic discourses, being equally redeemed as progressive and dismissed as reactionary, are a reflection of the tendency within television studies to situate the analysis of television within a series of binary oppositions. Hence, academically valued television is that which opens up spaces for resistance to dominant ideological structures through its treatment of themes and characters, while academically dismissed television is that which confirms dominant ideological structures through the representation of stereotyped characters and conventional narratives. What these case studies suggest is that such binary oppositions do not account for the often contradictory textual representations within television programmes and the often contradictory pressures on television production.

In the production discourses surrounding these series, the representation of the fantastic is negotiated in relation to broader institutional discourses about the varying aesthetic and economic pressures on television production. The negotiation of the economic and the aesthetic is industrially and historically specific, shifting quite dramatically from the 1950s and 1960s to the 1990s, and from the UK to the US. In particular, it is bound up with nationally specific notions of the social and aesthetic role of television as a medium, which is in part legitimised by the different industrial structures within which television is situated. However, while the commercial system in the US places a greater emphasis on economic profit than the public service system in the UK, Chapters 2 and 4 in particular have been concerned with complicating any easy dichotomies between these two industrial systems. The production of *The Prisoner* and the production of *The X-Files* are both concerned with aligning the aesthetic and the economic. However, in the former case, this is an attempt to create aesthetically valuable 'public service' television that will also appeal to a wide (and international) audience, while in the latter case, the turn to the aesthetic functions as a specific economic strategy to appeal to a particular 'quality' demographic.

What these case studies suggest, therefore, is that the representation of the fantastic is a particularly rich site for challenging the established dichotomies in television studies. Rather than evidencing a model of television aesthetics that privileges the spoken word over the

image, that constructs the television viewer as distracted, and that draws particular attention to television's intimacy through reference to its small screen, poor sound and image
quality, these case studies paint a more complex picture. The centrality of the display of visual
style to these series threatens the notion of television spectatorship as distracted and suggests that these series pertain to a distinctiveness that attempts to separate them from the
'flow' of everyday television. While studies such as Siegel's (1984), have argued for an aesthetics of television science fiction in which visual style and spectacle should be rejected in
favour of the development of character, complex storytelling and the treatment of contemporary social concerns, these case studies demonstrate that the dichotomies established by
Siegel (action versus character, spectacle versus narrative complexity) are false ones. Each
chapter has revealed that the tendency towards visual display need not be understood as
opposed to narrative complexity, character development, continuity or intimacy. Rather, the
representation of the fantastic challenges these dichotomies because it suggests the possibility of adopting a dialectical position, in which texts can be experimental and formulaic,
spectacular and intimate, economically successful and aesthetically valued. Furthermore,
each of these case studies has demonstrated that the adoption of such a position is a particularly desirable production strategy. However, it has also been a problematic strategy and
one that reveals some of the key discourses in television production within these different
contexts.

History: Exploring Telefantasy through Historical Case Studies

Chapter 1 explored the discourses that arose in relation to the representation of the fantastic in the *Quatermass* serials, which were primarily concerned with the ways in which the
fantastic offered the opportunity to experiment with the formal possibilities of television.
Reacting against the intimate model of television which predominated in the early days of
British television production, Nigel Kneale and Rudolph Cartier created three serials that
stressed the importance of the image to the narrative. In each of these serials, there is a build-
up to revealing the fantastic, which places an emphasis on the sheer spectacle of seeing
images represented that confound socio-cultural verisimilitude. However, this representation
of the fantastic as spectacle is not opposed to the notion of television as an intimate domestic medium. Rather, moments of spectacle are constructed as much to *exploit* the 'intimate'
screen as to *expand* it. The representation of the fantastic therefore functions as a means of
enabling *experimentation* with, rather than a *rejection* of the dominant television aesthetic
of the early 1950s. The construction of intimately spectacular moments is facilitated by the
serial structure that embeds these serials within the weekly routines of everyday life, encouraging identification with the recurring characters. The combination of experimentation and
familiarity which was an integral part of *The Quatermass Experiment* was understood to be
exemplary of the potential for BBC television drama following the introduction of competition in 1955 and became an integral part of the *Quatermass* format in the second and third
serials.

Chapter 2 explored how such discourses of experimentation are negotiated in relation to
the production of *The Prisoner*, as part of an attempt to reconcile the conflicting demands of
commercial and public service television in the UK in the late 1960s. The representation of the

fantastic functions in *The Prisoner* to combine the demands of appealing to a 'mass' audience with the call for television drama that fulfils traditional criteria of aesthetic value (single author-ship, formal and narrative experimentation and so on). In attempting to negotiate a position as 'serious entertainment', *The Prisoner* uses the evocation and disruption of socio-cultural and generic verisimilitude in the representation of the fantastic to occupy a seemingly contradic-tory position between the familiar pleasures of generic entertainment and the formally disruptive strategies of the avant-garde. However, over the course of its seventeen episodes, the series struggles to maintain this dialectical position, as its disruptive strategies are embed-ded in its repetitive serial structure. While in the *Quatermass* serials, the dialectic between experimentation and formula is contained within the serial structure, *The Prisoner*'s initial experimentation with existing representational strategies finally becomes a rejection of them, as the series abandons the generic and narrative expectations upon which it had been premised.

In the *Quatermass* serials and *The Prisoner*, the dialectic between disruption of and depen-dence upon generic expectations in the representation of the fantastic functioned (to varying degrees) as a means of challenging existing representational and production strategies. By contrast, Chapter 3 demonstrated how in *Star Trek* this dialectic functioned as an integral part of the dominant aesthetic. For the producers of *Star Trek*, the representation of the fan-tastic fulfilled two primary requirements in the production of primetime network series television – product differentiation and story latitude – while functioning within the expec-tations of the action-adventure series, the dominant series form at that time. While the representation of the fantastic did offer the opportunity to experiment with new technologies (particularly colour television) and new series formats (futuristic space travel), this experi-mentation was used to fulfil the commercial demands on network television to provide 'regulated innovation' rather than to challenge or disrupt existing practices. However, the series' dependence upon and disruption of socio-cultural verisimilitude, in constructing a fic-tional world that is both fantastic and plausible, does enable it to be read as both a progressive and a reactionary text.

Although product differentiation and story latitude remained key in the 1990s, Chapter 4 demonstrated that within this industrial environment, the strategies used to fulfil these requirements were distinctly different. While *Star Trek* was produced for a broadly defined 'mass' primetime audience, by the 1990s, the US network primetime audience had been reconceived as a series of 'taste markets' to which specific programmes could be marketed. In appealing to a range of differently defined (although not mutually exclusive) taste markets, *The X-Files* and *Buffy the Vampire Slayer* displayed a pronounced generic hybridity that had a further function as a marker of distinctiveness. While generic hybridity has always been a feature in television programmes, here it was exploited as an economic strategy to maximise profits by giving each series a clear visual signature which could be exploited through brand-ing to reach a range of markets. It also functioned as an aesthetic strategy that endeavoured to construct these series as aesthetically valuable (individually authored, thematically and for-mally challenging) in order to appeal to a 'quality' demographic. The attempt to combine the commercial and aesthetic demands of television production recalled the attempt to conflate extant generic expectations and experimental representational strategies in *The Prisoner*. However, here its function as a production and a textual strategy was quite different. *The*

Prisoner was produced within an industrial environment within which the economic, social and aesthetic demands of television production were still understood to be in conflict. By contrast, in the industrial environment of 1990s US network television production, an appeal to 'quality' was not understood to be opposed to commercial or economic demands. 'Quality' functions here at the service of the economic, as distinctiveness functions as a valuable marketing strategy. However, the alignment of the aesthetic and the economic in the production of these series has proved problematic in analyses of the aesthetics of contemporary US television, as it threatens the previous dichotomies upon which aesthetic criteria such as quality and distinctiveness were based.

While Chapter 4 demonstrated that, in the 1990s, US network television production increasingly depended upon the construction of series to appeal to specific (and frequently multiple) taste markets, Chapter 5 argued that UK terrestrial television at this time maintained an emphasis on catering to a broadly defined national audience. This proved particularly problematic for the scheduling of series like *Buffy the Vampire Slayer*, whose mixed address is not easily accommodated into the scheduling practices of UK terrestrial television. Attempts to create British terrestrial series that respond to the increasing number of US telefantasy series transmitted in the UK have also been problematic. *Randall and Hopkirk (Deceased)* reworked the format of a 1960s British telefantasy series with two popular alternative British comedians, Vic Reeves and Bob Mortimer, in the central roles. The discourses surrounding the representation of the fantastic in *Randall and Hopkirk (Deceased)* are concerned with aligning the series with its US contemporaries by adopting a self-conscious display of visual style. The series uses the representation of the fantastic to challenge the dominant expectations of British television as less 'sophisticated' than its US counterpart. However, this attempt to react to the predominance of US telefantasy in the late 1990s is difficult to reconcile with the public service requirements of the BBC. The series emphasised the display of visual style combined with the anarchic and surreal performance style of Reeves and Mortimer, over the narrative consistency and generic expectations of the original series. Although the series was popular with younger viewers, its lack of success with older viewers was understood as a failure to fulfil the public service requirements of the BBC1 primetime Saturday-evening slot in which it was scheduled, to provide entertainment for a broad family audience. While on US network television, telefantasy has been critically and commercially successful in the 1990s, in the UK the production and scheduling of telefantasy remains problematic to the public service environment of British terrestrial television.

These historical case studies reveal that, in order to understand how the representation of the fantastic functions as a production and a textual strategy, it is necessary to situate each series within its specific industrial contexts. Through these case studies, it is possible to identify the ways in which the debates surrounding both public service and commercial television have developed across the US and the UK and the impact that US television has had on British terrestrial television. By following these debates concerning public service broadcasting in the UK, it is apparent that, while from the 1950s the demands of competition have been problematic for public service broadcasting, these become particularly strained in the 1990s with the expansion of television service providers. Furthermore, the expansion of television in the UK and the development of VCR/DVD technology have increased the influence of US television on British television, both because US television is more visible, and because it has become an increasingly important market for television production. However, despite this, proclamations of the end of public service television in the UK certainly seem premature, as the demands of public service broadcasting continue to be a significant factor in the production of British terrestrial television in the new millennium.

These case studies also reveal the development of the debates concerning US network television and enable a comparison between the different responses of the British and US industries to the expansion of the television industry in the 1980s and 1990s. In the US, these industrial changes can also be seen to threaten the established network system. However here, this has led to the development of production and textual strategies that are concerned specifically with combining the aesthetic and economic demands of television production. This is not to suggest that US television in the 1950s, 1960s and 1970s was not concerned with aesthetics. Rather, it is to suggest that in the 1980s and 1990s, the aesthetic becomes a central economic strategy in the production of US network television, in response to the increasing fragmentation of the television industry.

Histories of Television: Methodology and Theory

Finally I want to explore the implications of this study for the current debates in television studies. As the US and the UK television industries struggle to negotiate the rapidly changing terrain of television production, television scholars have been exploring the impact of these shifts for the barely established discipline of television studies. There has been an increasing interest in television production as a site of analysis,[2] as well as attempts to delineate the dominant paradigms in television and to explore how they are challenged by the industrial changes of the 1980s and 1990s.[3] These debates are inevitably bound up with the histories of television studies as a discipline, a field that has been dispersed (and sometimes marginalised) across a range of more established fields (film studies, cultural studies, sociology, media studies and so on).[4] As television studies has struggled to emerge as a singular discipline and to establish its place within academia, analyses of television have been inevitably concerned with the value of television as an object of study. Explorations centred on the effects of this seemingly pervasive social phenomenon were replaced by an increasing shift towards studying the viewing practices of actual audiences. These studies were concerned with exploring the social and psychological value of television as a medium in the broader practices of everyday life. Similarly, textual studies of television increasingly embraced popular forms and asserted the value of studying television as a popular medium. Historically, the study of television has also been concerned with differentiating television as a medium from other forms of media in order to establish the debates that arise specifically in relation to television. Television is understood to have had a profound effect on our personal and public lives, bringing the very definition of the personal and the public into question. It has been understood as a medium that is essentially embedded in the everyday domestic sphere, a medium whose value can be found in its social function. As a consequence, television's aesthetic has been defined in terms of its specificity, its difference from other media. It has been conceptualised as a domestic medium, whose small screen intimately addresses viewers in the private space of their own homes. Television programmes have been understood as ephemeral texts existing in a flow of programmes which enter the home and become integrated in the routines of everyday life.

However, as Western television studies struggles to make sense of the rapid changes that have occurred in the US and UK television industries over the past two decades, the previous paradigms for understanding television have become increasingly problematic. Visually and technologically, television has become increasingly aligned with cinema. Television dramas are frequently shot on film; home cinema attempts to replicate the cinematic experience in the domestic space; and television is increasingly the primary site for the consumption of movies. With the development of the VCR (and later the DVD player) and the expansion of television channels, television is no longer ephemeral and is no longer exclusively embedded in our everyday domestic routines. As these changes challenge the dominant paradigms for conceptualising television, they suggest the inadequacy of such essentialist models for understanding historical change in television.

The case studies in this book suggest that such generalising 'grand theories' of television's specificity are unable to account fully for the historical and national diversity of television as a medium. At the level of production and at the level of text, these case studies demonstrate that television can only be fully understood through analyses that are historically situated.[5] However, as this book has argued, to offer historically embedded and contextualised analyses of television texts need not necessitate a rejection or avoidance of the broader theories concerning television as a medium. Rather, such work can provide an historical specificity that explores the consequences of broad shifts within specific contexts and can thus complicate the existing paradigms for understanding television as a medium.

In this book, this approach has been adopted in relation to the representation of the fantastic across five historically and nationally specific instances. These five case studies represent a very small section of the total production of telefantasy and of television as a whole. One of the problems with such an approach is that it elevates certain programmes that (in the context of this book) have already received a significant amount of academic attention. As such, this book is in danger of contributing to a distorted understanding of television history in which those programmes which (for whatever reasons) have yet to be extensively academically studied remain outside of both theory and history. Yet, at the same time, by focusing on programmes that are already somewhat canonised in television studies, this book points to the inadequacy of the dominant paradigms of television as a medium for fully understanding these programmes within their historical contexts of production. While the challenge that these series present to the dominant paradigms within television studies may have led to their characterisation as 'unique' cultural phenomena, this book suggests that the production of these series can be understood as part of a broader set of strategies designed to respond to the historical circumstances within which they were produced. The tendency to remove these series from the historical context within which they were produced is not, therefore, a consequence of their unique cultural status, but rather a reflection of the inadequacy of our historical and contemporary understanding of the aesthetics of television as a medium. This has profound implications for the ways in which television studies approaches the current industrial changes in the UK and US television industries. By undermining the adequacy of these paradigms for exploring the *Quatermass* serials, *The Prisoner* and *Star Trek*, this book suggests that we cannot go on to use these paradigms as a barometer for exploring the impact of the current industrial upheaval in the UK and US television industries. If television studies is to understand the implications of the current changes in the television industry, it must approach television in ways that acknowledge the historical specificity of what television is and has been, before it can fully assess what television could or should be.

Notes

1. This book focuses on the representation of the fantastic as a link between these series. However, a different set of generic expectations could form the focus of such an approach. Following this methodology, it is perfectly possible that the *Quatermass* serials, *The Prisoner*, *The X-Files*, *Buffy the Vampire Slayer*, *Angel* and *Randall and Hopkirk (Deceased)* could be combined with other series which make use of the generic expectations of the detective genre in order to explore a different set of discourses.
2. See, for example, Born (2000).
3. See, for example, Frith (2000) and Ellis (2000).
4. The diverse and obtuse nature of television as a medium – a collection of texts, a series of industries, a rapidly developing technology, a social phenomenon and so on – has inevitably contributed to the dispersal of television studies across so many different academic disciplines (see Brunsdon, 1998).
5. While this book has explored each text within its historical context of production, these texts can also be understood within other historical contexts. As the analysis of the scheduling of *Buffy the Vampire Slayer* in the UK demonstrated, television texts can operate quite differently within specific historical, national and industrial contexts.

BIBLIOGRAPHY

Aldiss, Brian, *Billion Year Spree: The History of Science Fiction* (London: Weidenfeld and Nicolson, 1973).

Alexander, David, Star Trek *Creator: The Authorized Biography of Gene Roddenberry* (London: Boxtree, 1994).

Alvey, Mark, 'The Independents: Rethinking the Television Studio System', in Lynn Spigel and Michael Curtin (eds), *The Revolution Wasn't Televised: Sixties Television and Social Conflict* (London: Routledge, 1997).

Amis, Kingsley, *New Maps of Hell: A Survey of Science Fiction* (London: Victor Gollancz, 1961).

Anderson, Christopher, *Hollywood TV: The Studio System in the Fifties* (Austin: University of Texas Press, 1994).

Bacon-Smith, Camille, *Enterprising Women: Television Fandom and the Creation of Popular Myth* (Philadelphia: University of Pennsylvania Press, 1992).

Bakewell, Joan and Garnham, Nicholas, *The New Priesthood: British Television Today* (London: Allen Lane, 1970).

Barnouw, Erik, *Tube of Plenty: The Evolution of American Television*, rev. edn (New York: Oxford University Press, 1982).

Barnouw, Erik, *Tube of Plenty: The Evolution of American Television*, 2nd rev. edn (New York: Oxford University Press, 1990).

Barr, Charles, 'Broadcasting and Cinema 2: Screens within Screens', in Charles Barr (ed.), *All Our Yesterdays: 90 Years of British Cinema* (London: BFI, 1986).

Barr, Charles, '"They Think It's All Over": The Dramatic Legacy of Live Television', in John Hill and Martin McLoone (eds), *Big Picture, Small Screen: The Relations between Film and Television* (Luton: John Libbey Media, 1997).

BBC Handbook 1967 (London: BBC, 1967).

Bellon, Joe, 'The Strange Discourse of *The X-Files*: What It Is, What It Does, and What Is at Stake', *Critical Studies in Mass Communication*, 16(2), 1999, pp.136–54.

Bernardi, Daniel Leonard, Star Trek *and History: Race-ing towards a White Future* (New Brunswick, NJ: Rutgers University Press, 1998).

Bick, Ilsa J., 'Boys in Space: *Star Trek*, Latency, and the Neverending Story', *Cinema Journal*, 35(2), 1996, pp. 43–60.

Bilby, Kenneth, *The General: David Sarnoff and the Rise of the Communications Industry* (New York: Harper and Row, 1986).

Biskind, Peter, *Seeing Is Believing: How Hollywood Taught Us to Stop Worrying and Love the Fifties* (New York: Pantheon Books, 1983).

Boddy, William, 'The Seven Dwarfs and the Money Grubbers: The Public Relations Crisis of US Television in the Late 1950s', in Patricia Mellencamp (ed.), *Logics of Television* (London: BFI, 1990).

Boddy, William, *Fifties Television: The Industry and Its Critics* (Urbana and Chicago: University of Illinois Press, 1993).

Booker, M. Keith, *Strange TV: Innovative Television Series from* The Twilight Zone *to* The X-Files (Westport, CT and London: Greenwood Press, 2002).

Born, Georgina, 'Inside Television: Television Studies and the Sociology of Culture', *Screen*, 41(4), 2000, pp. 404–24.

Briggs, Asa, *The History of Broadcasting in the United Kingdom, Volume IV: Sound and Vision* (Oxford: Oxford University Press, 1979).

Briggs, Asa, *The History of Broadcasting in the United Kingdom, Volume V: Competition* (Oxford: Oxford University Press, 1995).

Brown, Les, 'The American Networks', in Anthony Smith (ed.), *Television: An International History*, 2nd edn (Oxford: Oxford University Press, 1998).

Brunsdon, Charlotte, 'Television: Aesthetics and Audiences', in Patricia Mellencamp (ed.), *Logics of Television* (London: BFI, 1990).

Brunsdon, Charlotte, 'What Is the "Television" of Television Studies?', in Christine Geraghty and David Lusted (eds), *The Television Studies Book* (London: Arnold, 1998).

Buckland, Warren, 'Between Science Fact and Science Fiction: Spielberg's Digital Dinosaurs, Possible Worlds, and the New Aesthetic Realism', *Screen*, 40(2), 1999, pp. 177–93.

Buxton, David, *From* The Avengers *to* Miami Vice*: Form and Ideology in Television Series* (Manchester: Manchester University Press, 1990).

Caldwell, John Thornton, *Televisuality* (New Brunswick, NJ: Rutgers University Press, 1995).

Carrazé, Alain and Oswald, Hélène, The Prisoner*: A Televisionary Masterpiece*, trans. Christine Donougher (London: W. H. Allen, 1990).

Carroll, Noël, *Engaging the Moving Image* (New Haven, CT and London: Yale University Press, 2003).

Carter, Meg, 'Rolling Back the Years', *Broadcast*, 26 May 2000a, pp. 20–1.

Carter, Meg, 'Judging the Critical Effect', *Broadcast*, 16 June 2000b, pp.18–19.

Cartier, Rudolph, 'A Foot in Both Camps', *Films and Filming*, September 1958, pp. 10, 31.

Caughie, John, 'Before the Golden Age: Early Television Drama', in John Corner (ed.), *Popular Television in Britain: Studies in Cultural History* (London: BFI, 1991a).

Caughie, John, 'Adorno's Reproach: Repetition, Difference and Television Genre', *Screen*, 32(2), 1991b, pp. 127–53.

Caughie, John, *Television Drama: Realism, Modernism and British Culture* (Oxford: Oxford University Press, 2000).

Cawelti, John G., *Adventure, Mystery, and Romance: Formula Stories as Art and Popular Culture* (Chicago, IL: University of Chicago Press, 1976).

Chapman, James, '*The Avengers*: Television and Popular Culture During the "High Sixties"', in Anthony Aldgate, James Chapman and Arthur Marwick (eds), *Windows on the Sixties: Exploring Key Texts of Media and Culture* (London: I. B. Tauris, 2000).

Chapman, James, *Saints and Avengers: British Adventure Series of the 1960s* (London and New York: I. B. Tauris, 2002).

Coe, Steve, 'Networks Take a Walk on the Weird Side', *Broadcasting and Cable,* 125(43), 1995, pp. 56–7.

Cooke, Lez, *British Television Drama: A History* (London: BFI, 2003).

Cornell, Paul, Day, Martin and Topping, Keith, *The Guinness Book of Classic British Television* (Enfield: Guinness, 1993).

D'Acci, Julie, *Defining Women: Television and the Case of* Cagney and Lacey (Chapel Hill and London: University of North Carolina Press, 1994).

Davis, Anthony, 'The Extraordinary Mr McGoohan', *TV Times*, Southern edn, 14–20 October 1967, p. 30.

Davis, Anthony, 'Patrick McGoohan Talks . . .', *TV Times*, Southern edn, 3–9 February 1968a, p. 5.

Davis, Anthony, 'Ad Lib', *TV Times*, Southern edn, 17–23 February 1968b, p. 11.

Davis, Glyn and Dickinson, Kay, 'Introduction', in Glyn Davis and Kay Dickinson (eds), *Teen TV: Genre, Consumption and Identity* (London: BFI, 2004).

De Moras, Lisa, 'The Sound and the Fury', *The Hollywood Reporter 1997–98 TV Preview*, September 1997, pp. 10–11.

Department of Trade and Industry and Department of Culture, Media and Sport, 'A New Future for Communications', in Bob Franklin (ed.), *British Television Policy: A Reader* (London and New York: Routledge, 2001).

Duncan, Jodi, 'Hide It in Shadow, Hide It in Light', *Cinefex*, 74, 1998, pp. 112–35.

Elliott, Katy, 'Backstage Comic', *Broadcast*, 24 March 2000, p. 21.

Ellis, John, *Visible Fictions: Cinema, Television, Video* (London: Routledge and Kegan Paul, 1982).

Ellis, John, *Seeing Things: Television in the Age of Uncertainty* (London: I. B. Tauris, 2000).

Ferrante, Anthony C., '*Buffy the Vampire Slayer*: The Monstrous Makeup', *Fangoria*, 177, 1998, pp. 44–8 and 82.

Feuer, Jane, 'The MTM Style', in Jane Feuer, Paul Kerr and Tise Vahimagi (eds), *MTM: 'Quality Television'* (London: BFI, 1984).

Feuer, Jane, 'Genre Study and Television', in Robert C. Allen (ed.), *Channels of Discourse Reassembled: Television and Contemporary Criticism* (London: Routledge, 1992).

Feuer, Jane, Kerr, Paul and Vahimagi, Tise (eds), *MTM: 'Quality Television'* (London: BFI, 1984).

Fox, Paul, *This Is BBC1* (BBC Lunchtime Lecture Seventh Series – 4, 1969).

Fox, Paul, 'Is BBC1 Too Popular', *In the Public Interest: A Six-part Explanation of BBC Policy* (London: BBC, 1971).

Franklin, Bob (ed.), *British Television Policy: A Reader* (London and New York: Routledge, 2001).

Frith, Simon, 'The Black Box: The Value of Television and the Future of Television Research', *Screen*, 41(1), 2000, pp. 33–50.

Garnham, Nicholas, *Structures of Television* (London: BFI, 1978).

Gibberman, Susan, Star Trek: *An Annotated Guide to Resources on the Development, the Phenomenon, the People, the Television Series, the Films, the Novels and the Recordings* (Jefferson, NC and London: McFarland, 1991).

Gitlin, Todd, *Inside Prime Time* (London and New York: Routledge, 1994).

Golden, Christopher and Holder, Nancy, Buffy the Vampire Slayer: *The Watcher's Guide* (New York: Pocket Books, 1998).

Gray, Innes, '*The Prisoner*'s Secret Revealed', *TV Times*, Southern edn, 28 October– 3 November 1967, pp. 18–19.

Gregory, Chris, *Be Seeing You ...: Decoding* The Prisoner (Luton: John Libbey Media, 1997).

Gregory, Chris, Star Trek: *Parallel Narratives* (Basingstoke: Macmillan, 2000).

Gross, Edward, 'Joss Whedon: Vampire Master', *TV Zone*, 155, 1999, pp. 16–21.

Halloran, James D., *The Effects of Mass Communications, with Special Reference to Television*, Television Research Committee Working Paper No. 1 (Leicester: Leicester University Press, 1964).

Harley, Denis, 'Parents, Children and Television: Whose Finger on the Switch?', *TV Times*, Southern edn, 11–17 November 1967, pp. 13–14.

Harrison, Taylor, Projansky, Sarah, Ono, Kent A. and Helford, Elyce Rae (eds), *Enterprise Zones: Critical Positions on* Star Trek (Boulder, CO: Westview Press, 1996).

Harvey, Sylvia, 'Channel Four Television: From Annan to Grade', in Edward Buscombe (ed.), *British Television: A Reader* (Oxford: Oxford University Press, 2000).

Head, Sydney W., Sterling, Christopher H. and Schofield, Lemuel B., *Broadcasting in America: A Survey of Electronic Media*, 7th edn (Boston, MA: Houghton Mifflin, 1994).

Helford, Elyce Rae, '"A Part of Myself No Man Should Ever See": Reading Captain Kirk's Multiple Masculinities', in Taylor Harrison, Sarah Projansky, Kent A. Ono and Elyce Rae Helford (eds), *Enterprise Zones: Critical Positions on* Star Trek (Boulder, CO: Westview Press, 1996).

Helmore, Edward, 'The World: Girl Power Rules as Teen TV Takes Over', *The Observer*, 1 November 1998, p. 27.

Higson, Andrew, 'A Wee Trendy Channel', *Screen*, 30(1–2), 1989, pp. 80–91.

Higson, Charlie, 'Randall and Hopkirk Resurrected', *Radio Times*, 18–24 March 2000, pp. 18–22.

Hill, Annette and Calcutt, Ian, 'Vampire Hunters: The Scheduling and Reception of *Buffy the Vampire Slayer* and *Angel* in the UK', *Intensities: The Journal of Cult Media*, <www.cult-media.com/issue1/Ahill.htm>, 2001, World Wide Web publication, accessed June 2001.

Hills, Matthew, 'From *The Radio Times* to *Cult Times*: Market Segmentation in TV Consumption', paper presented at the 'Consuming Markets, Consuming Meanings' Conference, University of Plymouth, September 1999.

Hills, Matt, *Fan Cultures* (London and New York: Routledge, 2002).

Hilmes, Michele, *Hollywood and Broadcasting: From Radio to Cable* (Urbana, IL: University of Illinois Press, 1990).

Holben, Jay, '*The X-Files*: Cinematographer: Bill Roe', *American Cinematographer*, 81(3), 2000, pp. 88–91.

Holliss, Richard, 'TV Zone', *Starburst*, 58, June 1983, p. 40.

Hudson, Heather E., 'Satellite Broadcasting in the United States', in Ralph Negrine (ed.), *Satellite Broadcasting: The Politics and Implications of the New Media* (New York and London: Routledge, 1988).

Hunter, I. Q., 'Introduction: The Strange World of the British Science Fiction Film', in I. Q. Hunter (ed.), *British Science Fiction Cinema* (London: Routledge, 1999).

Hutchings, Peter, ' "We're the Martians Now": British SF Invasion Fantasies of the 1950s and 1960s', in I. Q. Hunter (ed.), *British Science Fiction Cinema* (London: Routledge, 1999).

Huyssen, Andreas, *After the Great Divide: Modernism, Mass Culture and Postmodernism* (Hampshire and London: Macmillan, 1988).

ITA: Annual Report and Accounts 1955–56 (HMSO, 1956).

ITA: Annual Report and Accounts 1957–58 (HMSO, 1958).

ITA: Annual Report and Accounts 1961–62 (HMSO, 1962).

ITA: Annual Report and Accounts 1962–63 (HMSO, 1963).

ITA: Annual Report and Accounts 1963–64 (HMSO, 1964).

ITA: Annual Report and Accounts 1965–66 (HMSO, 1966).

ITA: Annual Report and Accounts 1966–67 (HMSO, 1967).

ITA: Annual Report and Accounts 1967–68 (HMSO, 1968).

ITV 1967: A Guide to Independent Television (ITA, 1967).

Jackson, Rosemary, *Fantasy: The Literature of Subversion* (London: Methuen, 1981).

Jacobs, Jason, *The Intimate Screen: Early British Television Drama* (Oxford: Oxford University Press, 2000).

Jancovich, Mark and Lyons, James (eds), *Quality Popular Television: Cult TV, the Industry and Fans* (London: BFI, 2003).

Jenkins, Henry, '*Star Trek* Rerun, Reread, Rewritten: Fan Writing as Textual Poaching', in Constance Penley, Elisabeth Lyon, Lynn Spigel and Janet Bergstrom (eds), *Close Encounters: Film, Feminism, and Science Fiction* (Minneapolis: University of Minnesota Press, 1991).

Jenkins, Henry, *Textual Poachers: Television Fans and Participatory Culture* (London: Routledge, 1992).

Kahn, Frank J. (ed.), *Documents of American Broadcasting* (Englewood Cliffs, NJ: Prentice Hall, 1984).

Kaveney, Roz (ed.), *Reading the Vampire Slayer: An Unofficial Critical Companion to* Buffy *and* Angel (London: Tauris Parke, 2002).

Kellner, Douglas, '*The X-Files* and the Aesthetics and Politics of Postmodern Pop', *Journal of Aesthetics and Art Criticism*, 57(2), 1999, pp. 161–75.

Kennedy Martin, Troy, 'Nats Go Home: First Statement of a New Drama for Television' reprinted under the collective title, 'Television Drama – Is This the Way Ahead?', *Screenwriter*, 15, 1964, pp. 18–25.

Killick, Jane, 'Charlie Higson: Resurrecting the Dead', *TV Zone*, 33, 1999, pp. 8–9.

Kneale, Nigel, 'To a New Wilderness', *Radio Times*, 14 October 1955, p. 7.

Kneale, Nigel, 'Not Quite So Intimate', *Sight and Sound*, 28(2), 1959, pp. 86–8.

Kneale, Nigel, *Quatermass II* (London: Arrow Books, 1979).

Knight, Peter, 'Angry Viewers Left in the Dark on *Prisoner*', *Daily Telegraph*, 5 February 1968, p. 13.

Kutzera, Dale, 'Buffy, Vampire Slayer: Bubbly Buffy Has Her Own TV Series, a High School Horror Show', *Cinefantastique*, 28(11), 1997, pp. 54–5.

Lane, Andy, *Randall and Hopkirk (Deceased): The Files* (London: Boxtree, 2001).

Lavery, David, Hague, Angela and Cartwright, Marla (eds), *"Deny All Knowledge": Reading The X-Files* (Syracuse, NY: Syracuse University Press, 1996).

Lewis, Lisa A. (ed.), *The Adoring Audience* (London: Routledge, 1992).

Litman, Barry, 'Network Oligopoly Power: An Economic Analysis', in Tino Balio (ed.), *Hollywood in the Age of Television* (Boston, MA: Unwin Hyman, 1990).

Lowry, Brian, *The Truth Is Out There: The Official Guide to* The X-Files (London: HarperCollins, 1995).

Lury, Celia, *Cultural Rights: Technology, Legality and Personality* (London: Routledge, 1993).

Lury, Karen, *British Youth Television: Cynicism and Enchantment* (Oxford: Oxford University Press, 2001).

Lyttle, John, 'Do We Need *The X-Files*?: The TV Phenomenon about Strange Phenomena Has Taken International Hold of Paranoid Minds. It Could Be a Conspiracy', *Independent*, 6 May 1996, pp. 8, 17.

MacDonald, J. Fred, *One Nation under Television: The Rise and Decline of Network Television* (Chicago, IL: Nelson-Hall, 1990).

MacDonald, J. Fred, *Blacks and White TV: African Americans in Television since 1948*, 2nd edn (Chicago, IL: Nelson-Hall, 1992).

MacMurraugh-Kavanagh, M. K., 'The BBC and the Birth of *The Wednesday Play*, 1962–66: Institutional Containment Versus "Agitational Contemporaneity"', *Historical Journal of Film, Radio and Television*, 17(3), 1997, pp. 367–81.

McCabe, Janet, 'Diagnosing the Alien: Producing Identities, American "Quality" Drama and British Television Culture in the 1990s', in Margaret Llewellyn-Jones (ed.), *Frames and Fictions on Television: The Politics of Identity within Drama* (Exeter: Intellect Books, 2001).

McLean, Adrienne L., 'Media Effects: Marshall McLuhan, Television Culture, and *The X-Files*', *Film Quarterly*, 51(4), 1998, pp. 2–11.

McLoone, Martin, 'Boxed In?: The Aesthetics of Film and Television', in John Hill and Martin McLoone (eds), *Big Picture, Small Screen: The Relations between Film and Television* (Luton: John Libbey Media, 1997).

Martinez, Jose, 'An Interview with Chris Carter and Howard Gordon', *Creative Screenwriting*, 2(3), 1995, pp. 20–3.

Melly, George, 'Violence for Fun', *The Observer*, 8 October 1967, p. 25.

Melly, George, 'Turning Fantasy into Reality', *The Observer*, 21 January 1968, p. 28.

Millar, Peter, 'Aliens Battle for the Sci-fi Viewer', *The Sunday Times*, Culture Section, 12 April 1998, p. 2.

Miller, Jeffrey S., *Something Completely Different: British Television and American Culture* (Minneapolis: University of Minnesota Press, 2000).

Minow, Newton, 'Address by Newton Minow to the National Association of Broadcasters, Washington, D. C. May 9 1961', in Frank J. Kahn (ed.), *Documents of American Broadcasting* (Englewood Cliffs, NJ: Prentice-Hall, 1984).

Moores, Shaun, *Interpreting Audiences: The Ethnography of Media Consumption* (London: Sage, 1993).

Moretti, Franco, *Signs Taken for Wonders*, rev. edn (London: Verso, 1988).

Moseley, Rachel, 'The Teen Series', in Glen Creeber (ed.), *The Television Genre Book* (London: BFI, 2001).

Moss, Gabrielle, 'From the Valley to the Hellmouth: *Buffy's* Transition from Film to Television', *Slayage: The On-Line International Journal of Buffy Studies*, 2, <www.slayage.tv>, 2001, World Wide Web publication, accessed January 2001.

Myles, Lynda and Petley, Julian, 'Rudolph Cartier', *Sight and Sound*, 59(2), 1990, pp. 126–9.

Neale, Steve, *Hollywood and Genre* (London: Routledge, 2000).

Neale, Steve, 'Genre and Television', in Glen Creeber (ed.), *The Television Genre Book* (London: BFI, 2001).

'New on Southern This Week', *TV Times*, 30 September–6 October 1967, p. 4.

Newcomb, Horace, *Television: The Most Popular Art* (New York: Anchor, 1974).

Newcomb, Horace, 'From Old Frontier to New Frontier', in Lynn Spigel and Michael Curtin (eds), *The Revolution Wasn't Televised: Sixties Television and Social Conflict* (London: Routledge, 1997).

Newman, Kim, '*The Quatermass Conclusion*', *Monthly Film Bulletin*, 56(662), 1989, pp. 94–5.

Oppenheimer, Jean, 'Young Blood', *American Cinematographer*, 10(6), 1999, pp. 90–101.

O'Reilly, John, 'Arts: A Jump-Cut above the Rest', *Independent*, 6 September 1996, pp. 6–7.

Osgerby, Bill, 'So *You're* the Famous Simon Templar': *The Saint*, Masculinity and Consumption in the Early 1960s', in Bill Osgerby and Anna Gough-Yates (eds), *Action TV: Tough Guys, Smooth Operators and Foxy Chicks* (London and New York: Routledge, 2001).

Osgerby, Bill and Gough-Yates, Anna (eds), *Action TV: Tough Guys, Smooth Operators and Foxy Chicks* (London and New York: Routledge, 2001).

Osgerby, Bill, Gough-Yates, Anna and Wells, Marianne, 'The Business of Action: Television History and the Development of the Action Television Series', in Bill Osgerby and Anna Gough-Yates (eds), *Action TV: Tough Guys, Smooth Operators and Foxy Chicks* (London and New York: Routledge, 2001).

Parrinder, Patrick, 'Science Fiction and the Scientific World-view', in Patrick Parrinder (ed.), *Science Fiction: A Critical Guide* (London: Longman, 1979).

Petley, Julian, '*The Quatermass Conclusion*', *Primetime*, 9, 1984–5, pp. 22–5.

Petley, Julian, 'The Lost Continent', in Charles Barr (ed.), *All Our Yesterdays: 90 Years of British Cinema* (London: BFI, 1986).

Pierson, Michele, 'CGI Effects in Hollywood Science-Fiction Cinema 1989–95: The Wonder Years', *Screen*, 40(2), 1999, pp. 158–77.

Pirie, David, 'In the Cold', *Sight and Sound*, N.S.6(4), 1996, pp. 22–3.

Pixley, Andrew, 'Grave Situation: Quatermass Enters ...', *TV Zone*, 106, September 1998, pp. 38–43.

Pounds, Michael C., *Race in Space: The Representation of Ethnicity in* Star Trek *and* Star Trek: The Next Generation (Lanham, MD: Scarecrow Press, 1999).

Probst, Chris, 'Darkness Descends on *The X-Files*', *American Cinematographer*, 76(6), 1995, pp. 28–32.

Rakoff, Ian, *Inside* The Prisoner*: Radical Television and Film in the 1960s* (London: B. T. Batsford, 1998).

Reeves, Jimmie L., Rodgers, Mark C. and Epstein, Michael, 'Rewriting Popularity: The Cult Files', in David Lavery, Angela Hague and Marla Cartwright (eds), *"Deny All Knowledge": Reading* The X-Files (Syracuse, NY: Syracuse University Press, 1996).

Report of the Committee on Broadcasting 1960 (Cmnd. 1753, London: HMSO, 1962).

Richardson, David, 'Ghost of the Past', *Starburst*, 24(7), 2000, pp. 44–51.

Robinson, Hubbell, 'Television's Purpose', *Television Quarterly*, 1(1), 1962, pp. 35–40.

Rogers, Dave, The Prisoner *and* Danger Man (London: Boxtree, 1989).

Scannell, Paddy, 'Public Service Broadcasting: The History of a Concept', in Edward Buscombe (ed.), *British Television: A Reader* (Oxford: Oxford University Press, 2000).

Schoeffter, Conrad, 'Scanning the Horizon: A Film Is a Film Is a Film', in Thomas Elsaesser and Kay Hoffmann (eds), *Cinema Futures: Cain, Abel or Cable? The Screen Arts in the Digital Age* (Amsterdam: Amsterdam University Press, 1998).

Scholes, Robert and Rabkin, Eric S., *Science Fiction: History, Science* (New York: Oxford University Press, 1977).

Sconce, Jeffrey, *Haunted Media: Electronic Presence from Telegraphy to Television* (Durham, NC and London: Duke University Press, 2000).

Sendall, Bernard, *Independent Television in Britain, Volume 2: Expansion and Change, 1958–68* (London: Macmillan, 1983).

Siegel, Mark, 'Towards an Aesthetics of Science Fiction Television', *Extrapolation*, 25, 1984, pp. 60–75.

Sobchack, Vivian, *Screening Space: The American Science Fiction Film* (New Brunswick, NJ: Rutgers University Press, 1987).

Solow, Herbert F. and Justman, Robert H., *Inside* Star Trek*: The Real Story* (New York: Pocket Books, 1996).

Sontag, Susan, *Against Interpretation and Other Essays* (New York: Farrar Straus & Giroux, 1966).

Spigel, Lynn, 'White Flight', in Lynn Spigel and Michael Curtin (eds), *The Revolution Wasn't Televised: Sixties Television and Social Conflict* (London: Routledge, 1997).

Spigel, Lynn, *Welcome to the Dreamhouse: Popular Media and Postwar Suburbs* (Durham, NC and London: Duke University Press, 2001).

'Statement from the Editorial Board', *Television Quarterly*, 1(1), 1962, p. 4.

Sutcliffe, Thomas, 'TV Review', *Independent*, 13 November 1996, p. 36.

Sydney-Smith, Susan, *Beyond* Dixon of Dock Green*: Early British Police Series* (London and New York: I. B. Tauris, 2002).

Thomas, Deborah, *Beyond Genre: Melodrama, Comedy and Romance in Hollywood Films* (Moffat, Dumfriesshire: Cameron and Hollis, 2000).

Thompson, Robert J., *Television's Second Golden Age: From* Hill Street Blues *to* ER (Syracuse, NY: Syracuse University Press, 1997).

Todorov, Tzvetan, *The Fantastic: A Structural Approach to a Literary Genre* (New York: Cornell, 1975).

Tulloch, John, 'Positioning the SF audience: *Star Trek*, *Dr Who* and the Texts of Science Fiction', in John Tulloch and Henry Jenkins, *Science Fiction Audiences: Watching* Doctor Who *and* Star Trek (London: Routledge, 1995).

Tulloch, John, *Watching Television Audiences: Cultural Theories and Methods* (London: Arnold, 2000).

Tulloch, John and Alvarado, Manuel, Doctor Who: *The Unfolding Text* (Hampshire and London: Macmillan, 1983).

Tulloch, John and Jenkins, Henry, *Science Fiction Audiences: Watching* Doctor Who *and* Star Trek (London: Routledge, 1995).

Turner, Graeme, 'Genre, Hybridity and Mutations', in Glen Creeber (ed.), *The Television Genre Book* (London: BFI, 2001a).

Turner, Graeme, 'Genre, Format and "Live" Television', in Glen Creeber (ed.), *The Television Genre Book* (London: BFI, 2001b).

Turnock, Rob, *Did ITV Revolutionise British Television?*, AHRB Report, <www.rhul.ac.uk/Media-Arts/staff/ellis/AHRB%20Report.doc.>, 2003.

Vahimagi, Tise, *British Television: An Illustrated Guide*, 2nd edn (London: BFI, 1996).

'Viewerpoint', *TV Times*, 17–23 February 1968, p. 16.

Walker, Cynthia W., 'Spy Programs', in Horace Newcomb (ed.), *Encyclopaedia of Television, Volume 3: Q–Z* (Chicago, IL: Fitzroy Dearborn, 1997).

Wee, Valerie, 'Selling Teen Culture: How American Multimedia Conglomeration Reshaped Teen Television in the 1990s', in Glyn Davis and Kay Dickinson (eds), *Teen TV: Genre, Consumption and Identity* (London: BFI, 2004).

Weldon, Huw, 'A Reply to Charges of Trivia in BBC TV Programmes', *In the Public Interest: A Six-part Explanation of BBC Policy* (London: BBC, 1971a).

Weldon, Huw, *Competition in Television*, Address to a joint meeting of the Faculty of Royal Designers for Industry and the Royal Society of Arts, 26 April 1971 (London: BBC, 1971b).

Wells, Paul, 'Apocalypse Then!: The Ultimate Monstrosity and Strange Things on the Coast ... An Interview with Nigel Kneale', in I. Q. Hunter (ed.), *British Science Fiction Cinema* (London: Routledge, 1999).

Wells, Paul, *The Horror Genre: From Beelzebub to Blair Witch* (London: Wallflower, 2000).

Wheatley, Helen, *Gothic Television*, PhD, University of Warwick, 2002, to be published by Manchester University Press, forthcoming: 2005.

Whitehouse, Mary, *Cleaning up Television: From Protest to Participation* (London: Blendford Press, 1967).

Whitfield, Stephen E. and Roddenberry, Gene, *The Making of* Star Trek (London: Titan Books, 1991 [1968]).

Williams, Raymond, *Television: Technology and Cultural Form*, 2nd edn (London: Routledge, 1994).

Woll, Allen L. and Miller, Randall M., *Ethnic and Racial Images in American Film and Television: Historical Essays and Bibliography* (New York and London: Garland, 1987).

APPENDICES

All transmission (tx.) dates refer to the first date of broadcast. The appendices for *The X-Files* and *Buffy the Vampire Slayer* also include initial transmission dates in the UK on Sky and on terrestrial television.

Appendix A

The Quatermass Experiment, UK, BBC, tx. 18 July 1953–22 August 1953.
Writ: Nigel Kneale, **Prod**: Rudolph Cartier.
Main Cast: Reginald Tate (Professor Bernard Quatermass), Isabel Dean (Judith Carroon), Duncan Lamont (Victor Carroon).
Episode list:
'Contact has been Established', Episode 1, tx. 18 July 1953.
'Persons Reported Missing', Episode 2, tx. 25 July 1953.
'Very Special Knowledge', Episode 3, tx. 1 August 1953.
'Believed to be Suffering', Episode 4, tx. 8 August 1953.
'An Unidentified Species', Episode 5, tx. 15 August 1953.
'State of Emergency', Episode 6, tx. 22 August 1953.

Quatermass II, UK, BBC, tx. 22 October 1955–26 November 1955.
Writ: Nigel Kneale, **Prod**: Rudolph Cartier.
Main Cast: John Robinson (Professor Bernard Quatermass), Hugh Griffiths (Dr Leo Pugh), Monica Grey (Paula Quatermass).
Episode list:
'The Bolts', Episode 1, tx. 22 October 1955, telerecorded repeat, tx. 24 October 1955.
'The Mark', Episode 2, tx. 29 October 1955, telerecorded repeat, tx. 31 October 1955.
'The Flood', Episode 3, tx. 5 November 1955, telerecorded repeat, tx. 7 November 1955.
'The Coming', Episode 4, tx. 12 November 1955, telerecorded repeat, tx. 14 November 1955.
'The Frenzy', Episode 5, tx. 19 November 1955, telerecorded repeat, tx. 21 November 1955.
'The Destroyers', Episode 6, tx. 26 November 1955, telerecorded repeat, tx. 28 November 1955.

Quatermass and the Pit, UK, BBC, 22 December 1958–26 January 1959.
Writ: Nigel Kneale, **Prod**: Rudolph Cartier.
Main Cast: André Morell (Professor Bernard Quatermass), Christine Finn (Barbara Judd), Cec Linder (Dr Matthew Roney), Anthony Bushell (Colonel Breen).
Episode list:
'The Halfmen', Episode 1, tx. 22 December 1958.
'The Ghosts', Episode 2, tx. 29 December 1958.
'Imps and Demons', Episode 3, tx. 5 January 1959.
'The Enchanted', Episode 4, tx. 12 January 1959.
'The Wild Hunt', Episode 5, tx. 19 January 1959.
'Hob', Episode 6, tx. 26 January 1959.

Appendix B

The Prisoner, UK, ITV, tx. 1 October 1967–4 February 1968.[1]
'Arrival', Episode 1, tx. 1 October 1967.
Writ: George Markstein and David Tomblin, **Prod**: David Tomblin, **Dir**: Don Chaffey
Main Cast: Patrick McGoohan (Number Six), Guy Doleman (Number Two).

'The Chimes of Big Ben', Episode 2, tx. 8 October 1967.
Writ: Vincent Tilsley, **Prod**: David Tomblin, **Dir**: Don Chaffey.
Main Cast: Patrick McGoohan (Number Six), Leo McKern (Number Two), Nadia Gray (Nadia).

'A, B and C', Episode 3, tx. 15 October 1967.
Writ: Anthony Skene, **Prod**: David Tomblin, **Dir**: Pat Jackson.
Main Cast: Patrick McGoohan (Number Six), Colin Gordon (Number Two), Sheila Allen (Number Fourteen).

'Free For All', Episode 4, tx. 22 October 1967.
Writ: Patrick McGoohan under the pseudonym Paddy Fitz, **Prod**: David Tomblin, **Dir**: Patrick McGoohan.
Main Cast: Patrick McGoohan (Number Six), Eric Portman (Number Two).

'The Schizoid Man', Episode 5, tx. 29 October 1967.
Writ: Terence Feeley, **Prod**: David Tomblin, **Dir**: Pat Jackson.
Main Cast: Patrick McGoohan (Number Six), Anton Rogers (Number Two).

'The General', Episode 6, tx. 5 November 1967.
Writ: Lewis Greifer under the pseudonym Joshua Adam, **Prod**: David Tomblin, **Dir**: Peter Graham Scott.
Main Cast: Patrick McGoohan (Number Six), Colin Gordon (Number Two), John Castle (Number Twelve).

'Many Happy Returns', Episode 7, tx. 12 November 1967.
Writ: Anthony Skene, **Prod**: David Tomblin, **Dir**: Patrick McGoohan under the pseudonym Joseph Serf.
Main Cast: Patrick McGoohan (Number Six), Georgina Cookson (Mrs Butterworth).

'Dance of the Dead', Episode 8, tx. 16 November 1967.
Writ: Anthony Skene, **Prod**: David Tomblin, **Dir**: Don Chaffey.
Main Cast: Patrick McGoohan (Number Six), Mary Morris (Number Two).

'Checkmate', Episode 9, tx. 3 December 1967.
Writ: Gerald Kelsey, **Prod**: David Tomblin, **Dir**: Don Chaffey.
Main Cast: Patrick McGoohan (Number Six), Peter Wyngarde (Number Two), Ronald Radd (The Rook).

'Hammer Into Anvil', Episode 10, tx. 10 December 1967.
Writ: Roger Waddis, **Prod**: David Tomblin, **Dir**: Pat Jackson.
Main Cast: Patrick McGoohan (Number Six), Patrick Cargill (Number Two).

'It's Your Funeral', Episode 11, tx. 17 December 1967.
Writ: Michael Cramoy, **Prod**: David Tomblin, **Dir**: Robert Asher.
Main Cast: Patrick McGoohan (Number Six), Derren Nesbitt (Number Two).

'A Change of Mind', Episode 12, tx. 31 December 1967.
Writ: Roger Parks, **Prod**: David Tomblin, **Dir**: Patrick McGoohan under the pseudonym Joseph Serf.
Main Cast: Patrick McGoohan (Number Six), John Sharp (Number Two).

'Do Not Forsake Me, Oh My Darling', Episode 13, tx. 7 January 1967.
Writ: Vincent Tilsley, **Prod**: David Tomblin, **Dir**: Pat Jackson.
Main Cast: Patrick McGoohan (Number Six), Nigel Stock (The Colonel/The Prisoner).

'Living in Harmony', Episode 14, tx. 14 January 1968.
Writ: David Tomblin, **Story**: David Tomblin and Ian Rakoff, **Prod**: David Tomblin, **Dir**: David Tomblin.
Main Cast: Patrick McGoohan (Number Six), Alexis Kanner (The Kid).

'The Girl who was Death', Episode 15, tx. 21 January 1968.
Writ: Terence Feeley, **Prod**: David Tomblin, **Dir**: David Tomblin.
Main Cast: Patrick McGoohan (Number Six), Justine Lord (Sonia), Kenneth Griffith (Schnipps).

'Once Upon a Time', Episode 16, tx. 28 January 1968.
Writ: Patrick McGoohan, **Prod**: David Tomblin, **Dir**: Patrick McGoohan.
Main Cast: Patrick McGoohan (Number Six), Leo McKern (Number Two).

'Fall Out', Episode 17, tx. 4 February 1968.
Writ: Patrick McGoohan, **Prod**: David Tomblin, **Dir**: Patrick McGoohan.
Main Cast: Patrick McGoohan (Number Six), Alexis Kanner (Number Forty-eight).

Appendix C

Star Trek, US, NBC, tx. 8 September 1966–3 June 1969.
Creator/Executive Prod: Gene Roddenberry.
Main Cast: William Shatner (Captain James T. Kirk), Leonard Nimoy (Mr Spock), DeForest
Kelley (Dr McCoy), James Doohan (Scotty), Nichelle Nichols (Lieutenant Uhura).
Season 1, tx. 8 September 1966–13 April 1967.
Season 2, tx. 15 September 1967–29 March 1968.
Season 3, tx. 20 September 1968–3 June 1969.

Specific episodes referred to in this book:
'Where No Man Has Gone Before', Season 1, Episode 3, tx. 22 September 1966.
Writ: Samuel A. Peeples, **Prod**: Gene Roddenberry, **Dir**: James Goldstone.

'The Naked Time', Season 1, Episode 4, tx. 29 September 1966.
Writ: John D. F. Black, **Prod**: Gene Roddenberry, **Dir**: Marc Daniels.

'The Enemy Within', Season 1, Episode 5, tx. 6 October 1966.
Writ: Richard Matheson, **Prod**: Gene Roddenberry, **Dir**: Leo Penn.

'The Menagerie: Part 1', Season 1, Episode 11, tx. 17 November 1966
Writ: Gene Roddenberry, **Prod**: Gene L. Coon, **Dir**: Marc Daniels.

'The Menagerie: Part 2', Season 1, Episode 12, tx. 24 November 1966
Writ: Gene Roddenberry, **Prod**: Gene Roddenberry, **Dir**: Robert Butler.

'Balance of Terror', Season 1, Episode 14, tx. 15 December 1966
Writ: Paul Schneider, **Prod**: Gene Roddenberry, **Dir**: Vincent McEveety.

'This Side of Paradise', Season 1, Episode 24, tx. 2 March 1967.
Writ: D. C. Fontana, **Story**: D. C. Fontana and Jerry Sohl under the pseudonym Nathan
Butler, **Prod**: Gene L. Coon, **Dir**: Ralph Senensky.

'The Devil in the Dark', Season 1, Episode 25, tx. 9 March 1967.
Writ: Gene L. Coon, **Prod**: Gene L. Coon, **Dir**: Joseph Pevney.

'Errand of Mercy', Season 1, Episode 26, tx. 23 March 1967.
Writ: Gene L. Coon, **Prod**: Gene L. Coon, **Dir**: John Newland.

'Mirror, Mirror', Season 2, Episode 4, tx. 6 October 1967.
Writ: Jerome Bixby, **Prod**: Gene L. Coon, **Dir**: Marc Daniels.

'A Piece of the Action', Season 2, Episode 17, tx. 12 January 1968.
Writ: David P. Harmon and Gene L. Coon, **Story**: David Harmon, **Prod**: John Meredyth Lucas, **Dir**: James Komack.

'Assignment: Earth', Season 2, Episode 26, tx. 29 March 1968.
Writ: Art Wallace, **Story**: Gene Roddenberry and Art Wallace, **Prod**: John Meredyth Lucas, **Dir**: Marc Daniels.

'Spectre of the Gun', Season 3, Episode 6, tx. 25 October 1968.
Writ: Gene L. Coon under the pseudonym Lee Cronin, **Prod**: Fred Freiberger, **Dir**: Vincent McEveety.

'Turnabout Intruder', Season 3, Episode 24, tx. 3 June 1969.
Writ: Arthur H. Singer, **Story**: Gene Roddenberry, **Prod**: Fred Freiberger, **Dir**: Herb Wallerstein.

Appendix D

Film Credits:
The X-Files: Fight the Future, Dir: Rob Bowman, Fox/10:13, 1998.

Television Series Credits:
The X-Files, US, Fox, tx. 10 September 1993–19 May 2002.
Creator/Executive Producer: Chris Carter, **Director of Photography**: John Bartley (seasons 1–3), Bill Roe (seasons 4–9).
Main Cast: David Duchovny (Fox Mulder), Gillian Anderson (Dana Scully), Robert Patrick (John Doggett) (seasons 8–9), Annabeth Gish (Monica Reyes) (seasons 8–9).

Season 1, US, Fox, tx. 10 September 1993–13 May 1994.
UK, Sky, tx. 26 January 1994–6 July 1994.
UK, BBC2, tx. 19 September 1994–9 March 1995.

Season 2, US, Fox, tx. 16 September 1994–19 May 1995.
UK, Sky, tx. 21 February 1995–9 August 1995.
UK, BBC2, tx. 28 August 1995–18 December 1995, BBC1, tx. 9 January 1996–27 February 1996.

Season 3, US, Fox, tx. 22 September 1995–17 May 1996.
UK, Sky, tx. 5 March 1996–13 August 1996.
UK, BBC1, tx. 12 September 1996–3 September 1997.

Season 4, US, Fox, tx. 4 October 1996–18 May 1997.
UK, Sky, tx. 12 January 1997–13 July 1997.
UK, BBC1, tx. 10 September 1997–4 March 1998.

Season 5, US, Fox, tx. 16 November 1997–17 May 1998.
UK, Sky, tx. 15 March 1998–5 July 1998.
UK, BBC1, tx. 3 October 1998–17 March 1999.

Season 6, US, Fox, tx. 8 November 1998–16 March 1999.
UK, Sky, tx. 7 March 1999–25 July 1999.
UK, BBC1, tx. 5 January 2000–12 August 2000.

Season 7, US, Fox, tx. 7 November 1999–21 May 2000.
UK, Sky, tx. 19 March 2000–13 August 2000.
UK, BBC2, tx. 15 November 2000–27 May 2001.

Season 8, US, Fox, tx. 5 November 2000–20 May 2001.
UK, Sky, tx. 15 February 2001–28 June 2001.
UK, BBC2, tx. 3 March 2002–25 August 2002.

Season 9, US, Fox, tx. 11 November 2001–19 May 2002.
UK, Sky, tx. 20 June 2002–26 September 2002.
UK, BBC2, tx. 3 November 2002–23 March 2003.

Specific episodes referred to in this book:

'Pilot', Season 1, Episode 1, tx. 10 September 1993 (Fox), tx. 26 January 1994 (Sky), tx. 19 September 1994 (BBC2).
Writ: Chris Carter, **Supervising Prod**: Daniel Sackheim, **Dir**: Robert Mandel.

'Squeeze', Season 1, Episode 3, tx. 24 September 1993 (Fox), tx. 8 February 1994 (Sky), tx. 3 October 1994 (BBC2).
Writ: Glen Morgan and James Wong, **Line Prod**: J. P. Finn, **Dir**: Harry Longstreet.

'E.B.E.', Season 1, Episode 17, tx. 18 February 1994 (Fox), tx. 18 May 1994 (Sky), tx. 19 January 1995 (BBC2).
Writ: Glen Morgan and James Wong, **Line Prod**: J. P. Finn, **Dir**: William Graham.

'Dod Kalm', Season 2, Episode 19, tx. 10 March 1995 (Fox), tx. 27 June 1995 (Sky), tx. 16
January 1996 (BBC1).
Writ: Howard Gordon and Alex Gansa, **Prod**: J. P. Finn, Kim Manners, Rob Bowman,
Dir: Rob Bowman.

Appendix E

Film Credits:
Buffy the Vampire Slayer, **Dir**: Fran Rubel Kuzui, Kuzui Enterprises/Sandollar
Productions/Fox, 1992.

Television Series Credits:
Buffy the Vampire Slayer, US, WB, tx. 10 March 1997–22 May 2001, UPN, tx. 2 October
2001–20 May 2003.
Creator/Executive Prod: Joss Whedon, **Director of Photography**: Michael Gershman.
Main Cast: Sarah Michelle Gellar (Buffy Summers), Nicholas Brendon (Xander Harris),
Alyson Hannigan (Willow Rosenberg), Anthony Stewart Head (Rupert Giles), David
Boreanaz (Angel) (seasons 1–3), Charisma Carpenter (Cordelia Chase) (seasons 1–3), James
Marsters (Spike) (seasons 2 and 4–7), Seth Green (Daniel 'Oz' Osborne) (seasons 3–4), Eliza
Dushku (Faith) (seasons 3 and 7), Marc Blucas (Riley Finn) (season 4), Emma Caulfield (Anya
Jenkins) (seasons 4–7), Michelle Trachtenberg (Dawn Summers) (seasons 5–7), Amber
Benson (Tara Maclay) (seasons 5–6).

Season 1, US, WB, tx. 10 March 1997–2 June 1997.
UK, Sky, tx. 3 January 1998–21 March 1998.
UK, BBC2, tx. 3 December 1998–31 March 1999.

Season 2, US, WB, tx. 15 September 1997–19 May 1998.
UK, Sky, tx. 28 March 1998–13 August 1999.
UK, BBC2, tx. 8 April 1999–16 March 2000.

Season 3, US, WB, tx. 29 September 1998–21 September 1999.[2]
UK, Sky, tx. 20 August 1999–26 November 1999.
UK, BBC2, tx. 30 March 2000–21 September 2000.

Season 4, US, WB, tx. 5 October 1999–23 May 2000.
UK, Sky, tx. 7 January 2000–28 May 2000.
UK, BBC2, tx. 28 September 2000–12 April 2001.

Season 5, US, WB, tx. 26 September 2000–22 May 2001.
UK, Sky, tx. 5 January 2001–1 June 2001.
UK, BBC2, tx. 23 August 2001–4 April 2002.

Season 6, US, UPN, tx. 2 October 2001–21 May 2002.
UK, Sky, tx. 10 January 2002–29 May 2002.
UK, BBC2, tx. 31 October 2002–5 June 2003.

Season 7, US, UPN, tx. 24 September 2002–20 May 2003.
UK, Sky, tx. 16 January 2003–12 June 2003.
UK, BBC2, tx. 28 October 2003–18 December 2003.

Specific episodes referred to in this book:

'Welcome to the Hellmouth', Season 1, Episode 1, tx. 10 March 1997 (WB), tx. 3 January
1998 (Sky), tx. 30 December 1998 (BBC2).
Writ: Joss Whedon, **Prod**: Gareth Davies, **Dir**: Charles Martin Smith.

'Ted', Season 2, Episode 11, tx. 8 December 1997 (WB), tx. 6 June 1998 (Sky), tx. 9
December 1999 (BBC2).
Writ: David Greenwalt and Joss Whedon, **Prod**: Gareth Davies, **Dir**: Bruce Seth Green.

'Tabula Rasa', Season 6, Episode 8, tx. 13 November 2001 (UPN), tx. 21 February 2002
(Sky), tx. 2 January 2003 (BBC2).
Writ: Rebecca Rand Kirshner, **Prod**: Douglas Petrie, David Solomon, Gareth Davies,
Dir: David Grossman.

Appendix F

Randall and Hopkirk (Deceased), UK, BBC1, Season 1, tx. 18 March 2000–22 April 2000,
Season 2, tx. 29 September 2001–24 November 2001.

Season 1:
'Drop Dead', Episode 1, tx. 18 March 2000.
Writ: Charlie Higson, **Prod**: Charlie Higson, **Dir**: Mark Mylod.
Main Cast: Vic Reeves (Marty Hopkirk), Bob Mortimer (Jeff Randall), Emilia Fox (Jeannie
Hurst), Charles Dance (Kenneth Crisby).

'Mental Apparition Disorder', Episode 2, tx. 25 March 2000.
Writ: Charlie Higson, **Story**: Mike Pratt and Ian Wilson, **Prod**: Charlie Higson, **Dir**: Rachel
Talalay.
Main Cast: Vic Reeves (Marty Hopkirk), Bob Mortimer (Jeff Randall), Emilia Fox (Jeannie
Hurst), Tom Baker (Wyvern), Hugh Lawrie (Dr Lawyer).

'The Best Years of Your Death', Episode 3, tx. 1 April 2000.
Writ: Charlie Higson, **Prod**: Charlie Higson, **Dir**: Mark Mylod.

Main Cast: Vic Reeves (Marty Hopkirk), Bob Mortimer (Jeff Randall), Emilia Fox (Jeannie Hurst), Tom Baker (Wyvern), Peter Bowles (Captain Graves).

'Paranoia', Episode 4, tx. 8 April 2000.
Writ: Charlie Higson and Paul Whitehouse, **Prod**: Charlie Higson, **Dir**: Charlie Higson.
Main Cast: Vic Reeves (Marty Hopkirk), Bob Mortimer (Jeff Randall), Emilia Fox (Jeannie Hurst), Tom Baker (Wyvern), Paul Rhys (Douglas Milton).

'A Blast from the Past', Episode 5, tx. 15 April 2000.
Writ: Charlie Higson, **Prod**: Charlie Higson, **Dir**: Rachel Talalay.
Main Cast: Vic Reeves (Marty Hopkirk), Bob Mortimer (Jeff Randall), Emilia Fox (Jeannie Hurst), Tom Baker (Wyvern), Paul Whitehouse (Sidney Crabbe).

'A Man of Substance', Episode 6, tx. 22 April 2000.
Writ: Charlie Higson, **Prod**: Charlie Higson, **Dir**: Mark Mylod.
Main Cast: Vic Reeves (Marty Hopkirk), Bob Mortimer (Jeff Randall), Emilia Fox (Jeannie Hurst), Tom Baker (Wyvern), Gareth Thomas (Dickie Bechard).

Season 2:
'Whatever Possessed You', Episode 1, tx. 29 September 2001.
Writ: Charlie Higson and Gareth Roberts, **Prod**: Charlie Higson, **Dir**: Metin Huseyin.
Main Cast: Vic Reeves (Marty Hopkirk), Bob Mortimer (Jeff Randall), Emilia Fox (Jeannie Hurst), Tom Baker (Wyvern), Hywel Bennett (James Whale).

'Revenge of the Bog People', Episode 2, tx. 6 October 2001.
Writ: Charlie Higson and Kate Woods, **Prod**: Charlie Higson, **Dir**: Charlie Higson.
Main Cast: Vic Reeves (Marty Hopkirk), Bob Mortimer (Jeff Randall), Emilia Fox (Jeannie Hurst), Tom Baker (Wyvern), Celia Imrie (Professor McKern), Mark Williams (Professor Doleman).

'O Happy Isle', Episode 3, tx. 13 October 2001.
Writ: Charlie Higson, **Prod**: Charlie Higson, **Dir**: Metin Huseyin.
Main Cast: Vic Reeves (Marty Hopkirk), Bob Mortimer (Jeff Randall), Emilia Fox (Jeannie Hurst), Tom Baker (Wyvern), George Baker (Berry Pomeroy).

'Marshall and Snellgrove', Episode 4, tx. 27 October 2001.
Writ: Charlie Higson, **Prod**: Charlie Higson, **Dir**: Metin Huseyin.
Main Cast: Vic Reeves (Marty Hopkirk), Bob Mortimer (Jeff Randall), Emilia Fox (Jeannie Hurst), Tom Baker (Wyvern), Shaun Parkes (Charlie Marshall), Colin McFarlane (Sebastian Snellgrove).

'Pain Killers', Episode 5, tx. 20 October 2001.
Writ: Gareth Roberts, **Prod**: Charlie Higson, **Dir**: Charlie Higson.

Main Cast: Vic Reeves (Marty Hopkirk), Bob Mortimer (Jeff Randall), Emilia Fox (Jeannie Hurst), Tom Baker (Wyvern), Dervla Kirwan (Petra Winters), Derek Jacobi (Colonel Anger).

'The Glorious Butranekh', Episode 6, tx. 3 November 2001.
Writ: Charlie Higson, **Prod**: Charlie Higson, **Dir**: Charlie Higson.
Main Cast: Vic Reeves (Marty Hopkirk), Bob Mortimer (Jeff Randall), Emilia Fox (Jeannie Hurst), Tom Baker (Wyvern), Pauline Quirke (Felia Siderova).

'Two Can Play at That Game', Episode 7, tx. 24 November 2001.
Writ: Mark Gatiss and Jeremy Dyson, **Prod**: Charlie Higson, **Dir**: Steve Bendelack.
Main Cast: Vic Reeves (Marty Hopkirk), Bob Mortimer (Jeff Randall), Emilia Fox (Jeannie Hurst), Tom Baker (Wyvern), Roy Hudd (Dicky Klein), John Michie (Stuart Boyle).

Notes

1. As transmission dates for *The Prisoner* in the UK varied from region to region, those given here relate to initial UK transmission in the Southern region only.
2. Season 3 of *Buffy the Vampire Slayer* was scheduled to complete its run on WB on 25 May 1999. However, due to the school shooting at Columbine, 'Earshot' was postponed from 27 April 1999 to 21 September 1999, and the season finale 'Graduation Day Part 2' was postponed from 25 May 1999 to 13 July 1999.

List of Illustrations

Whilst considerable effort has been made to correctly identify the copyright holders, this has not been possible in all cases. We apologise for any apparent negligence and any omissions or corrections brought to our attention will be remedied in any future editions.

The Quatermass Experiment, BBC; *Quatermass and the Pit*, BBC; *The Prisoner*, Everyman Films/ITC; *Star Trek*, Desilu Productions Inc./Norway Corporation/Paramount Television; *The X-Files*, 20th Century Fox Television/Ten Thirteen Productions; *Buffy the Vampire Slayer*, 20th Century Fox Television/Mutant Enemy Inc./Kuzui Enterprises/Sandollar Television; *Randall and Hopkirk (Deceased)*, Ghost Productions/Working Title Television.

INDEX

Page numbers in *italic* denote illustrations; *n* = endnote.